MICROCOMPUTER INTERFACING

FOR ELECTRONICS TECHNICIANS

EDWARD J. PASAHOW

San Diego Community College
San Diego, California

Gregg Division, McGraw-Hill Book Company

New York   Atlanta   Dallas   St. Louis   San Francisco   Auckland   Bogotá   Guatemala
Hamburg   Johannesburg   Lisbon   London   Madrid   Mexico   Montreal   New Delhi
Panama   Paris   San Juan   São Paulo   Singapore   Sydney   Tokyo   Toronto

In Memory of Tom Brereton: A Great Teacher; An Even Better Friend.

Sponsoring Editor: *Mark Haas*
Editing Supervisor: *Karen Sekiguchi*
Design Supervisor: *Caryl Spinka*
Production Supervisor: *Kathleen Morrissey*
Art Supervisor: *Howard Brotman*

Cover Designer: *David Thurston*

Library of Congress Cataloging in Publication Data

Pasahow, Edward.
    Microcomputer interfacing for electronics technicians.

    Bibliography: p.
    Includes index.
    1. Computer interfaces.   2. Microcomputers.
3. Microprocessors.   I. Title.
TK7887.5.P28   621.3819′592   80-14763
ISBN 0-07-048718-9

Microcomputer Interfacing for Electronics Technicians

    3 4 5 6 7 8 9 0   SMSM   8 8 7 6 5 4 3 2

CONTENTS

PREFACE

If you work with microcomputers, this book is for you. Sooner or later anyone associated with microprocessing equipment will need practical advice on interface construction. You may be confronted with having to know about the IEEE-488 bus standard, adding more memory to your computer, diagnosing why the computer will not output to the printer, or building a circuit to convert TTL levels to a teletype current loop. All of these topics and more are presented in this book.

As a companion volume to my *Microprocessors and Microcomputers for Electronics Technicians,* this book on interfacing brings you into the field of digital communications. You need not have read the other work to understand this one, however, because that material is reviewed in the opening chapters.

A background in high school algebra together with some experience with microprocessors is all that is needed to understand this book. With your efforts in studying each chapter, working the problems, and doing the experiments, this book can put you in the ranks of the most sought-after digital technicians.

This book is uniquely organized to integrate theory and experiments into one package. By reading the material and working the experiments, you will gain a thorough understanding of both hardware and software for microprocessor input and output. You will be able to analyze interface circuits and the signal flow between the computer and peripheral equipment to diagnose the cause of failures. Using the programs given in the text as examples, you will also be capable of writing diagnostic software to localize faulty components.

The circuits and experiments are based on the popular 8080A microprocessor, with direct applicability to the 8085 and Z80 as well. This selection of heavily used and readily available microprocessors allows you to actually try out these interfacing concepts. Early chapters present a selection of typical microcomputer applications to illustrate how widespread interfacing is. Then microprocessor architecture is discussed, mostly as a review, because you probably know something about it already. Memory and I/O port addressing methods are considered at that time also. Then peripheral equipment, such as terminals, keyboards, floppy disks, printers, and modems, is introduced.

Material specifically addressing interface circuitry begins in Chap. 4, which covers all variations of parallel input/output. Chap. 5 provides corresponding material for serial I/O channels. The electrical and mechanical characteristics of almost any interface you are likely to encounter are then described. The chapter on teletype current loops includes conversion to or from TTL logic and use of opto-isolators. The frequently used communications standards RS-232C and IEEE-488 are discussed in detail, together with implementation techniques. Computer buses, such as the hobbyist S-100 and the Multibus, receive a full treatment which extends to the problems you may come across in bussed equipment and how to resolve them.

An important area not previously presented in texts at this level is analog interfacing. Here analog circuits, with working applications of such devices as multiplying DACs and V/F converters, D/A and A/D converters, and sample-and-hold devices, receive a complete analysis.

Other ready-made solutions to common problems are considered in Chap. 11. Floppy disk controllers, sound generators, CRT and keyboard controllers, and the emerging technology of data encryption units are studied, and circuits showing how to use them in a microcomputer system are provided. Finally, the topic of troubleshooting is covered. A recommended approach to finding faults in a microcomputer is laid out and the functions and operation of test equipment, as applied to microcomputers, are described. The emphasis on servicing the computer in a step-by-step fashion will help you sharpen your troubleshooting skills in servicing equipment.

The ideas and suggestions of many co-workers have assisted a great deal in writing this book. The same can be said of manufacturers of the devices, whose technical publications were the starting point for this effort. The assistance of Myrna Davis with typing, and Rosemarie Pasahow with the myriad of manuscript preparation tasks, is gratefully acknowledged.

Edward J. Pasahow

MICROCOMPUTER INTERFACING

FOR ELECTRONICS TECHNICIANS

EDWARD J. PASAHOW

1

INTRODUCTION TO INTERFACING

Even the most powerful computers are useless if isolated from their environment. The computer must have a way to accept entry of programs and data, so a new job can be processed. The outcome of this processing must also be communicated to the person who requested the work. There is a further need for data and instruction paths between the processor and memory units within the computer.

Every time signals cross between pieces of equipment or major units, an interface is needed. Much of the day-to-day work on microcomputers involves the fabrication, use, or repair of interface circuitry. When confronted by the myriad of interface circuits that a microcomputer can use, a technician may experience considerable confusion, especially when dealing with combinations of analog, parallel, and serial interfaces.

In spite of the seemingly endless variety of interfaces, a few simple concepts are the basis for all of them. A grasp of these concepts will equip you with the understanding needed to troubleshoot even the most complicated microcomputer system.

CHAPTER OBJECTIVES

Upon completion of this chapter, you should be able to:

1. Explain the role that interfaces play in a microcomputer
2. Explain why software, as well as hardware, is an important component of the interface
3. List examples of commonly used interfaces
4. Discuss the importance of standardization for interfaces
5. Give several examples of interface designs

MICROPROCESSORS AND MICROCOMPUTERS

A *microprocessor* is an integrated circuit that contains the logic for the central processor of the computer. The processor is responsible for executing the program in a step-by-step fashion by obtaining the proper data, manipulating it as required, storing away answers, and sending or receiving information. The processor alone is not sufficient to perform all of these services. For a completely useful device, the microprocessor unit (MPU) must be combined with other elements to form a *microcomputer.*

A microcomputer is capable of stand-alone operation. We might say that a

$$\text{Microcomputer} = \text{MPU} + \text{memory} + \text{I/O} + \text{power supply} + \text{interfaces}$$

That is, in addition to the processor, we need memory to be used by the microprocessor to store the program and data. Input and output (I/O) circuitry are the links between the processor and external equipment that can send new information to the computer for processing and display the answers that result. Some single-chip microcomputers, such as the 8048, can perform all or almost all of these functions.

Most microcomputers work on 8-bit long binary quantities, though a rapidly growing number of 16-bit computers are coming on the market. The length of these quantities is the *word size* of the microprocessor. An 8-bit word is frequently called a *byte.* So we can describe a processor as having an 8-bit word size or a single-byte word and mean the same thing either way. In most cases a memory word has the same size as the processor word. One example of an exception is the 8088, with a 16-bit processor that uses an 8-bit memory word.

The components of the computer are bussed together. There are usually three *buses* of interest. The data bus is a bidirectional, three-state bus between the processor and other modules such as memory and I/O ports. The address bus is a single direction, often three-state, bus and it tells all other modules which one the processor has designated to carry out the required action. Finally, the control bus is a collection of the signals that command the memory or I/O ports, provide timing throughout the computer, and return status information to the MPU.

INTERFACES

Every time a device is connected to a bus or I/O port, an interface is created. An *interface* is simply a shared boundary between two systems or units. Obviously interfaces play an important role in any microcomputer. The method by which memory can be addressed to locate a particular cell is dependent upon its interface to the data, address, and control buses. Similarly an *I/O port* requires that the same types of signals be applied before data can be sent or received. In the chapters that follow you will gain an appreciation for the issues with which one must deal in building, troubleshooting, and maintaining microcomputer interfaces.

An important point to keep in mind is that interfacing almost always involves a computer program as well as circuitry. Therefore, we speak of both hardware and software interfacing. The relationship between the two is extremely important because the design of one interacts with the other. A particular hardware interface may make it quite difficult to write a properly running program for the computer. A minor change in the equipment interfacing technique can often dramatically reduce the complexity of the programming task. You may hear people talking of the hardware-software tradeoffs in discussions of these relationships.

Memory interfacing is divided into dealing with read-only and read-write memories. *Read-only memories* (ROM) do not allow the stored values to be changed. For that reason, ROM interfacing is simplified because no write circuitry is needed. *Read-write memories,* also called *random-access memories* (RAM), on the other hand, must be able to change the cell contents as well as read out their values. To further complicate the problem, there are dynamic and static RAMs. Static memories will hold the contents in each cell constant as long as power is applied. Dynamic memories, however, must be repeatedly refreshed. Refreshing writes the information back into each location several times per second. A refresh mechanism must be built into the interface of dynamic memories. The new bubble and charge-coupled device memories have their own unique interface requirements too. Input/output is most simply accomplished by an I/O port. Another straightforward I/O interface technique is *memory mapping.* More sophisticated systems may demand that interrupts be supported. *Interrupts* are signals from an external device that inform the computer of an unscheduled event in a real-time system. Interrupt processing requires that the MPU handle this signal immediately, yet still keep track of what it was doing before the interrupt came along. Because the computer can only perform one operation at a time, the work in progress must be stopped and enough detail about it saved to allow the processor to respond to the interrupt. Then the temporarily stored information is retrieved and the original sequence resumed.

If the speed of transfer between memory and the peripheral equipment is especially critical, *direct-memory-access* input/output can be used. With this arrangement, the I/O device can read or write memory contents just like the processor. Implementing any of these methods of data exchange is facilitated by the availability of integrated circuits that supply much of the logic needed to control and respond to signals on the buses.

So far we have only considered *parallel I/O* but the data can be sent serially, one bit at a time, as well. The rules for a *serial I/O* channel are specified in a *protocol*. If the data stream is an unbroken one, *synchronous* protocols are applicable. In contrast, a data stream that starts or stops is suited for *asynchronous* communications. Again, the job of designing, building, and repairing these interfaces is made easier by integrated circuit receivers and transmitters.

One of the most used peripheral devices for microcomputer I/O is the *teletype*. A special interface for this equipment, called a 20-milliamp (mA) current loop, is frequently encountered in microcomputer systems. By rearranging the elements of the current loop, the communications path between teletype and computer can be made one-way or two-way.

With the wide interest in computer communications, establishing common ways of exchanging data or *communication standards* is important for reliability and cost savings. The EIA-RS-232C standard provides for a serial interface between the data handling equipment and the computer. Another widely used standard is the IEEE-488 bus, which is well suited for instrumentation networks.

The buses within the computer are becoming standardized as well. Possibly one of the best known is the S-100 bus, which has been the basis for many "personal" microcomputers. Manufacturers of microprocessors are also establishing standards within their product lines, and organizations like the Institute for Electrical and Electronics Engineers are furthering standardization efforts.

All of these interfaces are fine if the computer is tied to another digital device, but most equipment is analog. When we want to use a computer to control or sense analog equipment, converters come into play. We can change the digital values to analog voltages or currents with a digital-to-analog converter. The continuously varying inputs from sensors can be made understandable to the computer with analog-to-digital converters.

This brief overview can only touch on the effects which interfacing has on a microprocessor-based system. The remainder of this book will help you develop an appreciation of these circuits, which are being used in an ever growing number of applica-tions. The technician who is prepared to work on interfacing circuits will find that the demand for his or her services can only increase as more and more reliance is placed on microcomputer-controlled equipment.

DESIGN EXAMPLES

The frequent need for interfacing can perhaps best be demonstrated by selecting some applications for microprocessors and then sketching out a design approach for each. Many ordinary products using microprocessors will resemble the ones described, but some simplifying assumptions have been made in these designs. Therefore do not expect to find that the "real" equipment works exactly in the manner suggested.

First, let us choose a word processor to make use of our microprocessor. Figure 1-1 shows a system that allows the typist to enter text at a terminal keyboard. While the typist may think that the cathode-ray tube (CRT) is displaying the characters by direct interaction with the keyboard, in fact the microprocessor is responsible. As a key is pressed, the microprocessor receives a notification and must decode its meaning. (The computer does not know that the keys represent letters, numbers, and punctuation marks.) The computer program selects the symbol for CRT display which matches that key and orders the output circuitry to send the symbol to the screen. When received by the terminal electronics, these commands are interpreted as orders to move the electron beam so that the desired character appears on the screen.

Among other actions that the word processor must supply is storing the text as it is typed. Temporary storage is accomplished using the memory, while bulk storage requires use of floppy disks. (Here we are assuming that two floppy disk drives are to be used.) Certainly most important to the typist

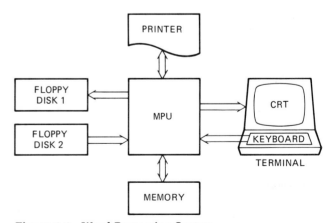

Figure 1-1. Word Processing System.

is the ability to have the text printed on paper. The printer does the hardcopy output.

How many interfaces can you identify in this design? One that is easy to overlook is a ROM interface. Without a program in memory the processor cannot do anything. As a minimum, a small program that can load other programs must be provided in ROM. Perhaps the entire program for our word processor is in read-only memory. If so, the typist does not need to reload the program before beginning to type. (Turning the machine off erases RAM contents.) Such a feature would be a good idea because operation is simplified.

Next we will look at a simple process controller. The problem, shown in Fig. 1-2, is to open a valve whenever the liquid level in a tank is above 10,000 gallons (gal) [2642 liters (L)] and close the valve when the level falls to 8000 gal (2114 L). Sensors in the tank monitor the two liquid levels. Through the isolation circuitry, the processor is informed when the output of either sensor changes. The processor can then order the valve actuator to open or close. What interfaces are present in the process control application that were not needed in our earlier example?

A slightly more demanding set of inputs is presented to the data acquisition system of Fig. 1-3. The inputs may be coming from a variety of sensors that are monitoring voltage, pressure, temperature, humidity, and many other parameters. Because the readings are arriving slowly (in comparison to computer speeds), they can all be channeled into a single analog multiplexer. Multiplexing is a means of reducing the amount of hardware by using it for several purposes. The program in a multiplexed system is more difficult to write, so we are not getting

something for nothing. The program must not only record the reading of the sensor, but must also figure out which sensor sent the information. The data is recorded on a cartridge magnetic tape unit for off-line analysis. The terminal is supplied so the operator can monitor what is happening and make changes in the frequency or types of measurements being recorded.

What if we have a system that is widely dispersed—perhaps there are miles between the individual stations that want to share their data? A distributed system, like the one in Fig. 1-4, can support communications between processors that are separated by large distances. Each processor has access to a serial communications channel; often telephone lines are used. Local control is exercised via the operator terminals. The processors can originate or respond to queries by any member of the network. Another advantage of distributed systems is that processors of many different types can be intermixed on the channel. Even large mainframe computers can communicate with microcomputers over the communications channel.

As a final example, let us consider an interactive graphics terminal that is controlled by a bit-sliced processor. Figure 1-5 is a block diagram of the system. Here two separate buses are used: a 32-bit graphics data bus that transfers the high-speed graphics information and a 16-bit bus for peripheral equipment communications.

In addition to the kinds of interfaces we have already seen, we note that there is an interface module to a host computer. For graphics applications, the host is usually a large computer with considerable capability. The program in the host computer writes instructions, called a display list,

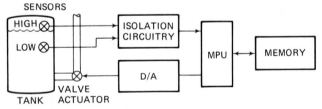

Figure 1-2. Process Controller.

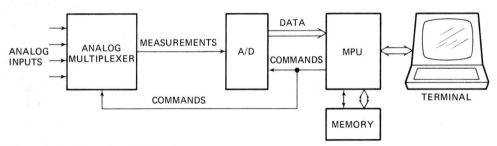

Figure 1-3. Data Acquisition System.

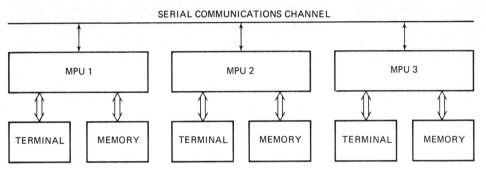

Figure 1-4. Distributed System.

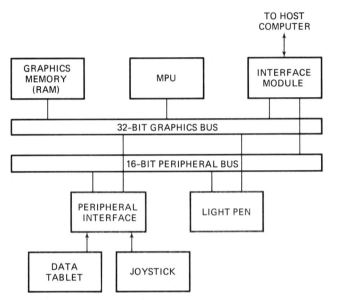

Figure 1-5. Interactive Graphics Processor
(Megatek Corp.).

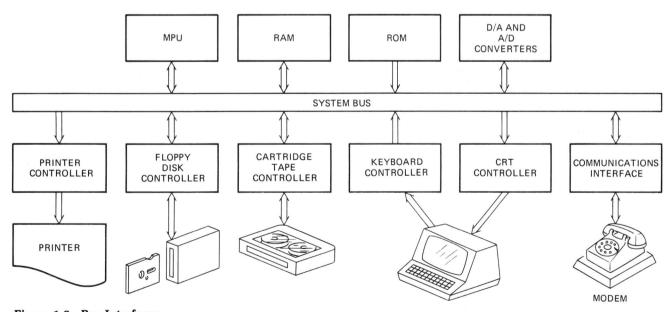

Figure 1-6. Bus Interfaces.

into the memory. The microprocessor then can read the memory contents to draw figures and refresh the display. As the drawing takes place, the host computer is free to proceed with other tasks. The figure stays on the screen until the host modifies some or all of the display list commands.

Figure 1-6 gives some idea of the many interfaces you may come across in your work on microcomputers. Of course, this is an extreme example. It is unlikely that any one microprocessor would need as many interfaces as shown, but the types of interfaces illustrated are the ones you will often be confronted with. In every case an interaction between the interface and bus occurs that will in some manner affect or be affected by the processor timing and operations. Because many of the interface operations are software-controlled, you must comprehend how the program can change the signal flow as well as understand what the hardware can do. Throughout the discussions to follow, an awareness of hardware and software requirements for interfacing will be emphasized.

CHAPTER REVIEW

1. To form a microcomputer, the microprocessor must be combined with memory, I/O circuits, interfaces, and a power supply.

2. Most microcomputers use three buses for internal communications. The data bus, address bus, and control bus provide the communications lines necessary to execute the computer program.

3. An interface is a shared boundary between two systems or units. The computer program is an important part of the hardware-software trade-offs in interfacing.

4. Different types of memories vary in their interface requirements. Read-only memories are the least demanding while dynamic RAMs have a need for read, write, and refresh circuitry. Static RAMs fall between these two in terms of the number of interfaces to be supported.

5. The simplest I/O techniques use ports or memory mapping. If the situation calls for faster responses, interrupts and direct memory access can be used.

6. Input and output can be serial or parallel. Synchronous or asynchronous I/O protocols are useful in serial data communications. The teletype loop is a specialized serial communications channel.

7. Standards for microcomputer data transmission have been established to simplify the job of interconnecting two pieces of equipment. Common interfaces considerably reduce the overall costs of the system.

KEY TERMS AND CONCEPTS

Microprocessor	Read-only memory (ROM)	Parallel I/O
Microcomputer	Read-write (or random-access) memory (RAM)	Serial I/O
Word size		Protocol
Byte	Memory mapping	Teletype loop
Buses	Interrupts	Communication standards
Interface	Direct memory access	Analog interfaces
I/O ports		

2

MICROPROCESSOR ARCHITECTURE

Understanding how any microcomputer interfaces with external devices requires a prior knowledge of the manner in which the processor performs its operations. The data paths and control sequences are entirely dependent upon the structure and instruction repertoire of the microprocessor. In this chapter we will consider how the microprocessor operates and how its data and control buses provide access to memory and I/O controllers.

Regardless of the particular model, all microprocessors must provide a certain set of communications capabilities. As an example of a typical microprocessor, the 8080A will be used to illustrate these concepts. Much of this material is directly applicable to the upward compatible 8085 and Z80 processors as well.

A review of the 8080A instructions is also provided in this chapter. These instructions will be used in examples, problems, and experiments to follow. As you will see, interfacing involves a combination of hardware and programs. In fact, we often have a choice whether the functions are to be implemented in hardware or in software. Therefore a thorough comprehension of the instruction set is an important prerequisite to your mastery of interfacing techniques.

CHAPTER OBJECTIVES

Upon completion of this chapter, you should be able to:

1. List the functions of the 8080A, 8224, and 8228 integrated circuits
2. Describe the programmable registers and stack of the 8080A
3. Discuss the functions of the arithmetic logic unit
4. Explain the control and timing of the 8080A by use of timing diagrams
5. Describe the interface between the 8080A and ROM or RAM and the method of address mapping
6. Define the purpose of bidirectional bus drivers in a microcomputer system
7. List the types of instructions used in the 8080A

ARCHITECTURAL CONCEPTS: 8080A ARCHITECTURE

In discussing the *architecture* of a computer, we refer to the structure of its internal components and the method of design used to route commands and data. Figure 2-1 shows the architecture of the 8080A. Immediately we can see that two types of lines interconnect the various components: Data paths are used to move the information being processed from one location to another, and the control lines supply the commands and timing signals needed to coordinate this movement.

Also apparent on the diagram are a number of registers. The register array and the accumulator are used to store data for most of the instructions. The arithmetic logic unit (ALU) is responsible for executing operations such as addition, subtraction, and Boolean combinations. Instructions are interpreted and timing sequences produced by the instruction decoder and microcode encoder logic.

The three buses used in communications outside the processor are indicated as well. The *data bus*

(D0 through D7) is the route for any values moving from memory or I/O devices to the processor. The *address bus* (A0 through A15) contains the value designating the specific memory location or I/O device to be used. Signaling between external devices and the MPU is accomplished by use of the *control bus.* Among other things, these signal lines permit the devices to request services from the processor and for the processor to provide acknowledgments when the requests are granted.

The 8080A provides all the processor features needed in a computer system, including arithmetic and logic, control and timing, and programmable registers. Three power-supply voltages are necessary to drive the chip: +5 volts (V), +12 V, and −5 V.

Data and Address Lines

Figure 2-2 is the pin assignment for the 8080A. As you can see, the 8080A is a 40-pin dual in-line (DIP) package. The purpose of each pin is described in Table 2-1. The address lines, A0 through A15, comprise the three-state address bus. Addresses set

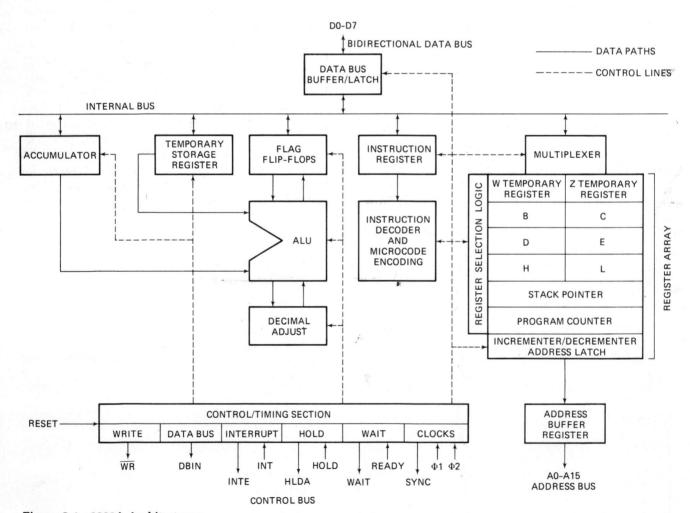

Figure 2-1. 8080A Architecture.

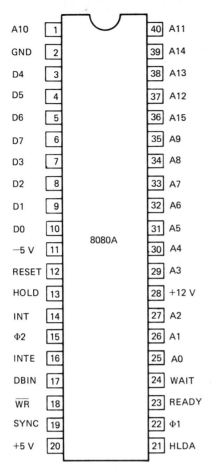

A10 [1]	[40] A11
GND [2]	[39] A14
D4 [3]	[38] A13
D5 [4]	[37] A12
D6 [5]	[36] A15
D7 [6]	[35] A9
D3 [7]	[34] A8
D2 [8]	[33] A7
D1 [9]	[32] A6
D0 [10]	[31] A5
−5 V [11]	[30] A4
RESET [12]	[29] A3
HOLD [13]	[28] +12 V
INT [14]	[27] A2
Φ2 [15]	[26] A1
INTE [16]	[25] A0
DBIN [17]	[24] WAIT
WR [18]	[23] READY
SYNC [19]	[22] Φ1
+5 V [20]	[21] HLDA

(center label: 8080A)

Figure 2-2. 8080A Integrated Circuit.

on these lines indicate the binary location in memory of data to be read or written. The address lines can also designate a particular I/O device to be used in data transfers external to the microcomputer. Consisting of three-state lines, the address lines can *float* (switch to the high impedance state) to allow

other users on the bus to exchange data without interfering with the MPU.

The bidirectional data lines form the data bus for the 8 bits of information being sent or received by the microprocessor. Input/output data to or from the processor is transferred by means of this bus also.

Timing Signals

Not every device can run as fast as the 8080A. When some peripheral cannot respond within the processor-dictated timing constraints, the peripheral can request that the MPU extend the interval. To request the delay, the peripheral sets the READY input low. (Refer to the control and timing section of Fig. 2-1.) This signal causes the 8080A to enter the wait state. The microprocessor signals this condition by setting the WAIT output high. While waiting, all MPU operations are suspended, but the address on the address bus remains stable. To return to normal operations, the peripheral pulls READY back to the high level.

The microprocessor can also be stopped between the completion of one instruction and the start of the next. Setting the HOLD input high produces this condition, which could be used for program debugging or computer maintenance. Another use for the hold state is to coordinate direct memory access (DMA). Upon receipt of the high HOLD signal, the processor floats both the data and address buses, allowing external logic to use the buses at will. The 8080A also sets HLDA high to acknowledge the input signal. This output signal is used by an external device to identify the beginning of the time that the buses are floating. When the HOLD signal is returned to the low state, the processor drops HLDA and continues its operation.

Table 2-1
8080A Signals

Signal name	Purpose	Type of data	Other characteristics
A0–A15	Address lines	Output	Three-state system bus
D0–D7	Data lines	Bidirectional	Three-state bus
DBIN	Data input strobe	Output	System bus
HOLD	Hold state request	Input	System bus
HLDA	Hold acknowledge	Output	System bus
INT	Interrupt request	Input	System bus
INTE	Interrupt acknowledge	Output	System bus
READY	Data input stable	Input	System bus
RESET	Reset MPU	Input	System bus
SYNC	Machine cycle Synchronizer	Output	
WAIT	MPU in wait state	Output	System bus
WR	Data output strobe	Output	System bus
Φ1, Φ2	Clock signals	Input	

If the RESET signal is held high for at least three clock periods, the microprocessor will zero all of its registers (except the status register, which remains unchanged). Because the program counter register has been zeroed, the computer will start by executing the program in cell 0000_{16} upon restart.

Data Bus Status

Two signals are provided to indicate the situation on the data bus. A high level for DBIN means that data from the addressed memory location or I/O device must immediately be placed on the data bus. This signal is a convenient input strobe for external logic. (Incidently, remember that input and output are always relative to the processor. An input command to a peripheral unit means that the device is to *send* data to the computer.)

The processor signals memory or other users that output data on the data bus is stable with the $\overline{WR}$ line. (The bar over the name of any signal means that the signal is true when it is low.) When $\overline{WR}$ is low, the receiving device should sample the data. This status line is usually used as the output, or write, strobe.

Interrupt Control

Two status lines are used to coordinate exchange of interrupt status: The INT line is set high by the external logic, and the processor uses INTE as a reply to indicate that the interrupt has been acknowledged.

Programmable Registers

There are ten *programmable registers* in the 8080A which are used by the programmer and controlled by use of processor instructions. See Fig. 2-3. The A register is the 8-bit primary accumulator. It is most commonly used in arithmetic, logic, and data transfer instructions. Certain aspects of arithmetic or logical results are indicated by *status flag* bits in the status register. The meaning of each bit in the status register is shown in Fig. 2-4.

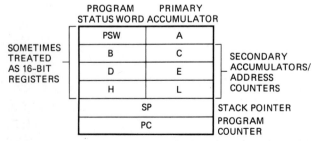

Figure 2-3. **Programmable Registers**

BIT NUMBER	7	6	5	4	3	2	1	0
	S	Z	–	A_C	–	P	–	C

Figure 2-4. **Flags.**

The flags reflect the outcome of the arithmetic and logical instructions. The sign flag is set if the A register holds a negative number; the flag is reset otherwise. If the value in the accumulator is 0, the zero flag is set. The parity flag is set to 1 if the parity of the accumulator is odd and to 0 if even. If the operation generated a carry from the most significant bit (MSB) position, the carry flag is set. The auxiliary carry operates the same as the carry indicator, but the A_C bit reflects carries out of bit position 3 into position 4 of the 8-bit result. This status flag is often used in binary coded decimal (BCD) operations. In some cases the A register is linked with the status register to form a 16-bit unit.

There are six general-purpose or *secondary accumulators:* B, C, D, E, H, and L. Each is an 8-bit register which can, in many cases, be used in the same manner as the A register. In addition these registers can be linked to be 16-bit address pointers or used for double-precision arithmetic. When used in this manner, they are referred to as the BC, DE, or HL *register pairs*. The HL register is used as the primary memory pointer.

The stack pointer (SP) is set to show the address for the top of the stack. The 8080A uses memory as the stack, so the programmer can have a stack 64K locations long if desired. Normally much shorter stack lengths are used. When the stack is popped, the contents of the memory cell on top of the stack, as addressed by the SP register, are obtained. New data is pushed on the stack also by using the address given in the stack pointer register.

The final register in the 8080A of interest to programmers is the program counter (PC). The program counter holds the address of the next instruction to be executed.

8080A Architecture Review

1. List the microprocessor functions performed by the 8080A.

2. Describe the purpose and type of signal applied to or sent by each pin of the 8080A.

3. Why are the data lines and address lines three-state buses? Why are only the data lines bidirectional?

4. How does the DBIN signal indicate to a peripheral device the proper time to send data to the processor? What signal does the processor use to indicate that output data is stable?

5. Describe the uses of the 10 programmable registers in the 8080A.

CONTROL

The control section of the 8080A executes instructions as timed by a sequence of *machine cycles* (MC), which are further subdivided into *clock periods* (T). An instruction may require from one to five machine cycles to complete its execution. Each of these machine cycles will be made up of three, four, or five periods (except MC1, which always is four or five periods in duration). Figure 2-5 summarizes the timing sequences. Specific instructions will be considered in this chapter to further illustrate how the processor timing is controlled by the machine cycles and clock periods.

Clock Phases

Two *clock phases*, Φ1 and Φ2, are used by the microprocessor to delineate the clock periods, T, of Fig. 2-5. These periods are derived from the two phases as shown in Fig. 2-6. The beginning of each period is indicated by the leading edge of Φ1.

A separate SYNC pulse is produced to identify T1 during every machine cycle. The SYNC signal rises on the leading edge of the first Φ2 pulse during each machine cycle and falls on the leading edge of the second Φ2 pulse. Arrows on the timing diagram show this cause and effect. As Φ2 goes

high the first time, it causes SYNC to switch to the high state. On the second Φ2 transition, SYNC returns to the original low level. While synchronizing clocking signals can be quite involved, they are easily generated using the 8224 clock-signal-generator integrated circuit.

Instruction Execution Timing

During any machine cycle, clock periods T1 through T3 are reserved from memory references. The use of these clock periods is illustrated in Fig. 2-7a. The remaining time periods in the machine cycle, T4 and T5, are available for MPU functions not involving memory or for use by external logic.

In addition, there is a special meaning of MC1 for any instruction: It is during this machine cycle that the instruction is fetched. As Fig. 2-7b shows, T1, T2, and T3 are used to obtain the instruction. This timing is a special case of memory referencing during the first three clock periods. It is in the T4 interval that the program counter will increment and the instruction be decoded. The remaining period T5 is optional; that is, for some instructions the MPU can use this time for other operations. Otherwise, T5 is cancelled.

IDENTIFYING OPERATIONS With all of the different tasks accomplished by the 8080A, how can external devices keep track of what is happening? Actually this seemingly complex problem is solved quite

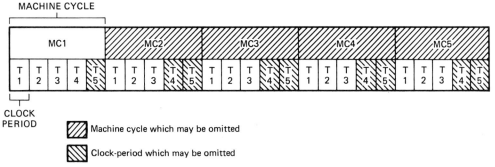

////// Machine cycle which may be omitted

\\\\\\ Clock-period which may be omitted

Figure 2-5. Machine Cycles.

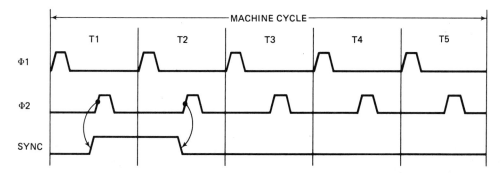

Figure 2-6. Clock Periods.

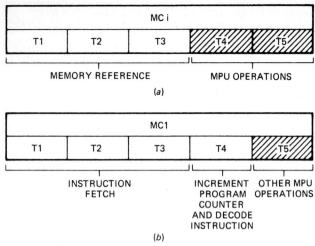

(a)

(b)

Note: Crosshatched clock periods may be omitted

Figure 2-7. Instruction Execution Timing (*a*) Other than MC1 (*b*) MC1.

simply. During T2 of every machine cycle, the processor signals the operation to be performed on the data bus. A code on the 8-bit data bus informs all devices of what is to take place.

A timing diagram of these signals is shown in Fig. 2-8*a*. The status signals are stable when both Φ1 and SYNC are high. From this fact the simple circuit, shown in Fig. 2-8*b*, can be constructed to trigger an external device to sample the data lines at the proper time. The "read status strobe" goes high only during the proper interval of T2.

The meaning of each bit in the status message is listed in Table 2-2. As you can see, each data bit (D0 through D7) is assigned a unique meaning in the status code. For example, if D1 is high, the instruction will use the data bus to transmit information to memory or an external device.

Each microinstruction sequence usually requires

more than one operation. Several status bits are set to provide a complete indication of the operations to be performed. As Table 2-3 shows, the code on the data lines uniquely identifies every microinstruction sequence. Consider the instruction fetch with its code of $A2_{16}$. Status bits 7, 5, and 1 are set. Referring back to Table 2-2, we see that these bits indicate memory reading, fetching the first byte of an instruction, and *not* writing. (Remember $\overline{WO}$ must be low to be true.) These three operations are those required for fetching an instruction.

To aid the hardware designer in the use of the status bits during T2, the 8228 system controller was developed. This integrated circuit (IC) automatically handles these status signals and converts them to command lines on the control bus.

INSTRUCTION FETCHING Let us analyze the instruction-fetching microprogram in more detail to gain a further understanding of the timing relationships in the MPU. The sequence of events is specified in Table 2-4. A timing diagram showing each period of MC1 is shown in Fig. 2-9. During T1, the clock phases and SYNC pulse indicate the start of a machine cycle. The WAIT line is low, allowing the processor to proceed without delay. Because this is a read operation, $\overline{WR}$ is held high.

At about the same time the processor sets the status code on the data lines for instruction fetching ($A2_{16}$ from Table 2-3). The memory address of the instruction is placed on the address lines. (The instruction address was obtained from the program counter.) In the next clock period the memory can anticipate an input operation by ANDing Φ1 with SYNC to generate a status read strobe. DBIN goes high, indicating that the data bus is ready to receive data; the processor floats the bus in preparation for the

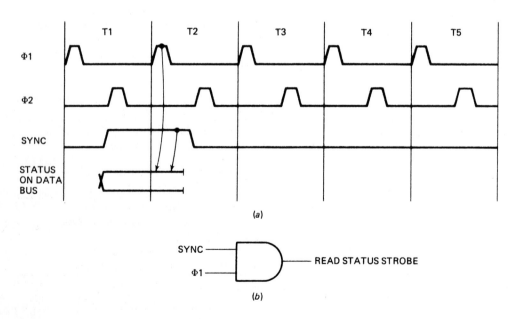

(a)

(b)

Figure 2-8. Status Signal Timing (*a*) Timing Diagram (*b*) Circuit.

Table 2-2
Status Bits Set During T2

Data bus bit	Status indication	Meaning
D0	INTA	Acknowledge signal for interrupt request.
D1	$\overline{WR}$	The data bus will be used for a write operation to either memory or an external device.
D2	STACK	The address bus now holds the stack pointer address.
D3	HLTA	Acknowledge signal for the HALT instruction.
D4	OUT	The address bus now indicates the output device that should accept data when $\overline{WO}$ is low.
D5	M1	MPU is in the fetch cycle of the first byte of an instruction.
D6	INP	The address bus now indicates the input device that should place data on the bus when DBIN goes high.
D7	MEMR	The data bus will be used for reading from memory.

data transfer. At the beginning of T3, memory data must be stable on the lines, so the processor can move the instruction into the instruction register. The data bus is floated by the memory after Φ2 of the third period to make it available to other users. It is in T4 that the processor counts up the program counter and also floats the address bus. T5 is an optional period in the machine cycle that may or may not be used, depending on the instruction.

READING MEMORY DATA The microprogram for reading memory uses practically the same procedures as the instruction-fetching sequence. There are only two changes. First, some machine cycle other than M1 would be used. Second, the status

Table 2-3
Status Codes for the Microinstructions

Type of microinstruction	Address bus status code (hexadecimal)
Instruction fetch	A2
Memory read	82
Memory write	00
Stack read	86
Stack write	04
Input read	42
Output write	10
Interrupt acknowledge	23
Halt acknowledge	8A or 0A
Interrupt acknowledge while halted	2B or 23

code set on the data lines during T1 would be 82_{16} because the M1 status bit (D5) is 0. Of course, every memory read operation adds one machine cycle to the instruction execution time.

Table 2-4
Single-Byte Instruction Fetching

T1: 1. Leading edge of Φ2 causes SYNC to rise, marking the period of T1.
2. WAIT is low, so the MPU is not in the wait state.
3. $\overline{WR}$ is high. Data is to be read (not written) from memory.
4. Data bits are set with the status code. $\overline{WO}$ (D1) high. The MPU is expecting an input. M1 (D5) high. The instruction is in the fetch cycle. MEMR (D7) high. Input from memory.
5. The appropriate memory address is set on the address lines, A0–A15.

T2: 1. Memory uses Φ1 ANDed with SYNC to read status from the data bus.
2. DBIN high causes the data bus to be ready to receive input. (The signal stays high until the rising edge of Φ2 during T3.)

T3: 1. MPU stores the instruction in the instruction register where the control section will interpret it.
2. The data lines are floated during T3, making it available to external logic.

T4: 1. The data bus is floated during T4.
2. The program counter is incremented.

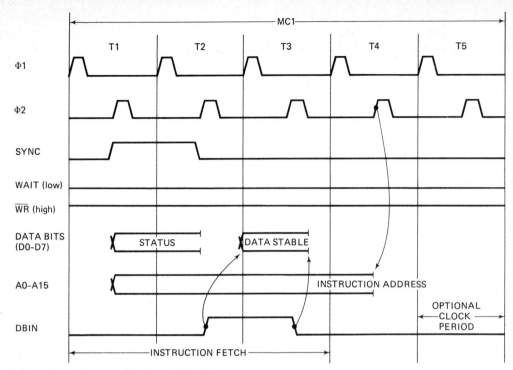

Figure 2-9. Instruction Fetch Timing.

WRITING MEMORY DATA The operations for sending a byte of data from the processor to memory have many similarities to those required for reading. The sequence is listed in Table 2-5 and a timing diagram provided in Fig. 2-10. The first difference occurs during step 4 of T1. The status code on the data lines is all 0s. With $\overline{WO}$ low, we know that this will be a write operation. During T2 the processor sets the data to be placed in memory on the data lines. (The memory already has the address available

on the address bus.) When $\overline{WR}$ goes low during T3, the memory accepts the data.

The Wait State

When an external device (a slow memory, for example) wants the MPU to provide more time for an input data transfer, the device signals its request by setting the READY signal low. As Fig. 2-11 shows, the *wait state* occurs between T2 and T3. If the READY signal remains low at $\Phi2$ of T2, the MPU enters the wait mode. Here the processor can be held for any number of clock periods until the peripheral device raises the READY line. The MPU indicates that no operations are being performed by setting the WAIT signal high; however, all output signals such as data and address lines remain unchanged. When the device finally sets READY high, the processor detects the condition on the first $\Phi2$ pulse after READY is high. The MPU then continues execution of the instruction at T3.

The Hold State

Be careful to distinguish the wait state from the *hold state*. During the wait state, the processor is held up in the middle of executing an instruction, but in the hold state the MPU is *between* instructions.

Another important difference is that during the hold state the system buses are floated, so that

Table 2-5
Writing Data in Memory

T1:	1. Leading edge of $\Phi2$ causes SYNC to rise, marking the period as T1.
	2. WAIT is low, so the MPU is not in the wait state.
	3. $\overline{WR}$ is high until the time to write.
	4. All data bits are zero.
	5. The appropriate memory address is set on the address lines, A0–A15.
T2:	1. Memory uses $\Phi2$ ANDed with SYNC to read status from the data bus.
	2. DBIN remains low.
T3:	1. $\overline{WR}$ goes low.
	2. The data is transferred from memory to the data bus and then to the processor.
T4:	1. The data and address buses are floated during T4.
	2. The program counter is incremented.

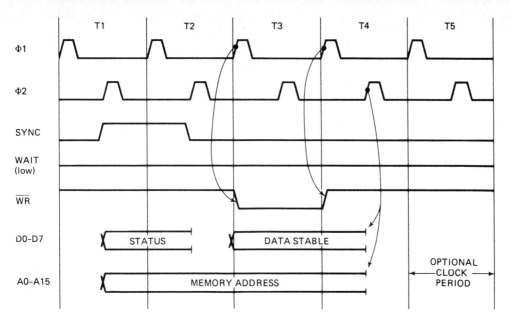

Figure 2-10. Memory Write Timing.

external logic can use them. (Output signals other than data and addresses are held constant.) Any number of clock periods may elapse between the machine cycles from the end of one instruction and the beginning of the next. Figure 2-12*b* shows the hold state situation, which should be compared with the wait state of Fig. 2-11.

The hold state basically allows the external logic to stop the MPU. The hold sequence is listed in Table 2-6. If the HOLD signal is detected high during T1, the microprocessor responds by setting the acknowledge, HLDA, high. If the current instruction was to read memory ($\overline{\text{WO}}$ high during T2), then HLDA goes high at the leading edge of Φ1 during T3. Had the current instruction been a write operation ($\overline{\text{WO}}$ is low during T2), the HLDA is set high on the leading edge of Φ1 of T4. Timing diagrams of these two situations are shown in Fig. 2-13*a* and *b*. When the external device drops HOLD, it is sensed on the leading edge of either clock phase by the processor, which terminates the hold state. The hold

state always ends at Φ1 of the next machine cycle, that is, during the next available T1 cycle. At that time the 8080A resets HLDA.

The Halt State

The programmer can cause the 8080A to stop by executing a halt instruction. The processor stops all operations and pauses with nothing to do until it is restarted. None of the system buses are floated in this *halt state.* Almost every program written for the microprocessor will contain at least one halt instruction. When the 8080A stops, the programmer knows the program has been completed.

The RESET Signal

The RESET signal is frequently used to restart the processor after a halt. When RESET goes high, the processor clears registers, as was previously ex-

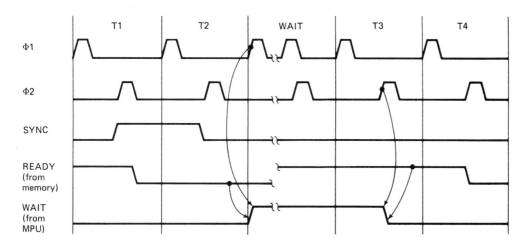

Figure 2-11. Wait State.

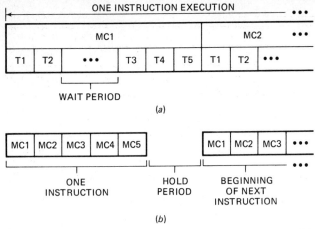

ONE INSTRUCTION EXECUTION

(a)

(b)

Figure 2-12. Wait and Hold States (*a*) Wait State (*b*) Hold State.

4. How does the processor use the data bus during T2 to tell other devices what the operation is to be?

5. Describe the use of the status bits in specifying the operations which comprise the microinstruction.

6. List the sequence of signals during MC1 to fetch an instruction. How does fetching data from memory differ?

7. Discuss the differences between control signals used to write and to read memory data.

8. How does an external device request more time for a reply? What signal does the 8080A use to acknowledge that the request is granted?

9. Contrast the hold state with the halt state.

10. Why does the processor execute the instruction in memory location 0000_{16} after the RESET line goes low?

plained. As long as RESET is high, the 8080A is in a suspended state; no operations are performed. When RESET falls, instruction execution begins with T1 at the next $\Phi1$ pulse. Because the program counter is 0, the instruction in memory location 0000_{16} is selected. When the 8080A is initially powered up, it must be reset. Otherwise all of the registers, including the program counter, will contain random data. Program execution would then erroneously start at some meaningless memory address.

Control Review

1. Distinguish between machine cycles, clock periods, and clock phases.

2. What is the purpose of T1 through T3 in any machine cycle? What is T4 used for during MC1?

3. In which clock period is an instruction fetched? When is it decoded so the processor knows the action to complete?

Table 2-6
Hold Sequence

1. The hold state is initiated by the HOLD input signal.
2. The MPU responds with HLDA high.
   a. If the hold was requested during a read operation, then HLDA is set high at the leading edge of $\Phi1$ of T3.
   b. If the hold was requested during a write operation, the HLDA is set high at the leading edge of $\Phi1$ of T4.
3. HOLD low is sensed at the leading edge of $\Phi1$ or $\Phi2$. The hold state is terminated at the starting of $\Phi1$ of the next machine cycle.
4. HLDA is reset by the processor.

THE 8224 CLOCK GENERATOR

The 8224 provides the 8080A with its $\Phi1$ and $\Phi2$ clock phases. This IC also creates READY and RESET inputs properly synchronized with $\Phi2$, as required by the MPU. The pin arrangement of the 8224 is shown in Fig. 2-14 and the signals described in Table 2-7.

The XTAL and TANK inputs are associated with the crystal that must be used to generate the clock phases. The 8224 produces the nonoverlapping $\Phi1$ and $\Phi2$ pulses which swing between +11 and +0.3 V. Because these voltages are not transistor-transistor logic (TTL) compatible, separate TTL level outputs of $\Phi2$ (TTL) and OSC are provided.

Timing Signals

The clock frequency of the 8224, and therefore the 8080A, depends on a crystal oscillator. The crystal frequency must be exactly nine times the required clock period. The standard clock period (and the one used in this book) for the 8080A is 500 nanoseconds (ns), which means that the crystal frequency should be 18 megahertz (MHz). Each clock period is divided into nine segments. Each segment is then equal to one crystal oscillation period. If a supporting LC network is used with an overtone mode crystal, the TANK input to the 8224 is used.

Control Signals

There are two sets of corresponding control signals handled by the 8224. The external-logic-supplied

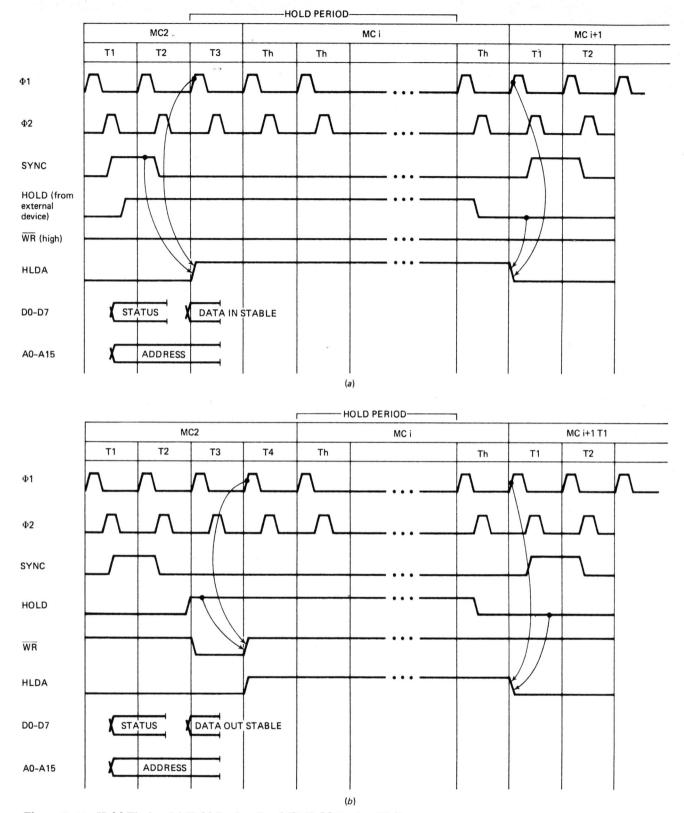

Figure 2-13. Hold Timing (a) Hold During Read (b) Hold During Write.

$\overline{\text{RESIN}}$ is converted to a synchronized RESET to be sent to the 8080A. Similarly, RDYIN from another device is translated to READY by the 8224. In addition, the 8224 sends a signal to the 8228.

RESET It would be difficult for external logic to synchronize the RESET signal input with $\Phi 2$, so the 8224 provides that service for the system. Furthermore, it converts a slowly varying input of $\overline{\text{RESIN}}$

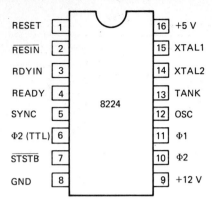

Figure 2-14. 8224 IC.

to a sharply rising RESET output by use of an internal Schmitt trigger. The output goes to the high level in synchronism with Φ2 when $\overline{\text{RESIN}}$ falls below a threshold value.

READY The 8224 will accept an asynchronous RDYIN signal also. RDYIN can arrive at any time in the interval between successive Φ2 pulses. The 8224 will generate a READY signal to coincide with the leading edge of the next Φ2 pulse.

STSTB A status strobe signal is sent from the 8224 to the 8228 system controller. This signal is produced as a result of the SYNC input from the 8080A. As long as the three ICs are being used to form the microcomputer, this signal is of little interest to the user.

8224 Review

1. Describe the purpose of each pin on the 8224.

2. How does the 8224 convert the external oscillator frequency to Φ1 and Φ2 clock pulses?

3. What is the purpose of the Schmitt trigger in the 8224?

4. Explain the conversion of RDYIN to a signal in synchronization with the leading edge of a Φ2 pulse.

THE 8228 SYSTEM CONTROLLER AND BUS DRIVER

The 8228 provides most of the bus signals in an 8080A based microcomputer. The 8228 is a bidirectional bus driver combined with signal generation logic. The pin configuration of this IC is shown in Fig. 2-15. Many of the signals are those provided by the 8080A or the 8224, which have already been described. The signals are summarized in Table 2-8. As we will see, the 8228 was developed to overcome the pin count limitation on the 8080A. To minimize the number of pins, control and data signals are multiplexed on the 8080A data bus. The 8228 basically acts as a demultiplexer for the signals.

Data Signals

The 8228 provides a bidirectional buffer for data moving between the 8080A and the system data bus. The 8080A internal microprocessor bus signals are designated D0 to D7. These bidirectional signals are passed through the bus driver to become the data on the system bus used by external logic. The corresponding system data bus lines are labeled DB0 through DB7.

Control Signals

The 8228 combines three 8080A control signals ($\overline{\text{WR}}$, DBIN, and HLDA) with status codes on the microprocessor data lines during T2 to generate the system control bus signals.

These signals are generated by combinatorial logic, as shown in Table 2-9. Note that all system bus signals use negative logic; that is, $\overline{\text{MEMR}}$, $\overline{\text{MEMW}}$,

Table 2-7
8224 Signals

Name	Purpose	Type
OSC	Crystal oscillator waveform	Output
RDYIN	Ready signal	Input
READY	Control signal to 8080A	Output
RESET	Control signal to 8080A	Output
$\overline{\text{RESIN}}$	Reset signal	Input
$\overline{\text{STSTB}}$	Sync signal	Output
SYNC	Control signal	Input
XTAL1, XTAL2, TANK	External crystal connections	Input
Φ1, Φ2	Clock signals	Output
Φ2 (TTL)	TTL-compatible clock	Output

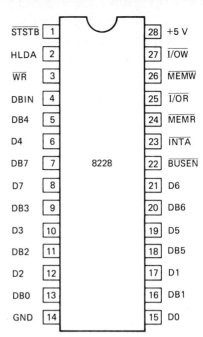

STSTB	1	28	+5 V
HLDA	2	27	$\overline{\text{I/OW}}$
$\overline{\text{WR}}$	3	26	$\overline{\text{MEMW}}$
DBIN	4	25	$\overline{\text{I/OR}}$
DB4	5	24	$\overline{\text{MEMR}}$
D4	6	23	$\overline{\text{INTA}}$
DB7	7	22	$\overline{\text{BUSEN}}$
D7	8	21	D6
DB3	9	20	DB6
D3	10	19	D5
DB2	11	18	DB5
D2	12	17	D1
DB0	13	16	DB1
GND	14	15	D0

Figure 2-15. 8228 IC.

$\overline{\text{I/OR}}$, $\overline{\text{I/OW}}$, and $\overline{\text{INTA}}$ are all true when low. The 8228 produces $\overline{\text{MEMR}}$ by ANDing MEMR (which is bit D7 on the data bus during T2) with DBIN from the 8080A. Other system bus signals are also derived from 8080A signals.

An example of the 8228 signals used for fetching an instruction from memory followed by writing into memory is shown in the timing diagram of Fig. 2-16. The signal to read, $\overline{\text{MEMR}}$, results from the MEMR bit being set in the status code during T1 and MC1 and DBIN going high during T2. (The 8228 must latch the status codes, so they will be available during T2.) The $\overline{\text{MEMR}}$ signal is synchronized with the input $\overline{\text{STSTB}}$ (from the 8224). The true state of $\overline{\text{MEMR}}$ is a read strobe for memory that places the data on the system data bus lines which the 8228 relays to the processor on the internal

Table 2-9
System Control Bus Signals

Inputs	System control bus output
MEMR (D7) AND DBIN	$\overline{\text{MEMR}}$
OUT (D4) AND WR	$\overline{\text{MEMW}}$
INP (D6) AND DBIN	$\overline{\text{I/OR}}$
OUT (D4) AND $\overline{\text{WR}}$	$\overline{\text{I/OW}}$
INTA (D0)	$\overline{\text{INTA}}$

data bus during T2 and T3 until $\overline{\text{MEMR}}$ goes high again. The writing of memory takes place in MC2. Then $\overline{\text{WR}}$ causes $\overline{\text{MEMW}}$ to become true (low) and memory accepts the data at the location specified by the address bus.

A system diagram for a complete microprocessor comprised of three ICs is shown in Fig. 2-17. The address bus, internal and system data buses, and system control bus are shown in the diagram. Three power-supply voltages are used by the 8080A, while the 8228 shares two of them, and the 8228 requires only +5 V. A common ground is also necessary for the three ICs.

8228 Review

1. Distinguish between the D0 to D7 and DB0 and DB7 pins on the 8228.

2. Explain why the 8228 must demultiplex signals sent on the internal microprocessor data bus.

3. What combination of signals causes $\overline{\text{MEMW}}$ to become true?

4. Describe the use of $\overline{\text{STSTB}}$ in causing $\overline{\text{MEMR}}$ to become true.

Table 2-8
8228 Signals

Name	Purpose	Type
$\overline{\text{BUSEN}}$	Data bus float/enable control	Input
DBIN	Data input strobe	Input
D0–D7	Microprocessor data bus	Bidirectional
DB0–DB7	System data bus	Bidirectional
HLDA	Hold acknowledge	Input
$\overline{\text{I/OR}}$	I/O read control	Output
$\overline{\text{I/OW}}$	I/O write control	Output
$\overline{\text{INTA}}$	Interrupt acknowledge	Output
$\overline{\text{MEMR}}$	Memory read control	Output
$\overline{\text{MEMW}}$	Memory write control	Output
$\overline{\text{STSTB}}$	Status strobe	Input
$\overline{\text{WR}}$	Data output strobe	Input

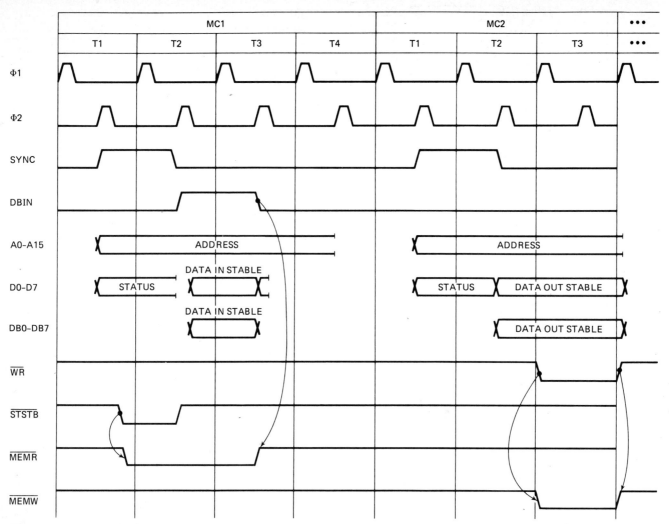

Figure 2-16. 8228 Timing.

MEMORY

There are so many memory locations available for use with the 8080A that it may be difficult to grasp the overall *memory organization*. A *memory map*, as shown in Fig. 2-18, is an effective way of picturing the memory space in the computer. The 64K memory is shown in 1K *memory blocks.* (The notation "1K" represents 1024 memory locations.) There is no requirement to equip the microcomputer with the entire 64K cells, so some of the blocks may be missing for a particular implementation. Eight blocks form a *memory bank.*

Furthermore, the memory in each block may be either ROM or RAM. For example, the RAM in Fig. 2-19 could be used in a block. The capacity of each memory IC will be the deciding factor in how many integrated circuits are required in the total memory. For example, if 256 × 8 ROMs are used, four ROM

ICs comprise one block. On the other hand, it would take eight 1K × 1 RAMS to form a block, because there are 8 bits in each word.

The address in memory does not depend on the type of memory used. Any address can be used for either ROM or RAM. In addition, it makes no difference if the ROM is mask-programmed by the manufacturer or if it is a programmable fusible link ROM (PROM) or ultraviolet erasable ROM (EPROM).

The address bits designate the bank and memory block, as indicated in Fig. 2-18. The selection of the correct block is a result of *address decoding.* For instance, let the address be $06BC_{16}$. Converting the hexadecimal address to binary, we see that bits A15, A14, and A13 are all 0s, causing bank 0 to be selected. The column of the block on the map depends on bits A12, A11, and A10, which are 001_2 in this case. The intersection of the bank 0 row with the 001_2 column is block 1, which contains

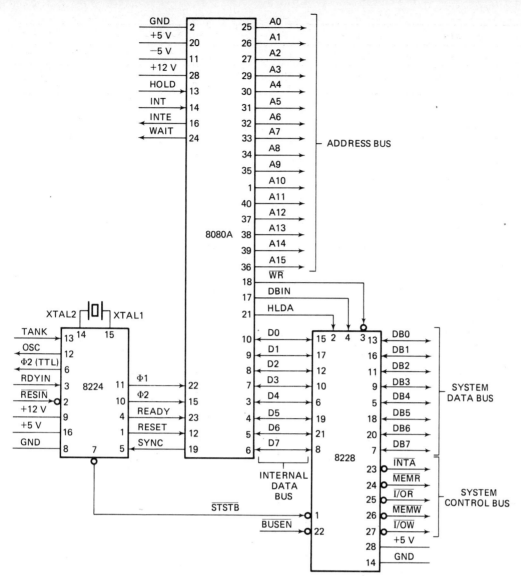

Figure 2-17. Microcomputer System.

addresses in the range of 0400_{16} to $07FF_{16}$. The remaining address bits A0 to A9 select the specific cell within the memory block.

A decoding circuit that uses the 8205 1-of-8 decoder is shown in Fig. 2-20. The 8205 has 3 address input pins (A0, A1, and A2) and 3 enabling pins (E1, E2, and E3). There are eight outputs, only one of which can be low at any time. When E3 is high and the other enable inputs low, the level of the output line corresponding to the binary value on the address lines is low and all others high. For example, when A2 to A0 levels are low, high, and low, respectively, (010_2) output line 2 is driven to its low state; all other outputs stay high.

Returning to Fig. 2-20, we see that the enable lines can be used to extend the address range of the 8205. Address bit 15 is ANDed with $\overline{MEMR}$ to

synchronize the addressing of memory with the true state of the latter signal. (The inverters on the AND gate inputs produce an output of the correct level to enable E3 when both inputs are low.) Bits A14 to A10 are properly connected to select the eight blocks of memory bank 0. (The entire 64K memory will require eight 8205 decoders in all.) When all inputs to the 8205 are low, pin 15 (output 0) goes low, making chip select $\overline{(CS)}$ true for block 0. The remaining bits on the address bus, A0 to A9, are applied to the 10 address pins on the ROM to read one of its 1024 memory cells. The data is available on the ROM output lines D0 to D7, which place the data on the system data bus.

Sequencing and timing signals used to read the ROM are shown in Fig. 2-21. The microprocessor ensures that the address is stable on the address

		ADDRESS BITS A12, A11, AND A10							
		000	001	010	011	100	101	110	111
ADDRESS BITS A15, A14, AND A13	000 BANK0	BLOCK0 0000– 03FF	BLOCK1 0400– 07FF	BLOCK2 0800– 0BFF	BLOCK3 0C00– 0FFF	BLOCK4 1000– 13FF	BLOCK5 1400– 17FF	BLOCK6 1800– 1BFF	BLOCK7 1C00– 1FFF
	001 BANK1	BLOCK8 2000– 23FF	BLOCK9 2400– 27FF	BLOCK10 2800– 28FF	BLOCK11 2C00– 2FFF	BLOCK12 3000– 33FF	BLOCK13 3400– 37FF	BLOCK14 3800– 3BFF	BLOCK15 3C00– 3FFF
	010 BANK2	BLOCK16 4000– 43FF	BLOCK17 4400– 47FF	BLOCK18 4800– 4BFF	BLOCK19 4C00 4FFF	BLOCK20 5000– 53FF	BLOCK21 5400– 57FF	BLOCK22 5800– 5BFF	BLOCK23 5C00– 5FFF
	011 BANK3	BLOCK24 6000– 63FF	BLOCK25 6400– 67FF	BLOCK26 6800– 6BFF	BLOCK27 6C00– 6FFF	BLOCK28 7000 73FF	BLOCK29 7400– 77FF	BLOCK30 7800– 7BFF	BLOCK31 7C00– 7FFF
	100 BANK4	BLOCK32 8000– 83FF	BLOCK33 8400– 87FF	BLOCK34 8800– 8BFF	BLOCK35 8C00– 8FFF	BLOCK36 9000– 93FF	BLOCK37 9400– 97FF	BLOCK38 9800– 9BFF	BLOCK39 9C00– 9FFF
	101 BANK5	BLOCK40 A000– A3FF	BLOCK41 A400– A7FF	BLOCK42 A800– ABFF	BLOCK43 AC00– AFFF	BLOCK44 B000– B3FF	BLOCK45 B400– B7FF	BLOCK46 B800– BBFF	BLOCK47 BC00– BFFF
	110 BANK6	BLOCK48 C000– C3FF	BLOCK49 C400– C7FF	BLOCK50 C800– CBFF	BLOCK51 CC00– CFFF	BLOCK52 D000– D3FF	BLOCK53 D400– D7FF	BLOCK54 D800– DBFF	BLOCK55 DC00– DFFF
	111 BANK7	BLOCK56 E000– E3FF	BLOCK57 E400– E7FF	BLOCK58 E800– EBFF	BLOCK59 EC00– EFFF	BLOCK60 F000– F3FF	BLOCK61 F300– F7FF	BLOCK62 F800– FBFF	BLOCK63 FC00– FFFF

Figure 2-18. Memory Map.

Figure 2-19. RAM Die. (*Intel Corporation*)

bus at the same time $\overline{\text{MEMR}}$ is set low. The 8205 decodes the upper six bits of the address, which causes $\overline{\text{CS}}$ to go low for one memory block. Data is unstable on the output lines during ROM access time, but eventually the information levels stabilize and the data can be read.

Accessing RAM is accomplished in much the same manner as ROM, except another control line must be provided to store data. Figure 2-22 shows another example of an address decoding circuit using 1K × 1 RAM. Of course the 8205 could also have been used with RAMs. Here the upper six bits for each block are decoded by a NAND gate for addresses in the range FC00_{16} to FFFF_{16}. In all, 64 gates would be needed for a full 64K memory. Appropriate inverters on the NAND perform the decoding function (0 bits in the address must be inverted). For example, if bits A15 to A10 for the address block to be selected were 110 101_2, address lines A13 and A11 would have to be inverted on the NAND inputs. Then the output of the gate $\overline{(\text{CS})}$ would be low only when the input was 110 101_2, and the proper memory block would be selected.

Each RAM in Fig. 2-22 provides 1 bit of the output data, so all eight must be enabled by the same low $\overline{\text{CS}}$ signal. The RAM knows whether to read or write data from the settings of $\overline{\text{MEMW}}$ and $\overline{\text{MEMR}}$.

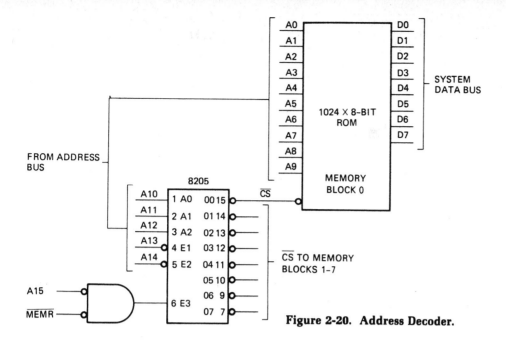

Figure 2-20. Address Decoder.

BIDIRECTIONAL BUS DRIVERS

Most microprocessor ICs can drive only limited loads, so *bidirectional bus drivers* are used to guarantee sufficient capacity. A three-state bus driver, such as the 8215 of Fig. 2-23, consists of two separate buffers; each is used to transmit data in its respective direction. The output of one buffer is tied to the input of the other, thus forming a system bus. For an 8-bit bus, two 8215 ICs would be used.

There are two control inputs to the driver. Chip selection is controlled by $\overline{CS}$ in the same way that we saw being used with memories. The direction of flow is determined by $\overline{DIEN}$. When this signal is low, data flows from the inputs (DI0 to DI3) to the system bus interface (DB0 to DB3). When $\overline{DIEN}$ is high, data flow is in the opposite direction (from DB0 through DB3 to DO0 through DO3).

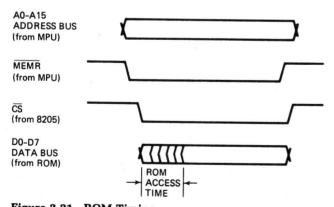

Figure 2-21. ROM Timing.

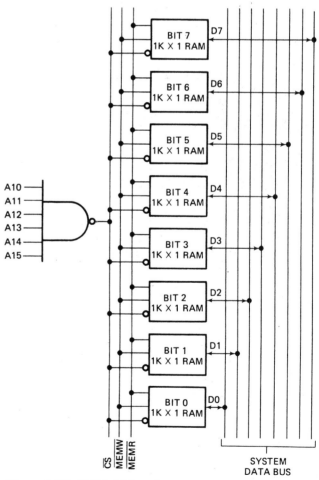

Figure 2-22. RAM Addressing.

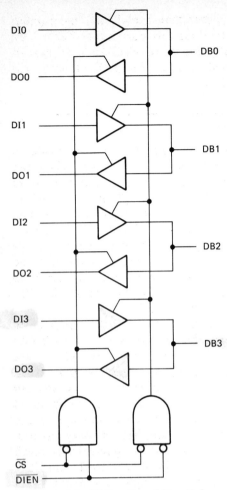

Figure 2-23. Bidirectional Bus Driver.

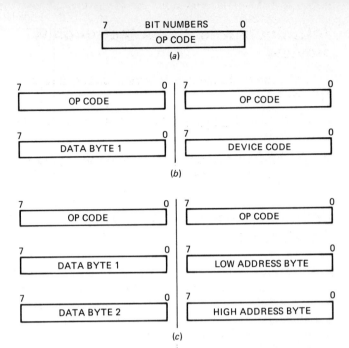

Figure 2-24. Instruction Formats (a) Single-Byte Instructions (b) Two-Byte Instructions (c) Three-Byte Instructions.

INTRODUCTION TO 8080A INSTRUCTIONS

Now that you have some background on the 8080A hardware, let us look at the instruction repertoire. Instructions for the 8080A can be categorized as data transfer, arithmetic, logical, branching, I/O, and miscellaneous. Data transfer operations move data between registers and memory locations. Arithmetic instructions involve addition or subtraction. Boolean functions such as AND and OR result from the logical instructions. Decision making in the program is supported by branching instructions.

All data is sent or received by means of input and output instructions. The remaining instructions are used for stack operations and control, such as halting the processor.

Instructions can also be categorized by *instruction format*. One, two, or three memory words may be used for an instruction, as Fig. 2-24 shows. Single-byte instructions consist only of the *operation code*. (op code.) The operation code is an 8-bit number that tells the processor what to do, such as transfer data, halt, input data, or perform addition. Every instruction, regardless of length, has the op code in its first byte.

The second word of a 2-byte instruction is used for either data or a device code. If the second byte is data, it is used as the *operand* of the instruction. For example, the data can be used for coded data as well as numbers, if the programmer desires. The data could represent two BCD digits or an American Standard Code for Information Interchange (ASCII) code for an alphanumeric character. In their coded form the processor can operate on decimal numbers or text, as well as on binary digits. The device code is only used for I/O instructions. The code specifies the input or output equipment to be used in the operation. The 8 bits of the device code provide the capability for addressing $256\ (2^8 = 256)$ different input devices and the same number of output devices.

There are also two formats for the 3-byte instructions. One format provides for 2 data bytes. This type of instruction allows the processor to work on data as 16-bit words. The other use of words 2 and 3 of the 3-byte instruction is to indicate the memory address of the operand. Word 2 is called the *low address byte*—the least significant 8 bits (bits A0 to A7) of the address. The *high address byte*, of course, provides the most significant 8 bits of the address (bits A8 to A15).

Introduction to 8080A Instructions

Review

1. List the six functional groups of 8080A instructions.

2. Describe the instruction formats used in the 8080A.

3. How is the 8-bit instruction word used to represent a 16-bit address?

MEMORY, REGISTER, AND I/O DEVICE NOTATION

All instructions and data are stored in the memory of the microcomputer. The program informs the processor of which cells contain instructions and which hold the information to be manipulated. Remember that the contents of every memory location simply represents an 8-bit number to the processor. The number $2A_{16}$ could mean to execute a particular operation; on the other hand, it could be just a hexadecimal quantity or the ASCII code for an asterisk. The processor treats that number precisely as the program dictates.

Working Registers

In regard to *register notation,* recall that there are seven working registers in the 8080A MPU. Each register is 1 byte in length. The registers were referred to as the A (accumulator), B, C, D, E, H, and L registers. When these registers are used in carrying out some processor action, the MPU must be told which register to use. The registers are assigned numbers, as listed in Table 2-10, which inform the processor that a particular register is involved in the instruction. For example, an instruction which is to move data to the accumulator provides the number 7 to specify the destination for the data. As you know, an operation may alternatively involve

Table 2-10
Working Registers and Memory Designation

Register	Numerical designation
B	0
C	1
D	2
E	3
H	4
L	5
M (memory)	6
A	7

a memory cell rather than a register. The number 6 has been reserved for this purpose, as Table 2-10 shows. (The particular memory cell to be addressed must be indicated as well. The method used will be described below.)

Register Pairs

Recall that some 8-bit registers could be linked to form a longer 16-bit capacity register. When the registers are linked, there are three ways to refer to them. Table 2-11 lists these options. The double-length BC register has its least significant 8 bits in the C register and most significant in the B register. The register pair is also referenced by a number or by the most significant register alone in some cases, that is, the "B register" pair. As the table indicates, the DE pair is also known as the "D" or "1" pair and HL as the "H" or "2."

The last row in the table requires a little more explanation. When the program status word (PSW) is linked to the accumulator, the two registers are designated as the "number 3" register pair in an instruction. The stack pointer is also sometimes given the same designator. Could the assignment of the same number to both cause confusion in the processor? The answer is no, because only instructions dealing with stack addressing refer to the stack pointer. Other instructions will only involve the PSW and the A register. (Even though the processor will not be confused by the assignment of the same designator to two register pairs, people may be. In the explanations to follow, carefully note which pair is specified in the descriptions for each instruction.)

Memory Designation

The entire memory address range of 65,536 (0000_{16} to $FFFF_{16}$) can be reached by the instructions. A common memory addressing error that can occur is referencing a nonexistent location. If the computer is not supplied with a full 64K memory, some locations are illegal. If the memory is actually only 32K in length (0000_{16} to $7FFF_{16}$), attempting to read location 8000_{16} or above would be wrong. The

Table 2-11
Register Pair Designation

Register Pair	Single-letter designation	Numerical designation
BC	B	0
DE	D	1
HL	H	2
PSW/A or SP	...	3

processor does not give any indication of this mistake, so it is the responsibility of the programmer to prevent it.

Memory Addressing Procedures

There are three ways of providing the processor with the 16-bit address of a memory cell. The memory address may be specified by 2 bytes of an instruction, the contents of a register pair, or the stack pointer.

ADDRESS SPECIFICATION BY INSTRUCTION

Many instructions supply the address explicitly and require 3 bytes to indicate the operation code as well as the data address. An instruction using the 3-byte format specifies the address in this manner. The operation code can be placed in any memory cell, say, memory cell 2020_{16}. The least significant address byte must be located at location 2021_{16}. The upper byte of the address then occupies cell 2022_{16}. (This somewhat cumbersome address designation is a carryover from the 8008 design. The designers were trying to maintain some downward compatibility between the 8080A and its predecessor.)

ADDRESS SPECIFICATION BY REGISTER PAIR

The main purpose for linking registers into pairs is to allow them to hold a 2-byte address. The HL pair is most frequently used, but some cases also employ the BC or DE pairs. The first register of the pair always holds the most significant address byte. Thus the designations for the H (high) register and L (low) register.

ADDRESS SPECIFICATION BY STACK POINTER

The 16-bit stack pointer can also provide the address. Only two instructions permit us to use the stack pointer in this manner: PUSH and POP. (See the discussion on miscellaneous instructions, which follows.)

I/O Devices

The 8080A can specify up to 256 independent input devices, and the same number of output devices. The input ports are numbered 00_{16} to FF_{16}. The output ports are identically designated.

Memory, Register, and I/O Device Review

1. List the 8080A microprocessor working registers and their numerical designations.

2. What register does a designation of 6 signify?

3. Which register pair has a numerical designation of 2? What is the single letter for the pair?

4. Distinguish between instruction address specification and register pair address specification.

ADDRESSING MODES

Now that we know how memory addresses are indicated, let us see how the address may be used. The mode of addressing depends on the instruction format of each instruction. The addressing mode selected must be either an implied address, direct address, register address, register transfer, or immediate address. Table 2-12 lists the modes for each instruction. As you read the descriptions below, note whether the instruction provides the data immediately or just points to the data by means of an address.

Direct Addressing

Direct addressing is used by instructions which transfer data from memory to a particular register or to write data from a register into memory. The instruction supplies the specific address to be used. When the direct addressing mode is used, the instruction always occupies 3 memory bytes. The address is in the two memory cells following the operation code.

Register Addressing

Register addressing is used with instructions involving only the data in a single register, such as moving data from one register to another. Others use a register pair to hold an address. If a single register is involved, the number of the register will be included in the instruction. Other instructions specify the register pair which contains the address. Instructions which use two 8-bit registers (moving data from one to the other, for example) must specify the register sending the information and the one receiving. The former is the *source register* and the latter the *destination register.*

Immediate Addressing

The instruction may also include the value to be used in the operation. In the *immediate addressing* mode, the byte following the op code is the quantity that will be used in executing the command. The data is obtained in conjunction with fetching the instructions.

Table 2-12
Addressing Modes

Instruction	Implied	Immediate	Register	BC	DE	HL	SP	Direct address
Move								
MOV D,S			X					
MOV M,S						X		
MOV D,M						X		
MVI D,B		X						
LDAX B				X				
LDAX D					X			
XCHG	X							
LXI D,BB		X						
LHLD								X
LDA								X
STAX B				X				
STAX D					X			
SHLD								X
STA								X
Arithmetic								
ADD S			X					
ADD M						X		
ADC S			X					
ADC M						X		
SUB S			X					
SUB M						X		
SBB S			X					
SBB M						X		
DAD				X	X	X	X	
INR S			X					
INR M						X		
INX				X	X	X	X	
DCR S			X					
DCR M						X		
DCX				X	X	X	X	
DAA	X							
CMA	X							
STC	X							
CMC	X							
ADI		X						
ACI		X						
SUI		X						
SBI		X						
Rotate								
RLC	X							
RRC	X							
RAL	X							
RAR	X							
Logical								
ANA S			X					
ANA M						X		
XRA S			X					
XRA M						X		
ORA S			X					
ORA M						X		
CMP S			X					
CMP M						X		

Table 2-12
Addressing Modes *(Continued)*

Instruction	Implied	Immediate	Register	BC	DE	HL	SP	Direct address
ANI		X						
XRI		X						
ORI		X						
CPI		X						
Jump								
JMP								X
JNZ								X
JZ								X
JNC								X
JC								X
JPO								X
JPE								X
JP								X
JM								X
PCHL						X		
Call								
CALL								X
CNZ								X
CZ								X
CNC								X
CC								X
CPO								X
CPE								X
CP								X
CM								X
Return								
RET	X							
RNZ	X							
RZ	X							
RNC	X							
RC	X							
RPO	X							
RPE	X							
RP	X							
RM	X							
Stack Operations								
PUSH				X	X	X	*	
POP				X	X	X	*	
XTHL						X		
SPHL						X		
Input/Output								
OUT		X						
IN		X						
DI	X							
EI	X							
RST	X							
Control								
NOP	X							
HLT	X							

Notes:
S is the source register.　　M is a memory location.　　BB is a 16-bit data quantity.
D is the destination register.　B is an 8-bit data quantity.　*Linked program status word and A register.

Addressing Modes Review

1. Define the terms "direct addressing" and "immediate addressing."

2. Why are 3 bytes required for a direct address instruction?

3. How is the register pair designated in an instruction?

ENCODING AND DECODING INSTRUCTIONS

Before we begin our study of specific instructions, we will consider the method used in writing an instruction. Because we are using machine code, every instruction will be an 8-bit binary string. We will write the code in hexadecimal for compactness. Every instruction must include two parts, or *fields.*

Operation Code Field

The *operation code (op code) field* uniquely identifies the machine function to be performed. In addition to the numerical op code, each instruction has a *mnemonic* associated with it. A mnemonic is a three- or four-letter abbreviation for the instruction intended to help the programmer remember the operation and document the program, but the computer cannot interpret the mnemonic. Examples of mnemonics are ADD for "addition" and LDA for "load accumulator direct." If an assembler is used to generate the program, the mnemonics can be used as inputs to the assembler.

Operand Field

The second part of the instruction is the *operand field.* The operand field designates the data to be manipulated as a result of the computer decoding and executing the instruction. The operand field may specify that data is

1. Immediate (part of the instruction)

2. Contained in some register

3. Contained in the memory cell indicated by a 16-bit memory address

4. Contained in the address indicated by a register pair

5. Contained in the address indicated by the stack pointer

The operand can be any value represented by binary numbers.

Label Field

The programmer can clarify the coding process by using a *label field*—that is, by assigning optional names to certain addresses in the program. These names, called *symbolic addresses,* are only useful to human beings. They appear on the coding sheet but are not meaningful to the computer. They help someone reading the program keep track of what is happening. Examples of two instructions, with all of the fields described in this section, are given in the table at the bottom of this page. The first instruction requires 3 bytes: one for the op code and two to specify the address of the operand (memory location 1000_{16}). The second instruction uses only 1 byte because the halt operation does not need any data. Memory location 2000_{16} was given the label START and cell 2003_{16} is labeled STOP. The mnemonics remind us that the first instruction means to load the accumulator using the direct addressing mode and the second instruction means to halt the processor.

Encoding and Decoding Instructions Review

1. What is the purpose of the operation code field?

2. Define the term "mnemonic." How does the use of mnemonics help the programmer?

3. List the locations that the operand field can designate as the source of data.

Label field	Mnemonic	Memory address	Operation code field	Operand field	Comments
START	LDA	2000	3A		First instruction
		2001	· · ·	00	
		2002	· · ·	10	
STOP	HLT	2003	76	· · ·	Second instruction

4. Which of the following cannot be operands for a computer instruction: I/O device codes, BCD codes, letters, binary numbers, or decimal numbers?

5. What is the purpose of the label field?

THE INSTRUCTION SET

Next we will briefly consider each group of instructions of the 8080A repertoire. A more detailed description of them is provided in the appendix. For each instruction a description of its operation, its effect on the flag bits, and the number of bytes for that format are given in the tables which follow. These listings use the notation indicated below. If the flag bit column is blank, the instruction does not change that flag. If the entry is an X, the flag is changed to reflect the new value in the accumulator.

S: source register
D: destination register
M: memory location
→: transfer to
( ): contents of register or memory location
B: an 8-bit data value
BB: a 16-bit data value
RP: register pair
A: accumulator
PC: program counter

Move Instructions

The instructions that transfer data to a register or memory cell are shown in Table 2-13. The MOV instructions carry the value from the source register or memory location to the destination. If a memory location is involved, its address is to be found in the HL register pair. The MVI command transfers a data byte in the second word of the instruction to the destination register.

Another way of specifying the memory address of data destined for the accumulator is used in the LDAX instructions. In this case either the BC or DE register pairs contain the address. The exchange instruction results in moving 4 bytes. The values in the H and D registers are interchanged, as are those in the L and E registers. A double register pair becomes the destination for the 2 data bytes of the LXI instruction. The LHLD works in a similar manner, but only the HL registers can receive the data. The LDA instruction places a value obtained from the memory cell addressed into the accumulator.

Data in the accumulator can be written into memory by use of the two STAX instructions. The only difference between them is that for one the BC register contains the address and for the second the DE registers are used. The H and L registers can be stored in sequential memory locations with the SHLD instruction. Storing the accumulator at the address given by the last two words of the instruction is the purpose of STA.

Arithmetic Instructions

The arithmetic instructions are listed in Table 2-14. Both single- and double-precision instructions are included in the repertoire. As Fig. 2-25 shows, single-precision arithmetic uses 8-bit operands. A double-length operand is used for double precision.

The ADD instructions provide the capability of summing the current value in the accumulator with a register or memory byte. The carry bit is also included in the sum with the ADC instructions. Subtraction is accomplished in much the same manner with SUB and SBB commands. An immediate byte serves as the second operand of ADI, ACI, SUI, or SBI.

The HL register pair can be added to another register pair using the DAD instruction. Frequently required for iterative processes, six instructions are provided to increment or decrement a register, register pair, or memory location. The decimal adjust instruction allows the 8080A to carry out BCD arithmetic correctly.

A 1's complement of the accumulator results from use of the CMA instruction. With STC and CMC, the carry status can be set or complemented.

Logical operations are supported by the AND, OR, and exclusive OR instructions. The operand for these

Table 2-13
Move Group*

Mnemonic	Description	Number of bytes
MOV D, S	(S) → D	1
MOV M, S	(S) → M	1
MOV D, M	(M) → D	1
MVI D, B	B → D	2
LDAX B	(M(BC)) → A	1
LDAX D	(M(DE)) → A	1
XCHG	(H) ↔ (D), (L) ↔ (E)	1
LXI D, BB	(BB) → RP	3
LHLD	(M) → L, (M + 1) → H	3
LDA	(M) → A	3
STAX B	(A) → M (BC)	1
STAX D	(A) → M (DE)	1
SHLD	(L) → M, (H) → M + 1	3
STA	(A) → M	3

*Flag bits are not affected by these instructions.

Table 2-14
Arithmetic Group

Mnemonic	Description	C	Ac	Z	S	P	Number of bytes
ADD S	(S) + (A) → A	X	X	X	X	X	1
ADD M	(M) + (A) → A	X	X	X	X	X	1
ADC S	(S) + (A) + (CARRY) → A	X	X	X	X	X	1
ADC M	(M) + (A) + (CARRY) → A	X	X	X	X	X	1
SUB S	(A) − (S) → A	X	X	X	X	X	1
SUB M	(A) − (M) → A	X	X	X	X	X	1
SBB S	(A) − (S) − (CARRY) → A	X	X	X	X	X	1
SBB M	(A) − (M) − (CARRY) → A	X	X	X	X	X	1
DAD	(HL) + (RP) → HL	X					1
INR S	(S) + 1 → S		X	X	X	X	1
INR M	(M) + 1 → M		X	X	X	X	1
INX	(RP) + 1 → RP						1
DCR S	(S) − 1 → S		X	X	X	X	1
DCR M	(M) − 1 → M		X	X	X	X	1
DCX	(RP) − 1 → RP						1
DAA	Decimal Adjust	X	X	X	X	X	1
CMA	(Ā) → A						1
STC	1 → CARRY	1					1
CMC	(CARRY) → CARRY	X					1
ADI	(A) + B → A	X	X	X	X	X	2
ACI	(A) + B + (CARRY) → A	X	X	X	X	X	2
SUI	(A) − B → A	X	X	X	X	X	2
SBI	(A) − B − (CARRY) → A	X	X	X	X	X	2
ANA S	(S) AND (A) → A	0	X	X	X	X	1
ANA M	(M) AND (A) → A	0	X	X	X	X	1
XRA S	(S) ⊙ (A) → A	0	X	X	X	X	1
XRA M	(M) ⊙ (A) → A	0	X	X	X	X	1
ORA S	(S) OR (A) → A	0	X	X	X	X	1
ORA M	(M) OR (A) → A	0	X	X	X	X	1
CMP S	COMPARE	X	X	X	X	X	1
CMP M	COMPARE	X	X	X	X	X	1
ANI	(A) AND B → A	0	X	X	X	X	2
XRI	(A) ⊙ B → A	0	0	X	X	X	2
ORI	(A) OR B → A	0	0	X	X	X	2
CPI	COMPARE	X	X	X	X	X	2

Boolean functions can be a register, memory cell, or immediate data. The compare instruction saves the accumulator in a temporary location, subtracts the operand (changing the status flag values), then restores the original accumulator contents. Comparisons made in this manner can be the basis for an efficient program, because data values do not have to be stored in memory to protect them.

Rotate Instructions

Refer to the rotate group that is shown in Table 2-15. The rotate, or shift, group rotates the accumulator right or left. An RLC instruction causes each bit in the A register to move one position to the left. The most significant bit is sent to the least significant bit position and also to the carry status flag. Rotating the accumulator right produces a reverse operation. Each bit rotates one place to the right, with the least significant bit ending up in the high-order position and in the carry bit. Rotating through the carry is equivalent to using a 9-bit register for the shifting. The RAL instruction rotates the accumulator left 1 bit and the high-order bit replaces the carry bit. The original carry bit takes the place of the low-order bit. For the RAR instruction, the accumulator shifts right and the most significant bit replaces the carry. The original carry

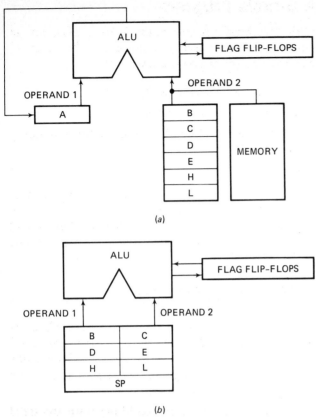

(a)

(b)

Figure 2-25. Arithmetic Instructions (a) Single Precision (b) Double Precision.

occupies the most significant bit after the instruction has been executed.

Jump, Call, and Return Instruction

Jump, call, and return instructions are shown in Table 2-16. This group of instructions includes both unconditional and conditional execution. For unconditional instructions the operation *always* is carried out. A *conditional* instruction causes the action to occur only if the stated condition is satisfied.

The unconditional JMP instruction always sets the program counter to the two-word address following the op code. The next instruction is therefore obtained from that location. The unconditional CALL instruction will reference a subroutine at the given address after first pushing the return address on to the stack. The unconditional RET will return to that address by popping the stack. A jump can also be forced with the PCHL instruction.

The conditional jumps, calls, and returns only complete the command if the status flag tested is in the correct state. The zero flag can be checked to determine if the last calculation produced a zero or nonzero result. The states of the carry, parity, or sign flags can be examined as well. If the flag is in the state specified by the instruction, a jump,

Table 2-16
Jump, Call, and Return Group*

Mnemonic	Description	Number of bytes
JMP	Jump	3
JNZ	Jump (zero) = 0	3
JZ	Jump (zero) = 1	3
JNC	Jump (carry) = 0	3
JC	Jump (carry) = 1	3
JPO	Jump (parity) = 0	3
JPE	Jump (parity) = 1	3
JP	Jump (sign) = 0	3
JM	Jump (sign) = 1	3
PCHL	(HL) → PC	1
CALL	Call	3
CNZ	Call (zero) = 0	3
CZ	Call (zero) = 1	3
CNC	Call (carry) = 0	3
CC	Call (carry) = 1	3
CPO	Call (parity) = 0	3
CPE	Call (parity) = 1	3
CP	Call (sign) = 0	3
CM	Call (sign) = 1	3
RET	Return	1
RNZ	Return (zero) = 0	1
RNC	Return (carry) = 0	1
RC	Return (carry) = 1	1
RPO	Return (parity) = 0	1
RPE	Return (parity) = 1	1
RP	Return (sign) = 0	1
RM	Return (sign) = 1	1

* Flag bits are not affected by these instructions.

Table 2-15
Rotate Group

Mnemonic	Description	Flags					Number of bytes
		C	Ac	Z	S	P	
RLC	Rotate A left	X					1
RRC	Rotate A right	X					1
RAL	Rotate A left through carry	X					1
RAR	Rotate A right through carry	X					1

call, or return will be made. Otherwise the next sequential instruction is fetched and executed.

I/O and Miscellaneous Instructions

I/O and miscellaneous instructions are shown in Table 2-17. The input and output instructions are discussed in the next chapter, so they need not be covered at this time. The stack operations allow a register pair to be placed on the stack (PUSH) or removed (POP). The XTHL instruction exchanges the values in the H and L registers with the contents of the memory bytes indicated by the stack pointer. The SPHL instruction loads the stack pointer from the HL pair. A no operation (NOP) instruction simply increments the program counter. The processor can be made to stop executing instructions with the HLT instruction.

Table 2-17
I/O and Miscellaneous Group*

Mnemonic	Description	Number of bytes
PUSH	(RP) → STACK	1
POP	(STACK) → RP	1
XTHL	(L) → (M(SP)), (H) → (M(SP + 1))	1
SPHL	(HL) → SP	1
NOP	(PC) + 1 → PC	1
HLT	HALT	1
OUT	OUTPUT	2
IN	INPUT	2
DI	0 → INTE	1
EI	1 → INTE	1
RST	RESTART	1

* Flag bits are not affected by these instructions.

Table 2-18
A Simple Program

Mnemonic	Address$_{16}$	Machine code$_{16}$	Comments
MVI A	0150	3E	Clear A
0	0151	00	Data byte
STA	0152	32	Store A
00	0153	00	Low address byte
02	0154	02	High address byte
ADI	0155	C6	Add to A
20	0156	20	Immediate data
STA	0157	32	Store A
01	0158	01	Low address byte
02	0159	02	High address byte
HLT	015A	76	Stop

A Simple Program

With that brief review of the instructions, let us put them to use in a simple program. The program will execute the following procedure:

1. Clear memory cell 0200_{16}
2. Add 20_{16} to the accumulator
3. Store the sum from the accumulator in memory cell 0201_{16}
4. Stop

The first step will have to be split into two actions, so that we can use the instructions to carry it out. First the accumulator must be cleared, then it will be stored in address 0200_{16}. The program is given in Table 2-18.

CHAPTER SUMMARY

1. The architecture of a computer describes the structure and the routing of data and commands between the components. Data paths are usually parallel, while command lines are a single discrete signal.

2. The 8080A is often combined with the 8224 system clock generator and 8228 system controller. The 8080A requires three supply voltages and has a 16-bit address bus and 8-bit data bus. The address and data buses use three-state logic.

3. There are 10 programmable registers in the 8080A. The A register is the primary accumulator. The status register provides flags of the results from the last operation. The six secondary accumulators can also be linked into 16-bit address counters. The stack pointer contains the top address on the stack. The program counter contains the address of the next instruction.

4. Timing and control of the microprocessor is based on a sequence of machine cycles which are subdivided into clock periods. The two clock phases, Φ1 and Φ2, delineate the limits of clock periods. The SYNC pulse marks T1 during each machine cycle. The 8224 clock signal generator produces all of these synchronized clock signals.

5. All memory references take place in T1 through T3 of any machine cycle. During MC1, T1 through T3 are used for instruction fetching and T4 for instruction interpretation.

6. The data bus status code during T2 informs all devices on the bus which operation will be performed. Because each microinstruction consists of a series of operations, usually the status code will have 2 or more bits set. The 8228 system controller handles the status signals and converts them to commands on the control bus.

7. The wait state permits external devices to request additional time in which to reply. The hold state causes the processor to pause between instructions.

8. The 8224 converts the external oscillator frequency to clock signals for the 8080A. The 8224 also processes control signals for the microprocessor IC and the 8228.

9. The 8228 demultiplexes status and data signals from the 8080A data bus and converts them to system data and control bus signals.

10. A memory map shows the organization of computer storage as banks and blocks. Address decoding logic in the memory selects the bank and block to be referenced. Address bits A13 to A15 designate the bank and bits A10 to A12 the block within the bank.

11. The working registers and memory to be used in many instructions are indicated by a 3-bit code.

12. Register pairs are referred to by a single letter in some instruction or by a 2-bit designator in other instructions.

13. Any memory address can be written or read. It is the programmer's responsibility to prevent attempts to write in ROM or to read nonexistent locations.

14. A memory address for an instruction can be supplied by the data in an instruction, a register pair, or the stack pointer.

15. A maximum of 256 independent input and output ports are available. The user must not reference nonexistent ports, because no error notification is provided by the processor.

16. Several addressing modes are used by the 8080A. Direct addressing supplies the location as part of the 3-byte instruction. When a register pair holds the address, or when only a single register is involved in the instruction, the register addressing mode is used. Immediate addressing uses a format which includes data with the instruction.

17. The instruction set of the 8080A provides for data transfer, arithmetic, Boolean logic, branching, and I/O. Instruction formats use one, two, or three words.

KEY TERMS AND CONCEPTS

Microprocessor	Reading memory data	Instruction format
Data bus	Writing memory data	High and low address bytes
Address bus	Wait state	Register notation
Control bus	Hold state	Direct addressing
Status codes	Halt state	Register addressing
Programmable registers (A, B, C, D, E, H, L, PSW, SP, PC)	RESET	Source register
Status flags (S, Z, A_C, P, C)	Memory organization	Destination register
Secondary accumulators	Memory map	Immediate addressing
Register pairs (BC, DE, HL)	Memory block	Operation code (op code) field
Machine cycles	Memory bank	Mnemonic
Clock periods	Address decoding	Operand field
Clock phases (Φ1 and Φ2)	Bidirectional bus drivers	Label field

2-1 How many memory banks are needed in a 32K memory? What is the range of addresses in the memory?

2-2 Draw a 16K memory map for a memory organized as follows:

Device	Address
256 × 8 ROM	2000–20FF
8 each 1K × 1 RAMs	3C00–3FFF
8 each 1K × 1 RAMs	3400–37FF
256 × 8 ROM	2200–22FF
8 each 1K × 1 RAMs	2C00–2FFF
1K × 8 ROM	3000–33FF
256 × 8 ROM	2300–23FF
8 each 1K × 1 RAMs	3800–3BFF
8 each 1K × 1 RAMs	2400–27FF
256 × 8 ROM	2100–21FF

Indicate the type of memory used in each block (some blocks will be vacant).

2-3 to 2-5

The initial conditions for Probs. 2-3 through 2-5 are stated below; that is, the register and memory locations are set to the given values before the instructions in each problem are executed. For each problem record the *changes only* in any register or memory location after the instructions are executed.

Program counter 4090
Registers

A	0F
B	00
C	01
D	02
E	A0
H	0F
L	0B

Stack pointer 2000
Memory

0000	00
0001	50
0002	AA
0003	7B
02A0	00
0B0F	50
A002	20
0F0C	07

(2-3)

Location	Contents	Mnemonic	Operand
4090	2A	LHLD	0001
4091	01		
4092	00		
4093	EB	XCHG	
4094	76	HLT	

(2-4)

Location	Contents
4090	0A
4091	32
4092	00
4093	00
4094	00
4095	76

(2-5)

Location	Contents
4090	22
4091	02
4092	00
4093	32
4094	03
4095	00
4096	76

2-6 Draw a circuit diagram using the 8205 decoder to decode addresses in memory bank 6. (Total memory capacity is 64K.) Your diagram will differ from the one in this chapter primarily in the use of inverters on some of the pins 1 through 6. (Refer to Fig. 2-20.)

2-7 What memory block is referenced by the following instructions when the operands are fetched?

a. Address$_{16}$	Machine Code$_{16}$
1010	32
1011	1B
1012	2F

b. Address$_{16}$	Machine Code$_{16}$
AC01	C6
AC02	32

2-8 Find the bug in the following program.

Location	Contents
4090	3A
4091	03
4092	00
4093	00
4094	32
4095	76
4096	76
4097	C3
4098	90
4099	40
409A	76

2-9 The following machine code program has run to completion. What value is in the accumulator?

Address$_{16}$	Machine Code$_{16}$
5020	C6
5021	71
5022	3E
5023	12
5024	76

5025	D3
5026	01
5027	C6
5028	00

2-10 What changes in memory are produced by this program?

Address	Mnemonic Code
F000	OUT
F001	03
F002	MVI, A
F003	04
F004	STA
F005	FF
F006	08
F007	ADI
F008	A1
F009	ADI
F00A	F0
F00B	STA
F00C	0C
F00D	AA
F00E	HLT

EXPERIMENT 1

PURPOSE: To introduce you to interfacing experiments. Performing the experiments in this book will increase your comprehension of interfacing concepts more than will any other method of study. The experiments use a minimum of equipment to reduce setup time, but demonstrate the key points of hardware and software operation. After completing an experiment, you may wish to go further by trying variations of the program. By all means do so, because software will not damage equipment—even if there are bugs in your program.

TOOLS AND TEST EQUIPMENT: Common hand tools, a voltmeter, breadboarding components, logic probe, pulser, and oscilloscope are necessary for the experiments which follow. Schematics for construction of a logic probe and pulser (see Fig. 2-26) that can serve in place of commercially manufactured ones are given below. The parts you will need to build them are listed here.

PARTS LIST:

Item	Quantity
7400	1
Light-emitting diode (LED)	1
330-Ω (ohm) resistor	1
900-Ω resistor	1
Single-pole double-throw (SPDT) slide switch (spring return)	1

LOGIC PROBE: Wire the circuit consisting of the 330-Ω resistor and LED. Touch the probe to ground. Did the LED light? If not reverse the LED leads in the socket and repeat the grounding. (The LED will not glow if it is reverse-biased.)

Next touch the probe to +5 V. What happens to the LED? It should be off. Now that you have checked out the probe, it can be used to determine whether a signal is high or low. The LED is off for a high, on for a low. If the signal is oscillating at a low frequency, about 10 Hz, the LED will glow more faintly. Of course this probe can only be used on signals that range between 0 and 5 V.

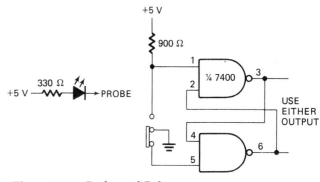

Figure 2-26. Probe and Pulser.

PULSER: After wiring the pulser circuit, touch the logic probe to pin 3 of the 7400. Now throw the switch keeping the probe in contact with pin 3. What happens? Initially the LED is on; but, when the switch is thrown, the LED goes off. If the switch is allowed to return to its initial position, the LED again illuminates. From these observations, we conclude that the first output of pin 3 is low. The output rises to a high when the switch is closed and falls again when the switch is opened. Try this experiment again using pin 6 instead. The results indicate that when pin 3 is high, pin 6 is low and vice versa.

PROCEDURE: Your instructor will introduce you to the microcomputer to be used in the experiments. Get familiar with its register display, memory, and I/O structure.

STEP 1. Record the range of memory addresses for your computer in both hexadecimal and decimal.

	Decimal		Hexadecimal	
	Low	High	Low	High
ROM				
RAM				

STEP 2. What I/O ports are assigned? How is each used?

Device Code	Purpose

STEP 3. How can you examine the contents of a register or memory cell? How can you change those contents?

3

PERIPHERALS

Once the microcomputer has calculated results, the output must be displayed in some way that a human being can understand. A method for entering data which the machine can read is also needed. Peripheral equipment is used for these functions, as well as to transmit data from one place to another and to store it offline. Equipment commonly encountered in microcomputer systems includes printers, CRT terminals and keyboards, modems and floppy disk drives, and cartridge or cassette recorders. In every case the information being exchanged must be coded in some manner. Coding is necessary because the processor has no way of dealing with letters, punctuation marks, pictures, or measurements from the physical world. All of these quantities or units must be translated to binary values before they can be accepted by a computer.

CHAPTER OBJECTIVES

Upon completion of this chapter, you should be able to:

1. Encode and decode characters using the binary coded decimal and ASCII codes
2. Explain the need for error detection and correction codes
3. List the most common error detection and correction codes
4. Describe the advantages and disadvantages of the various types of printers
5. Explain the principles of operation of a keyboard
6. Draw a block diagram for a CRT terminal
7. Explain why modems are needed in telecommunications
8. Distinguish between the various kinds of floppy disk drives available
9. Explain the operation of magnetic cartridge and cassette recorders

CODES

Much of the data that is processed by computers is nonnumeric. Text characters, shaft angles, and control signals are only a few types of information that can be manipulated by the processor. Because microprocessors are limited to storing only 1s and 0s, many *codes* have been developed to translate other forms of data into binary numbers.

Binary Coded Decimal

Binary coded decimal (BCD) is commonly used by input/output devices. Many numeric keyboards encode data into BCD. The encoded data represents the decimal digits in the range of 0 through 9 as 4-bit quantities. Table 3-1 lists the coded value for each digit.

While BCD is a good way of representing the decimal values, the coded versions of the numbers will not give the correct answer if used in normal arithmetic. This problem can easily be seen in the following example:

Decimal	BCD
19_{10}	0001 1001
$+1$	$+\ 0001$
$20_{10} = 1\ 0100_2$	0001 1010

But $\quad 1\ 0100_2 \neq 0001\ 1010_2$

The problem comes about because binary coded decimal cannot represent the true binary value of the sum. A correct solution results if the BCD is first converted to the true binary representation.

Decimal	BCD	Binary
19_{10}	0001 1001	$= 01\ 0011_2$
$+1_{10}$	$+\ 0001$	$= +0001_2$
$20_{10} = 01\ 0100_2 =$		$01\ 0100_2$

Table 3-1
Binary Coded Decimal

Decimal digit	BCD code
0	0000
1	0001
2	0010
3	0011
4	0100
5	0101
6	0110
7	0111
8	1000
9	1001

The American Standard Code for Information Interchange

The *American Standard Code for Information Interchange (ASCII)* is widely used by digital communications systems and computers. Shown in Table 3-2, it is a 7-bit code. The characters, their coded values, and the meaning of each character are listed in the table.

This code can be divided into subsets, if the application does not require all 128 characters. There are 64 of the codes (20_{16} to $5F_{16}$) used for upper-case letters, numbers and common punctuation marks, and the blank space (SP). Another 32 codes (60_{16} to $7F_{16}$) specify lower-case letters and the less common punctuation marks; these codes are not often used. The final codes (00_{16} to $1F_{16}$) specify machine commands such as linefeed (LF), carriage return (CR), and ring the bell (BEL). They do not appear in a message or in print, but they control the communications equipment from both ends of the line.

In practice, an eighth bit is usually appended to the MSB position. This bit can be used for error detection or may be always 0. The 8 bits of the complete code may be sent either serially, 1 bit at a time, or in parallel, all 8 bits at once.

The meanings of all of the control codes may not be obvious from Table 3-2. A brief description of each should clarify their use. The "start of heading" is used to begin a character sequence which includes the address and routing information, called the *message heading*. The "start of text" character terminates the heading and signals the start of the message. The message ends with the "end of text" character. When an entire transmission is concluded, the "end of transmission" character is sent.

An "enquiry" is used to request a response from a remote station, such as identification or status. "Acknowledge" is sent by the receiver as an affirmative response to the sender; "NAK" is used for a negative response.

Many of the characters control the message handling equipment. The BEL character sounds an alarm or buzzer. "Backspace," "linefeed," "horizontal" and "vertical tabulation," "form feed," and "carriage return" position the print head on the page. "Delete" is used to erase an unwanted character.

When one or more characters outside the standard ASCII set are to be sent, they are preceded by the "shift out" control. "Shift in" is sent after those codes have been transmitted. "Data link escape" and "escape" provide supplementary controls in data communications networks to change the meaning of a limited number of characters which follow. DLE and ESC are usually terminated by the "shift in" character.

Table 3-2
ASCII Code

Character	Code (hexadecimal)	Meaning	Character	Code (hexadecimal)	Meaning
NUL	00	All zero character	1	31	1
SOH	01	Start of heading	2	32	2
STX	02	Start of text	3	33	3
ETX	03	End of text	4	34	4
EOT	04	End of transmission	5	35	5
ENQ	05	Enquiry	6	36	6
ACK	06	Acknowledge	7	37	7
BEL	07	Bell	8	38	8
BS	08	Backspace	9	39	9
HT	09	Horizontal tabulation	:	3A	Colon
LF	0A	Linefeed	;	3B	Semicolon
VT	0B	Vertical tabulation	<	3C	Less than
FF	0C	Form feed	=	3D	Equal
CR	0D	Carriage return	>	3E	Greater than
SO	0E	Shift out	?	3E	Question mark
SI	0F	Shift in	@	40	Commercial at
DLE	10	Data link escape	A	41	A
DC1	11	Device controls	B	42	B
DC2	12	Device controls	C	43	C
DC3	13	Device controls	D	44	D
DC4	14	Device controls	E	45	E
NAK	15	Negative acknowledge	F	46	F
SYN	16	Synchronous idle	G	47	G
ETB	17	End of transmission block	H	48	H
CAN	18	Cancel	I	49	I
EM	19	End of medium	J	4A	J
SUB	1A	Substitute	K	4B	K
ESC	1B	Escape	L	4C	L
FS	1C	File separator	M	4D	M
GS	1D	Group separator	N	4E	N
RS	1E	Record separator	O	4F	O
US	1F	Unit separator	P	50	P
SP	20	Space			
!	21	Exclamation point	Q	51	Q
"	22	Quotation marks	R	52	R
#	23	Number sign	S	54	S
$	24	Dollar sign	T	54	T
%	25	Percent	U	55	U
&	26	Ampersand	V	56	V
'	27	Apostrophe	W	57	W
(	28	Opening parenthesis	X	58	X
)	29	Closing parenthesis	Y	59	Y
*	2A	Asterisk	Z	5A	Z
+	2B	Plus	[	5B	Opening bracket
,	2C	Comma	\	5C	Reverse slant
-	2D	Hyphen	]	5D	Closing bracket
.	2E	Period	^	5E	Circumflex
/	2F	Slant	_	5F	Underline
0	30	0	`	60	Accent grave

Table 3-2
ASCII Code *(Continued)*

Character	Code (hexadecimal)	Meaning	Character	Code (hexadecimal)	Meaning
a	61	a	q	71	q
b	62	b	r	72	r
c	63	c	s	73	s
d	64	d	t	74	t
e	65	e	u	75	u
f	66	f	v	77	v
g	67	g	w	77	w
h	68	h	x	78	x
i	69	i	y	79	y
j	6A	j	z	7A	z
k	6B	k	{	7B	Opening brace
l	6C	l			7C	Vertical line
m	6D	m	}	7D	Closing brace
n	6E	n		7E	Overline
o	6F	o	DEL	7F	Delete
p	70	p			

Device controls are used to switch teleprocessing devices on or off. "Synchronous idle" is used to provide a synchronism signal when there are no other characterss to be sent. The "end of transmission block" allows blocking of data for communications purposes. The "cancel" character indicates that erroneous data has been sent and should be disregarded. "End of medium" indicates the conclusion of useful data. "Substitute" is used in place of a character that has been found to be invalid. "File," "group," record," and "unit separators" can divide data into segments.

Error Detection and Correction Codes

When data is transmitted from one place to another in a digital system, the receiver may question the validity of the data. Noise, crosstalk, or malfunction may introduce errors in the received bit stream. Through the use of *error detection and correction (EDAC) codes,* data can be checked for the possibility of error, and it can be modified to restore the original message, if errors are found.

PARITY *Parity* is simply an indication of whether a binary number consists of an odd or even count of set bits. Here we will examine how parity can indicate inaccuracies in the data. Commonly an extra bit is appended to the ASCII code for a character to be used for parity checking. The *parity bit* is a form of redundancy that is part of the message. The redundancy has a price though. By increasing

the number of bits per character from 7 to 8, an overhead of 14 percent is incurred. The overhead of any error detection code is a measure of its *efficiency.*

Assume a capital E is the ASCII character to be transmitted. Therefore, the code 45_{16} represents the character. Let parity bit occupy the MSB position. We have a choice of using even or odd parity, so both possibilities will be investigated. Writing the code in binary $0100\ 0101_2$ shows that the parity is odd. By setting the parity bit ($1100\ 0101_2$), the overall parity for the 8 bits becomes even. Making the parity bit 0 is equivalent to giving the word odd parity (in this case).

Starting with the even-parity situation, we will look into the consequence of errors. Assume that the letter E is transmitted four times in a message: The first time it was sent with no errors; the second time bit 1 was read as a "1" because of noise on the line; the third time bit 2 became 0 and bit 4 became a 1; the last time bits 3, 4, and 5 were set erroneously. Summarizing the received characters, we have the following:

	Binary data received								Received parity
Bit number	7	6	5	4	3	2	1	0	
Case 1	1	1	0	0	0	1	0	1	Even
Case 2	1	1	0	0	0	1	1	1	Odd
Case 3	1	1	0	1	0	0	0	1	Even
Case 4	1	1	1	1	1	1	0	1	Odd

In case 1, the received character had even parity, as was expected. In case 2, the word was received with odd parity, but we know it was transmitted with even parity. Receiving a character which has improper parity implies that some bit changed state; either a 1 was reset or a 0 was set to 1 by noise. Case 3 has two errors, but the parity does not show any irregularity. Why? The reason is that even parity can only detect an odd number of bits in error. An even number of incorrect bits gives a seemingly correct even-parity indication. Case 4, with 3 bits in error, again shows the wrong parity, but we see that there is no way to distinguish between 1-bit or 3-bit errors. In fact, any odd number of incorrect bits will produce odd parity. While this parity code can detect an odd number of bit errors, it cannot indicate how many occurred or which bits are actually wrong.

Had we started with odd parity at the transmitter, the situation would just be reversed. An odd number of bits in error (1, 3, 5, . . .) would be received with even parity, but an even number (2, 4, 6, . . .) would be seemingly correct at the receiving station. Using more bits for parity strengthens the detection of multiple errors and can even indicate which bit (or bits) is (are) wrong. An elaborate theory for EDAC coding which can be used to assure reliable data communications has been developed.

CHECK SUMS Sometimes we are not concerned about the correctness of one word, but about that of an entire block of data composed of many words. An efficient code for verifying data blocks is the *check sum* (also called "hash totals"). Generation of the check sum requires that the transmitting station add all of the data codes and append the sum as a final word in the message. The receiving station also sums the data and compares its answer with the last word. If they agree, there is a high probability that the data is correct.

You may wonder why the receiving station cannot be sure the data was correct if the check sums agree. First, there may be compensating errors in the data, that is, one word may have been increased by the same amount another was decreased. Second, the addition is performed in an adder of finite length. In most microprocessors that would be 8 bits. This means that all carries from the MSB position are discarded and errors may occur which are hidden by this loss of information.

The data block shown below will be used to demonstrate the check-summing procedure. Each word in the block is 8 bits long. Adding the first two words gives 60_{16}, but when that partial sum is added to FF_{16} the result is $15F_{16}$. Because we are limited to 8 bits, the MSB of 1 is lost and the resulting sum is $5F_{16}$. Finally, adding $0E_{16}$ gives $6D_{16}$.

1. Generating the check sum

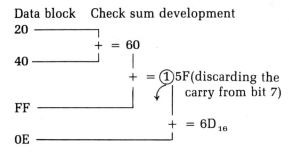

2. Transmission block

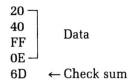

3. Correctly received data

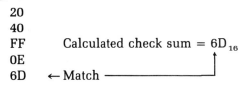

4. Incorrectly received data

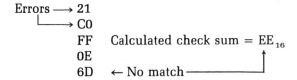

The data is blocked for transmission with the check sum in an extra word (not part of the data). In this case, the check sum has an efficiency of 25 percent (one code word per four data words.) If the data is received correctly, the check sum independently calculated by the receiver will match the last word in the block; however, bits that have changed will cause a different sum to be produced. No indication of which word has the error is provided, so the entire block must be retransmitted when a mistake is detected.

CYCLIC REDUNDANCY CHECK Another code that can be used to provide error detection capability on blocks of data is the *cyclic redundancy check (CRC)*. The CRC uses fewer bits than parity codes and has been implemented both in hardware and software. Integrated circuits are on the market that will automatically calculate the CRC bit pattern which is appended to the data block as an extra word, much like the check sum. Computer programs have also been written which can generate the same bit pattern. Almost all floppy disks and digital tape cassettes use the cyclic redundancy check when recording data.

The CRC is a bit pattern for a polynomial of degree 7. The pattern can be expressed as

$$D(x) = D_7 x^7 + D1_6 x^6 + D_5 x^5 + D_4 x^4 + D_3 x^3$$
$$+ D_2 x^2 + D_1 x^1 + D_0 x^0 \qquad (3\text{-}1)$$

where x = a dummy variable

A *generator polynomial* is used as the divisor of $D(x)$:

$$D(x)/G(x) = Q(x) + R(x) \qquad (3\text{-}2)$$

where $G(x)$ = the generator polynomial
$Q(x)$ = the quotient
$R(x)$ = the remainder

The purpose of the CRC, which is appended to the data, is to make the remainder in Eq. (3-2) become zero. By rewriting that equation, we can see how to accomplish this task:

$$D(x) - R(x) = Q(x)\, G(x) \qquad (3\text{-}3)$$

That is, if the remainder is used for the CRC word, the generator polynomial will exactly divide the total data string (which includes the CRC).

The CRC transmitted in the last word in the block is thus the remainder generator. When the receiving station divides by $G(x)$, it will find that there is a nonzero remainder if an error has occurred. If the remainder is zero, either the data has been correctly received or an error which cannot be detected has appeared in the data stream.

A simplified example will illustrate the CRC concept more concretely. Let

$$D = 1000\ 0101_2$$

Then
$$D(x) = (1)(x^7) + (0)(x^6) + (0)(x^5) + (0)(x^4)$$
$$+ (0)(x^3) + (1)(x^2) + (0)(x^1) + (1)(x^0)$$
$$D(x) = x^7 + x^2 + 1$$

Using $G(x) = x^2 + 1$ gives

$$B(x)/G(x) = x^5 - x^3 + x + 1$$

with a remainder of $-x$.

Using Eq. (3-3) to obtain an exact dividend:

$$D(x) - R(x) = x^7 + x^2 + 1 - (-x)$$
$$= x^7 + x^2 + x + 1$$

so $-x$ corresponds to the CRC bits. Because x is a dummy variable, we can arbitrally assign the value of 1 to x. That assignment would make the CRC bits FE_{16} in an 8-bit, 2's complement.

Codes Review

1. List the common codes used in digital communications.

2. When would use of BCD instead of binary cause an incorrect result?

3. List the ASCII codes for the following characters: T, ?, $, 7.

4. What are the meanings of the control characters DLE, SOH, ENQ, and LF?

5. Why does a single parity bit, used to check ASCII codes, for instance, seem correct when there are two received errors in the code?

6. Compare the efficiency of parity bits with check sums. Which would be more efficient for a 1000-word-long data block?

7. How do CRC bits make the bit pattern $D(x)$ exactly divisible by the generator polynomial?

PRINTERS

A printer converts electrical codes to commands for the print head that impresses the character on paper. These hardcopy units are either *serial printers* (one character at a time) or *line printers.* The serial printer has a single print head which moves horizontally across the page. As the head moves to the next position, one character is printed. This type of printer receives the characters one by one from the microcomputer. A line printer has a number of print actuators (heads or hammers). Normally there will be one actuator in each print column. When they print, all of the actuators hit the paper at once. This printing method means that enough characters must be stored in the print buffer to allow an entire line to be composed. Therefore, the computer transmits several characters between each print operation. Figures 3-1 and 3-2 show two printer configurations. The printer in Fig. 3-2 can also punch or read paper tape.

A print line consists of from 48 to 128 characters, depending on the model of printer. Most printers can take paper of varying widths. The print rate can range from a slow 30 characters per second (char/s) to thousands of lines per minute (lines/min). Most printers accept at least a subset of the ASCII code, though other character codes are sometimes encountered.

Printers are further characterized by their printing mechanisms. Either impact or nonimpact heads are used. *Impact printers* employ front-striking typefaces that press the ribbon against the paper to print or rear-striking type mechanisms that have a hammer which forces the paper and ribbon against a type chain. Front-striking impact printers include spherical, daisy wheel, cylinder, and dot matrix heads which can run at speeds up to 60 char/s. The

Figure 3-1. Printer *(Heath Co.)*.

Figure 3-2. Printer with Paper Tape Reader/Punch *(Teletype Corp.)*.

rear-striking printers require drum, belt, band, or train print mechanisms and can exceed 3000 lines/min. Such high speed is not normally required for microprocessor output.

Nonimpact printers do not have a type face that presses an image onto the paper. Ink-jet printers can produce up to 45,000 lines a minute on plain paper; photocopier printers also use plain paper. Treated papers which change color when subjected to heat or electric fields are necessary for thermal, electrostatic, and electrosensitive printers. A shortcoming of nonimpact printers is their inability to make multiple copies. Table 3-3 summarizes the various types of printers.

Some of the most economical models are the serial impact printers. Because of the cost advantage, these are the types you are most likely to find in a microcomputer installation. For this reason, we will discuss them in greater detail.

Printers with a cylindrical print head have the character set embossed as a series of rings around the cylinder. The head rotates and shifts up or down to move the selected character into position. Then a hammer strikes the cylinder against the ribbon and paper.

The spherical head, sometimes called the "golf-ball," has its character set arranged on a ball. The sphere rotates on its axis to position the character. It then strikes the ribbon.

Imagine a wagon wheel with 96 spokes, each terminated with a print character to picture the daisy wheel head. This printer rotates the wheel rapidly to place the character to be printed at the topmost point. Then tip of the arm is struck to print.

A matrix head uses a column of pins to construct the required character as a series of dots. The character is printed one column at a time as the head moves across the page. The pins are retracted or extended to create the proper pattern for the column

Table 3-3
Printer Summary

Type	Speed	Print quality	Cost	Comments
Cylinder	10 char/s	Poor	Low	Noisy
Ball	15 char/s	Excellent	Low	Changeable fonts
Daisy wheel	30–55 char/s	Excellent	Medium	Changeable fonts
Matrix	30–330 char/s	Good to poor	Medium	Graphics capability
Thermal	30–120 char/s	Medium	Low	Low noise
Electrosensitive	160–2200 char/s	Poor	Low	Paper wrinkles easily
Electrostatic	300–18,000 lines/min	Excellent	High	Not suited for microcomputers
Photocopier	4000–14,000 lines/min	Excellent	High	Not suited for microcomputers
Ink jet	30 char/s–45,000 lines/min	Good to poor	Low to high	Quiet

being printed. A large variety of fonts can easily be produced by this type of head. Lines can also be compressed or expanded by a control on the printer, as Fig. 3-3 shows.

Printers Review

1. Distinguish between serial and line printers.

2. Characterize the following as either impact or nonimpact print mechanisms: daisy wheel, ink jet, cylinder, matrix, thermal, and photocopier.

3. Which printer would be faster, one with a spherical print head or one with an ink jet?

4. Which printers require treated paper?

KEYBOARDS

A *keyboard* is simply a matrix of normally open key switches. The matrix is crisscrossed by a series of row and column sense lines. When a key is depressed, the row and column intersecting that position become connected (either by grounding or capacitive coupling), so that a voltage applied to the column can be sensed at the appropriate row. By strobing the columns sequentially and scanning the rows, the depressed key can be detected. Keyboards are manufactured in a variety of price ranges based on differing technologies.

The simplest keyboards use mechanical contact switches. Low cost and ease of construction characterize these keyboards. Because they are not sealed, they are subject to contact contamination from dust or moisture. Contact bounce takes a considerable amount of time to settle out, so *debouncing* logic or software must be provided to delay until solid closure is established. With gold contacts on the switches, these keys can provide 5 to 10 million operations.

Reed switches use reed relays sealed in glass for contacts. They are open and closed by the movement of a small magnet toward or away from the contact. Not being exposed to air, the contacts do not become contaminated. Bounce time is also shorter than mechanical switches because the small reeds have a high resonant frequency.

Keyboards built from saturable core switches use magnetic toroid transformers, similar to those used in computer memories. When no key is pressed,

THIS IS AN EXAMPLE OF COMPRESSED TYPE

THIS IS AN EXAMPLE OF EXPANDED TYPE

Figure 3-3. Matrix Fonts.

the transformers are saturated, so little of the energy from a high-frequency oscillator is coupled through the transformer. Pressing a key causes a magnet to be displaced, so the toroid is no longer saturated. Then the oscillator energy appears as a voltage at the output. These keyboards are noted for their high reliability.

Another magnetic technology is employed with Hall effect switches. Here a magnet is attached to a plunger on each key. Moving the magnet toward or away from a Hall effect transducer chip produces two output states. These keyboards are high power users because a dc current is needed at all times. Their payoff is that the keyboard is good for more than 100 million operations.

Capacitive switch keyboards have plates under every key, which increase the coupling of other plates connected between an oscillator and amplifier when a key is pressed. As the coupling becomes greater, a much higher output signal is produced. These keyboards are also long-lasting.

Keyboards with membrane switches can be manufactured at the lowest cost. A conductive pattern is laid down on a printed circuit board which is overlaid with a Mylar film. The film has holes in it at the key positions. The conductive elastomer sheet on top penetrates these holes when pushed by someone's finger. Contact is made with that portion of the pattern underneath. The keyboards can be formed into thin, sealed assemblies with good reliability.

Keyboards Review

1. Explain how a keyboard is scanned to detect a depressed key.

2. What are the major shortcomings of mechanical contact switches?

3. How are reed switches opened and closed?

4. Which keyboard resembles core memory of a computer?

5. True or false? Hall effect switches require a magnetic field for operation.

6. Explain how capacitive coupling can be used in a keyboard.

CRT TERMINALS

CRT terminals provide a fast scan display, often accompanied by a keyboard for data input. See Fig. 3-4. Any combination of alphanumeric characters can be displayed on the CRT screen, and some models

Figure 3-4. CRT Terminal and Keyboard *(Southwest Technical Products Corp.).*

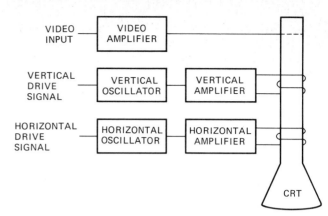

Figure 3-6. Monitor Circuits.

also provide a graphics capability. The major component of terminal is, of course, a cathode-ray tube.

The evacuated glass tube has a phosphorescent coating on the inner surface of the flat screen, as shown in Fig. 3-5. The filament in the neck of the tube heats a cathode, which then produces a flow of electrons by thermionic emission. A high potential between the cathode and screen accelerates the electrons toward the positive screen. When they strike the phosphor, light is emitted.

The beam is positioned under control of electromagnetic coils, as shown in the figure, or by deflection plates. If coils are used, the current through the coil produces a magnetic field which deflects the beam horizontally or vertically. With electrostatic plates, a voltage is applied across the vertical or horizontal deflection plates. Electrons are attracted toward the more positive plate, causing the beam to move in that direction.

A *monitor* is a CRT together with the necessary electronic circuitry needed to position the beam. As Fig. 3-6 shows, the horizontal oscillator moves the beam across the CRT screen from left to right, then the beam returns rapidly to the left-hand side and repeats the scan. The time that the beam is moving back to the left is called the *horizontal*

retrace. The vertical oscillator deflects the beam vertically, resulting in the raster pattern shown in Fig. 3-7. To display a character, the beam intensity must be turned on for the bright areas and off in the dark areas. The video amplifier controls this beam intensity, depending on the input to the amplifier.

If we combine the monitor with memory to store display information, we have a *terminal*. The terminal will also contain input/output logic so it can communicate with the computer. Sometimes a keyboard and light pen are also supplied with the terminal.

The terminal display *format* is specified by the maximum number of characters that can be written across the screen and the number of rows of characters on the screen. For example, a terminal may permit 80 characters to be displayed in 64 rows. This arrangement is referred to as the *display page.* Some terminals can store several pages in memory, but only one can be viewed at a time.

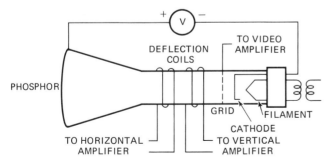

Figure 3-5. CRT Circuits.

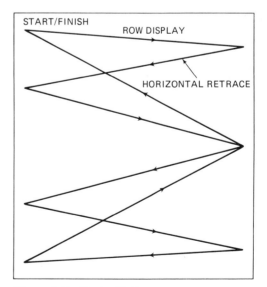

Figure 3-7. Raster Pattern.

To keep the image from blinking, the terminal beam refreshes the display many times a second. A 60-hertz (Hz) *refresh rate* is typical. The total time necessary to draw a full page is then

$$T_{tot} = 1/60 \text{ Hz} = 16.67 \text{ milliseconds (ms)}$$

This time can also be expressed in terms of the number of rows:

$$T_{tot} = T_{row} N + T_{vb} \qquad (3\text{-}4)$$

where T_{row} = time to refresh one row
N = number of rows
T_{vb} = vertical blanking time

If the row refresh time is 246 microseconds (μs) and vertical blanking time is 900 μs:

$$T_{tot} = (246 \text{ μs})(64) + 900 \text{ μs} = 16.64 \text{ ms}$$

Some terminals will automatically shift the display upward by one row after a page has been filled and another line is transmitted by the computer. This *scrolling* action ensures that the latest information will be viewable for the maximum period of time, though the computer is capable of sending data at a faster rate than we can read even with scrolling.

CRT Terminals Review

1. Describe the operation of the two types of CRT deflection circuitry.

2. True or false? A monitor contains memory and can communicate with the computer.

3. How is the intensity of the electron beam controlled?

4. Define the term "page."

MODEMS

Modems, or modulators/demodulators, convert digital data to analog signals for transmission over telephone lines. Medium-speed modems [1200 bits per second (bps)] use *frequency shift keying (FSK)* for modulation. (Frequency modulation, which has a higher signal-to-noise ratio and requires a wider bandwidth, is used in higher-speed modems.) In FSK, digital values are converted to one of two frequencies by the modulation: a *mark* (1) is represented by a 1200-Hz tone while a *space* (0) is transmitted as a 2200-Hz tone. These frequencies can readily be transmitted within the 3-kilohertz (kHz) bandwidth of a telephone channel. See Fig. 3-8.

Either dial-up or leased phone lines can be used for the communications channel. Dial-up lines require that either a person or originating computer dial the phone number of the receiving (answering) computer. With leased lines the computers are permanently connected. The computer interfaces with the modem using one of the digital exchange protocols such as EIA-RS-232C, IBM, MIL-STD-188C, International Telegraph & Telephone Consultative Committee (CCITT), or Bell Telephone. A *simplex* interface can transmit data in one direction only. One computer acts as the transmitting unit and the other as the receiver. Both can transmit with a *half-duplex* interface, but not simultaneously. A *full-duplex* interface allows for two-way transmission at the same time.

Modems Review

1. Explain how the name "modem" is formed.

2. What is FSK?

3. True or false? A mark representing 0 is transmitted at 1200 Hz.

4. How does a computer interface to the modem?

5. Distinguish between full-duplex and half-duplex communications.

FLOPPY DISK DRIVES

A *floppy disk* is a circle of plastic coated with a magnetic surface used for recoding digital data. A drive spins the disk much like a phono record. The disk is permanently sealed in its jacket, and is highly polished to prevent abrasion from damaging the surface. Figure 3-9 shows two of the common sizes of disks. The standard disk is 8 inches (in) [20.3 centimeters (cm)] in diameter, while the minidisk has a diameter of 5.25 in (13.3 cm). Other sizes that you may encounter are the 4.12-in (10.5-cm) Eurodisk, 3.25-in (8.3-cm) IBM disk, and the 2.55-in (6.5-cm) Olivetti minidisk. Comparing the two most common disks, the 5.25-in mini is smaller and its drive requires less power, but the 8-in disk has four times as much data capacity.

There are several types of 5.25-in disks. As listed in Table 3-4, these are the standard, double-density, two-sided, and double-track/double-density disks. The double-density disks can store twice the information of a standard disk. The two-sided disk has twice the number of *tracks* and the double-track/double-density disk almost as many.

A *disk drive* provides the mechanical handling for the disk, a drive motor to spin it, and electronics to read or record. Figure 3-10 shows the drive

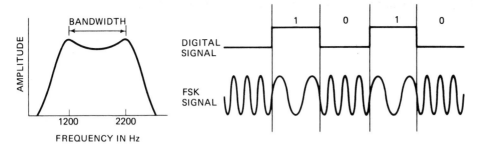

Figure 3-8. FSK Modulation.

components. The spindle hub engages the center of the disk and imparts the drive motor motion to it. The stepper motor moves the head assembly in or out to position it over the correct track. An index sector LED shines light on the disk, which has an index hole in it to allow the light to pass through to the detector as the hole rotates into position. A write protect switch senses whether the write protect notch on the disk envelope is covered or not. If a disk is write protected, the computer cannot record on it. Write protection prevents any incorrect recording action that could destroy the information previously put on the disk. Electronic circuits provide control of reading and writing as well as of the drive and stepper motors. A controller permits the microprocessor to select any one of four disk drives to use for reading or writing.

A dc drive motor with a servo speed controller and built-in tachometer comprises the drive mechanism. The motor cannot rotate until the interlock in the door latch is closed, to make sure that the disk is properly inserted. The head is made of ceramic material and is mounted on the head assembly. The entire assembly is positioned by a cam which is driven by the stepping motor in discrete increments. Each step corresponds to the track-to-track spacing on the disk. The control electronics have many tasks to perform, including detection of the sector index hole, positioning the head over the correct track, loading the head (pressing it against the disk), generating read or write signals, detecting a write protected disk and informing the computer, and selecting the proper drive for a given operation.

Standard Disk Formats

Disks are formatted to split the surface into blocks of a usable size. All disks are divided into *sectors* like pieces of a pie. Each sector begins at a particular point measured from the index hole. Furthermore, *hard-sectored disks* have an additional index hole to mark the beginning of each sector. *Soft-sectored* disks have only one timing hole. All other sectors begin at a sector mark recorded on the disk by the computer program. Because soft-sectored disks must use part of the surface area for sector marks, they cannot hold as much information as the same size hard-sectored disks.

Information is stored in concentric, circular *tracks* on the disk surface. There are 40 tracks in all on one side, with the same number of tracks on the other surface of a double-sided disk. The identically numbered upper and lower tracks of a double-sided

(b)

Figure 3-9. 8 in and 5.25 in Floppy Disks (*a*) Controller with Four Drives (*b*) 8 in and 5.25 in Disks.

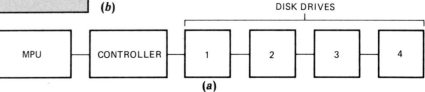

(a)

Table 3-4
5.25-in Floppy Disks

	Standard	Double density	Two sided	Double track/ Double density
Encoding	FM*	MFM†	FM	MFM
Data rate (kbps)	125	250	125	250
Number of tracks	40	40	80	77
Capacity (bytes)	125,000	250,000	250,000	481,250

*Frequency modulation.
†Modified FM.

floppy disk are sometimes called a "cylinder." The number of sectors that a track is divided into varies; there can be 8, 15, or 26 sectors per track. Depending on the number of sectors, there are then 512, 256, or 128 bytes in a sector. Sectors are also called the "track length."

A sector will always contain a record or part of a record. If the record is too short, the remainder of the bytes in the sector will be filled with zeros. If the record is too long, it will overlap into as many sectors as are needed to hold that number of data bytes. Because of this record-to-track assignment, good practice requires that data be blocked into the correct number of bytes to completely fill a sector before writing out. When reading, an entire sector is received at one time.

The IBM soft-sector format is illustrated in Fig. 3-11. With it, track 00 is always used as a system label track identifying the entire floppy disk. Tracks 01 through 74 are used to record data, and tracks 75 and 76 are available as alternates for bad tracks. If track 04, for example, is bad, the data intended for that track is automatically placed on track 75. Whenever a command to read track 04 is issued, track 75 is read instead.

The fields required in an IBM formatted disk are shown in Fig. 3-12. The identification (ID) field specifies the track number, head number, sector number, and sector length to the disk controller. In addition, a sync field is provided for timing synchronization. The CRC allows error checking on the other fields of identification. There are also sync and CRC fields in the data area.

Gaps on the recording surface separate the index hole gap from other sectors and the ID and data recordings. These gaps provide the electronics with a delay to switch from reading to writing. The gaps also compensate for speed errors between two drives, if the floppy disk was written on a different drive from the one reading it.

Minidisk Formats

A typical format for a mini floppy disk is shown in Fig. 3-13. Here the surface can hold 40 tracks and is divided into 10 soft sectors. Each sector has a length of 256 bytes so a track holds

$$10 \times 256 = 2560 \text{ bytes} = 20,480 \text{ bits}$$

Because there are forty tracks, the disk capacity is

$$2560 \text{ bytes/track} \times 40 \text{ tracks} = 102,400 \text{ bytes}$$

The disk spins at 300 revolutions per minute (rpm), so the sector hole passes under the sensor five times a second. At this speed, we can compute the average time to access a random track:

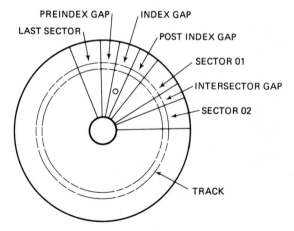

Figure 3-10. Floppy Disk Drive.

Figure 3-11. IBM Soft Sectored Format.

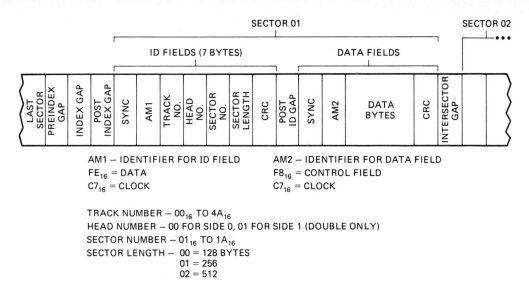

AM1 — IDENTIFIER FOR ID FIELD AM2 — IDENTIFIER FOR DATA FIELD
FE_{16} = DATA $F8_{16}$ = CONTROL FIELD
$C7_{16}$ = CLOCK $C7_{16}$ = CLOCK

TRACK NUMBER — 00_{16} TO $4A_{16}$
HEAD NUMBER — 00 FOR SIDE 0, 01 FOR SIDE 1 (DOUBLE ONLY)
SECTOR NUMBER — 01_{16} TO $1A_{16}$
SECTOR LENGTH — 00 = 128 BYTES
                01 = 256
                02 = 512

Figure 3-12. Floppy Disk Fields.

$$T_r = T_{seek} + T_{sector} + T_{data} \qquad (3\text{-}5)$$

where $\quad T_r$ = random-access time

T_{seek} = average seek time to move head over the track

T_{sector} = average time for the desired sector to rotate under the head

T_{data} = time to read the data

A particular disk drive, for example, has a T_{seek} of 450 ms, a T_{sector} of 100 ms, and T_{data} of 20 ms. Therefore, the random-access time is

$$T_r = 450 + 100 + 20 = 570 \text{ ms}$$

More than half a second is consumed in reading the data in a random way. A more efficient input procedure is to arrange the data to be read sequentially, which eliminates most of the seek and sector time delays.

Floppy Disk Drives Review

1. Which disk can hold more data, a double-density or two-sided disk?

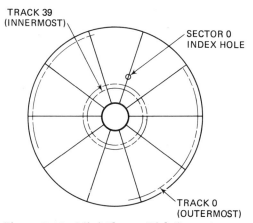

Figure 3-13. Mini Floppy Disk Format.

2. Explain the head movement mechanism of a floppy disk drive.

3. How is the index mark detected?

4. What is the purpose of the write protection notch?

5. Explain the difference between hard- and soft-sectored disks.

6. What is another name for the track length?

MAGNETIC TAPE RECORDERS

Cassette and cartridge recorders are peripherals often used to record and store microcomputer data offline. The recording medium is a coated tape that is magnetized in one of two states to represent a 1 or 0. Digital recording usually saturates the tape at its positive or negative limits. Saturation results in about 12 decibels (dB) higher output than audio recording on the same tape. This gain is realized because audio recording uses only 25 percent of the magnetic moment of the tape coating.

In addition to recording 1s and 0s, the digital signals must intermix error detection and correction codes (such as parity or CRC) and timing data. The resulting data stream is shaped and converted to an analog signal in the recording process. The writing actually takes place at the trailing edge of the head gap where the flux density is highest. The number of bits recorded per inch significantly affects the error rate. Only a single bit error in 10^7 bits would be expected when recording at 800 bits per inch (bpi), but the error rate increases to one in a thousand at 1200 bpi using the identical coding scheme.

As mentioned above, timing is recorded along with data on the tape. There are two methods for recording the clock: using a separate clock track or employing a self-clocking data code. Microcomputer tape recorders are limited to a single track, so only the latter method is of interest. The clock rate is important because a tape recorded on one machine and read by another should be reliable with as much as 4 percent difference in speed between the two.

Self-clocking codes transition from one level to another at the same time as the clock pulse, so the level changes of the signal allow the reading machine to reconstruct the proper timing. With most codes, a preamble is required to establish synchronization between the read clock and the signal on the tape. The preamble is simply a known bit pattern recorded ahead of the data.

One code suitable for this application is the return-to-zero, or *RZ code.* A positive transition in flux represents a 1 and a negative change a 0. When no bits are being recorded, the head does not put out a signal, leaving the tape in its unmagnetized state. The RZ code is suited for low-density recording. A disadvantage of this type of coding is that unmagnitized tape must be used because no signal is recorded between bits. If a signal were already on a tape (which is quite likely when tapes are used more than once), a confused recording would result. Bulk erasing of the tapes before each use will demagnetize them.

A more practical code is the *biphase code.* There are many variations on this scheme, such as Manchester, phase encoding, and frequency modulation codes. A binary 1 is recorded as two changes in flux direction, while no change in direction represents a 0. A distinct advantage of biphase recording is its insensitivity to drive motor speed changes.

Magnetic Tape Recorders Review

1. Why is the output from digital recording higher than analog recording?

2. How does recording density affect error rate?

3. Explain the method used to record the clock.

4. What is the purpose of a preamble?

5. What problem might you encounter in recording a second set of data on a used tape with the RZ code?

6. True or false? Manchester and frequency modulation are RZ codes.

CHAPTER SUMMARY

1. Codes are used to represent data that is not already in binary form. With encoding, letters, numbers, angles, and special symbols can be processed in the computer. Both BCD and ASCII are frequently used codes.

2. Error detection and correction codes make it possible to send information reliably over noisy communications channels.

3. Serial printers type one character at a time, while line printers can type an entire line at once. Print heads in the form of cylinders, balls, daisy wheels, and matrices are used in impact printing mechanisms. Ink-jet, photocopy, electrosensitive, electrostatic, and thermal printers have nonimpact heads.

4. The rows and columns of a keyboard are scanned to detect a depressed key. Switches operating on several different principles are used in the manufacture of keyboards. The technology used in building the keyboard determines its reliability, operating characteristics, and cost.

5. CRT terminals are based on a monitor, together with memory and I/O electronics to interface with the computer. The rows and columns of characters on the screen make up the display page.

6. Modems convert digital data to analog with a modulation scheme before sending, then demodulate the signals at the receiving end of the channel. A binary 1 is encoded as a mark and a 0 as a space. For medium-speed modems, FSK is usually the means of modulation used.

7. Floppy disks are an economical media for recording data for microcomputers. Sizes most often seen are the 8-in standard disks and 5.25-in minidisks. The disk drive must spin the disk, step the read head to the correct track, record or read data, and control the process. Disks are formatted into tracks and sectors to organize the information written on the magnetic surface.

8. Magnetic cassette and cartridge recorders are also used with microprocessors. As well as preserving the binary values, the coding for data provides timing information. Biphase codes are a widely used scheme for these recorders.

Codes	Impact printers	Space
Binary coded decimal (BCD)	Nonimpact printers	Floppy disk
American Standard Code for Information Interchange (ASCII)	Keyboards	Disk drive
	CRT terminals	Sectors
Error detection and correction (EDAC) codes	Monitor	Hard-sectored disks
	Display page	Soft-sectored disks
Parity	Refresh rate	Tracks
Check sum	Scrolling	Cassette and cartridge recorders
Cyclic redundancy check (CRC)	Modems	Self-clocking codes
Generator polynomial	Frequency shift keying (FSK)	RZ code
Serial printers	Mark	Biphase code
Line printers		

PROBLEMS

3-1 How much time is needed to refresh the CRT display if the row refresh time is 200 μs and there are 40 rows? The vertical blanking time is 800 μs.

3-2 How many rows are there to a page if the vertical blanking time is 900 μs, the row refresh time is 492 μs, and the refresh cycle is 120 Hz?

3-3 A CRT terminal page can display 2048 characters. If there are 32 rows to a page, how many characters are displayed on a line?

3-4 For the display in Prob. 3-3, what is the page refresh time if each character takes 26 μs to be refreshed? The vertical blanking time is 900 ms.

3-5 If a minidisk could hold 512 bytes in each of its 10 sectors, what would the bit capacity of the disk be? *40,960*

3-6 How long does it take for an entire sector on a standard minidisk to pass under the read head?

(Assume that the beginning of the sector is now under the head.)

3-7 On the average, what is the random-access time for track 16 of a minidisk drive with a sector time of 150 ms, data time of 18 ms, and head seek time of 380 ms?

3-8 How much time is saved if data is arranged in two sequential sectors of one track rather than in the random sectors used for the disk drive of Prob. 3-7?

3-9 How long does it take to move the head into position for a 300-rpm minidisk drive if random-access time is 475 ms? The mean sector time is 85 ms and the data read time is 12 ms.

3-10 What ID fields for track number, head number, sector number, and sector length would be read in the following situation?

Single-sided, 15-sector IBM format
Sector 13
Track 34

EXPERIMENT 2 _____

PURPOSE: To develop a time-delay computer program.

PROCEDURE:

STEP 1. Using any instructions that you like, write a program that puts the computer in a loop for 1 s then halts. *Hint:* A NOP instruction can be executed in 2 µs and a JMP in 5 µs. Design a nested loop to provide the correct time delay. Table A-4 in the Appendix to this book lists the execution time for all instructions.

STEP 2. Using a watch, test your program by calling it as a subroutine the number of times listed below. Record the time delay it produces.

Number of times called	Time delay
10	
20	
60	
100	
200	

4

PARALLEL INPUT/OUTPUT

Even the most powerful computer would be useless if data could not be accepted and answers could not be retrieved. The input/output circuitry and software provide these facilities. As you will see, the transfer of data between the microprocessor and external devices requires a greater awareness of the hardware interactions with software than any other computer operation. The proper timing and sequencing of the signals on the system buses is crucial to the transfer of data. A processor, such as the 8080A, usually can perform the data transfer in several different manners. The use of accumulator I/O, interrupts, and direct memory access to move parallel data back and forth together with the circuitry required will be explored in this chapter.

CHAPTER OBJECTIVES

Upon completion of this chapter you should be able to:

1. Distinguish between accumulator and memory-mapped I/O
2. Explain the function of the 8080A input and output instructions
3. Describe how the 8095 three-state buffer and 8212 I/O port can be used to transfer data to the 8080A
4. Discuss the use of interrupts in data transfer
5. Distinguish between single, multiple, and vectored interrupt architectures
6. Analyze the operation of the 8259 priority interrupt control unit
7. Define the term "direct memory access"
8. Show how the 8257 direct memory access controller is used in a microcomputer circuit

INPUT/OUTPUT CONCEPTS

Before starting the study of specific I/O methods, let us briefly consider the various methods of exchanging data between the microcomputer and the external devices, often referred to as *peripheral equipment.* Such devices might include printers (Fig. 4-1), CRT terminals (Fig. 4-2), or floppy disk drives (Fig. 4-3).

Data can move in either direction to the computer, as shown in Fig. 4-4. The direction is always relative to that computer. That is, output means that the computer is sending and input that the computer is receiving. This convention prevents the confusion that sometimes arises when discussing the exchange from the peripheral equipment point of view. That equipment must receive output data and send input data. Notice in Fig. 4-4 that every device need not handle two-way data exchange. Only device 3 has that ability. Device 1 accepts output data only, like a printer. Device 2 can only send data, a temperature sensor for example.

The 8080A microprocessor can accept or send data by using either *accumulator I/O* instructions or by *memory-mapped I/O* techniques. The input and output instructions and an *I/O port* are used in the former situation, while the peripheral is treated as part of memory in the latter case. An external device, suitably equipped, can notify the processor when it has input data to transmit or of any other special event by means of *interrupt signals.* The microprocessor must be able to process this signal at any time. An even more sophisticated I/O device can cause the microcomputer memory to allow that device to read or write data by mimicking the processor on the system buses. The microprocessor and *direct memory access (DMA)* device share memory accesses in this scheme. The following sections in this chapter will more fully explain these techniques.

Figure 4-2. CRT Terminal *(Hewlett-Packard Co.)*

ACCUMULATOR INPUT/OUTPUT

Accumulator I/O permits transfer of data between the microprocessor and the external device in either direction. Special instructions in the repertoire use the accumulator to send or receive data. Outgoing data must be in the A register before the output instruction is executed, and input data is placed in the accumulator upon instruction completion.

Figure 4-3. Floppy Disk Drive *(Billings Computer Corp.)*

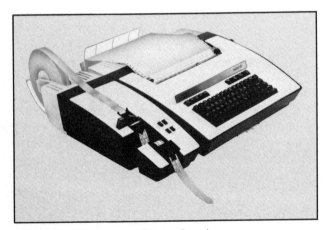

Figure 4-1. Printer *(Teletype Corp.)*

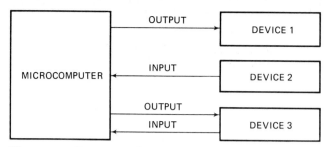

Figure 4-4. Data Transfer Directions.

Accumulator I/O is most similar to the data transfer operations of minicomputers. Many microprocessors do not provide this capability, but the 8080A does support it. An I/O port already mentioned above, is used with accumulator I/O.

The I/O port is a buffer which is connected to the system buses. Figure 4-5 shows a generalized I/O port. Only eight of the address bus lines need be decoded, for reasons that will become apparent when the instructions are discussed. Also, only the appropriate control bus signals need be accepted. In this situation only $\overline{I/OR}$ (input) and $\overline{I/OW}$ (output) are used by the I/O port.

The port must access the system bus at the proper time in the instruction cycle to prevent confusing other users of the buses. By proper sharing of the time available, many I/O ports can be attached to one MPU. The MPU selects the I/O port it wants to access in a manner not too different from reading or writing memory.

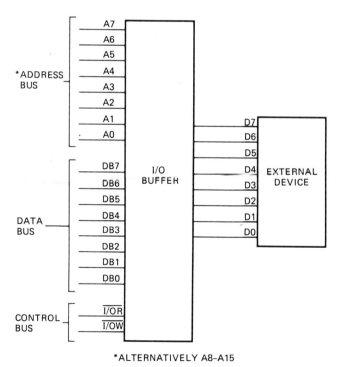

Figure 4-5. I/O Port.

I/O Instructions

There are two instructions available for accumulator I/O: one for input and the other for output. Each instruction can select up to 256 independent devices. Therefore, we can input from a maximum of 256 devices and output to another 256. Some of the devices (device 3 in Fig. 4-4, for example) would need both input and output, while others would require only one or the other. The number associated with each input or output device is called the *device code (DC)*.

The device code is an 8-bit number which uniquely addresses one peripheral device. Examples might be:

14_{16} (output)	Printer device code
02_{16} (input)	Temperature sensor
02_{16} (output) and $F6_{16}$ (input)	CRT terminal

Note that the input and output device codes need not be the same, as the CRT terminal assignment shows. Furthermore, the same code number may be used for input and output, as above, without any interference between the two.

INPUT The input instruction causes the 8-bit data byte to be read from the I/O port with the device code found in the second word of the instruction. The data is placed in the accumulator. There is no need to clear the A register before this instruction because all bits are changed by reading the input data. No status bits are affected by this instruction. A timing diagram is shown in Fig. 4-6. The first machine cycle is a normal instruction fetch. During MC2 the device code is obtained from memory. This will be a hexadecimal value from 00_{16} to FF_{16}. Data transfer occurs during MC3. During the first clock period of that machine cycle the device code is set on bits A0 to A7 of the address bus. The same code is also placed on bits A8 to A15 of the address bus, so the device need only decode 8-bits. Either the upper or lower byte may be used. The device must recognize its code and hold data stable on the data bus during the portion of T2 and T3 when DBIN is high. The processor accepts the data during this interval. By the end of T3 the external device drops the data and the device code is removed from the address bus.

Operation code	DB
Mnemonic	IN
Addressing mode	Immediate
Status bits affected	None

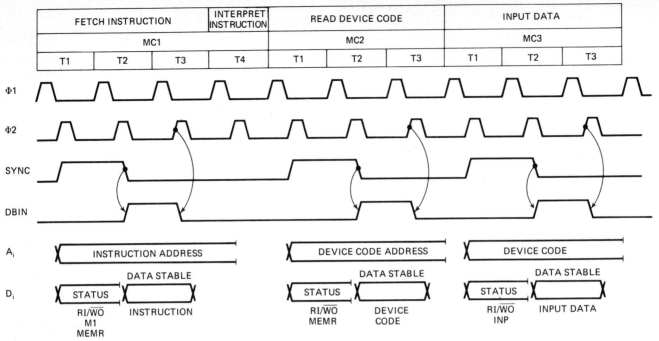

FETCH INSTRUCTION			INTERPRET INSTRUCTION	READ DEVICE CODE			INPUT DATA		
MC1				MC2			MC3		
T1	T2	T3	T4	T1	T2	T3	T1	T2	T3

Figure 4-6. Input Instruction Timing.

Clock periods	10		Operation code	D3
Execution time	5 μs		Mnemonic	OUT

Format

Bit numbers

7 6 5 4 3 2 1 0

Memory cell m | 1 1 0 1 1 0 1 1 |

m + 1 | Device code |

Addressing mode Immediate

Status bits affected None

Clock periods 10

Execution Time 5 μs

Format

Bit numbers

7 6 5 4 3 2 1 0

Memory cell m | 1 1 0 1 0 0 1 1 |

m + 1 | Device code |

□ EXAMPLE

Before execution		After execution	
Program counter	1406	Program counter	1408
A register	03	A register	4A
Memory	1406 DB	Memory	1406 DB
	1407 02		1407 02

The device on I/O port number 02_{16} has transmitted $4A_{16}$ to the processor, changing the value of the accumulator.

OUTPUT This instruction sends the current accumulator contents to the equipment connected to the I/O port indicated by the device code. A timing diagram of the output sequence is shown in Fig. 4-7. The instruction is fetched during MC1 and the device code during MC2. Just as in the input instruction, the device code is set on A0 to A7 and A8 to A15 during MC3. The device recognizes its address and samples the data bus when $\overline{WR}$ goes true (low).

□ EXAMPLE

Before execution		After execution	
Program counter	350A	Program counter	350C
A register	22	A register	22
Memory	350A D3	Memory	350A D3
	350B 14		350B 14

The A register value (22_{16}) is sent out I/O port number 14_{16}.

Programmed I/O Review

1. List four types of I/O used with microprocessors.

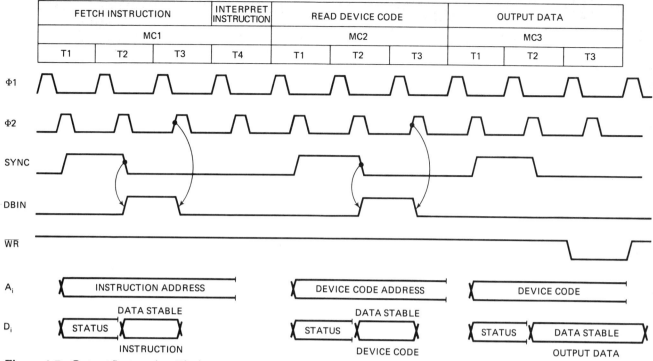

Figure 4-7. Output Instruction Timing.

2. Which method of input/output uses an I/O port?

3. Why is it unnecessary for the device to decode more than eight address lines?

4. Where is the device code obtained?

5. What operation occurs during T2 of machine cycle 3 of the input instruction?

6. When is the data sampled by the external device during output instruction execution?

I/O DEVICES

The 8080A is supported by a family of integrated circuits which help to solve the problems of *interfacing* the microprocessor with the I/O equipment. There are also general-purpose ICs which can be used as well. When connecting any device to the 8080A, the output drive capability must be considered.

The fan-out of the 8080A is such that the device can drive a maximum current of 1.9 mA. The fan-in of the 7400 series TTL is 1.6 mA—very close to the limit. A better choice for interfacing logic would be the 74LS low-power Schottky logic with 0.2 to 0.34 mA fan-in, or the 74L series with 0.1 to 0.16 mA fan-in. Other alternatives are the specially designed 8080A devices such as the 8205 decoder and 8212 8-bit I/O port with fan-in of 0.15 to 0.25 mA.

If the signals must travel more than 3 in (7.6 cm),

the outputs should be *buffered.* The 8228 system controller can be used to satisfy this requirement. When signal runs are over 12 in (30.5 cm), special *bus drivers* and *termination networks* are necessary.

Address Selection

Interpreting every bit of a device code or an address is referred to as *fully decoded address selection.* Otherwise, using *linear selection,* only certain bits can be decoded to generate the device select pulse. For example, if only the device codes 00_{16} through 07_{16} are used, then only address bits A0 through A2 need be examined. The shortcoming of this latter approach is that someday one may want to expand the system, and increasing the number of bits in the device code might require a major rebuild.

A fully decoded address selection decoder can be constructed using the 74LS30 eight-input NAND gate shown in the Fig. 4-8b. The device code used is $B6_{16}$. The pin assignment for the 74LS30 is shown in Fig. 4-8a. The output for this particular NAND may be expressed as

$$\overline{A7 \cdot \overline{A6} \cdot A5 \cdot A4 \cdot \overline{A3} \cdot A2 \cdot A1 \cdot \overline{A0}} \quad (4\text{-}1)$$

and only an input of $B6_{16}$ will produce a low output, $\overline{ADDR}$. Assuming we want to use the decoder with an output device, the chip select signal can be generated by ORing this output ($\overline{ADDR}$) with the processor output strobe ($\overline{I/OW}$) as shown in Fig. 4-8c. A low output from the OR gate selects the device.

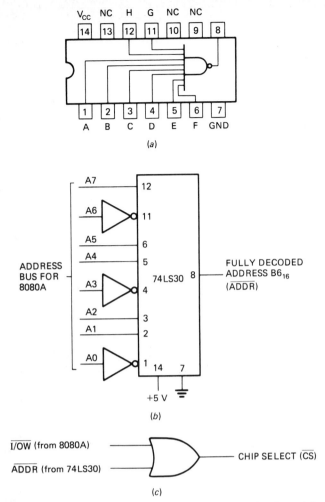

(a)

(b)

(c)

Figure 4-8. 8-Bit Fully Decoded Address Selection. (a) 74LS30 (b) Decoder (c) Generating Chip Select Strobe.

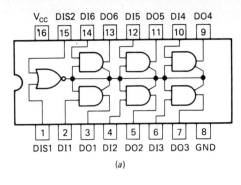

(a)

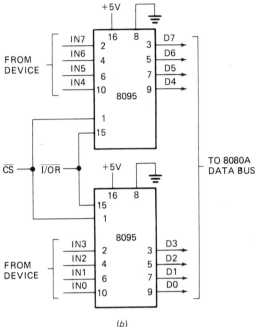

(b)

Figure 4-9. Input Buffer (a) 8095 (b) 8-Bit Data Input.

Buffering

Either input or output signals can be buffered to supply the necessary signal stability. A frequently used IC in 8080A applications is the three-state *8095 buffer.* Because it is a three-state device, several such buffers can be attached to the data bus, but only one will send an input to the 8080A at any given time. Good design practice calls for absolutely decoding the device code.

The buffer IC is shown in Fig. 4-9a. A low input on pins 1 and 15 (DIS1 and DIS2) enable the buffer to transfer data. The chip select ($\overline{CS}$), from a decoder similar to Fig. 4-8, and the processor input ($\overline{I/OR}$) signal are applied to the enabling inputs. When $\overline{I/OR}$ and $\overline{CS}$ go low, *data jamming* occurs: Data is sent, or *jammed,* into the MPU.

Two 8095s can be used to provide a full 8-bit data input, as shown in Fig. 4-9b. The external device first places the data on the input lines. When the $\overline{CS}$ and $\overline{I/OR}$ signals go low, the three-state AND gates are enabled, passing the signals through to the MPU.

I/O Ports

Input/output ports are well suited for small microprocessor systems or for the special needs of larger systems. The ports usually consist of data latches, buffers, and interrupt logic. The 8212 I/O port is an 8-bit port with eight D flip-flops for the latches. The Q outputs of the flip-flops are connected to three-state, noninverting output buffers, as shown in Fig. 4-10a. A pin assignment diagram for the port is shown in Fig. 4-10b.

From Fig. 4-10 and with a little Boolean algebra, we can readily determine

$$ENB = \overline{DS1} \cdot DS2 + MD$$
$$CK = STB \cdot \overline{MD} + MD \cdot \overline{DS1} \cdot DS2$$
$$SET = \overline{\overline{CLR} + (\overline{DS1} \cdot DS2)}$$
$$= \overline{CLR}(DS1 + \overline{DS2}) \text{ by DeMorgan's theorem}$$

A brief description of the 8212 input and output signals is given in Table 4-1.

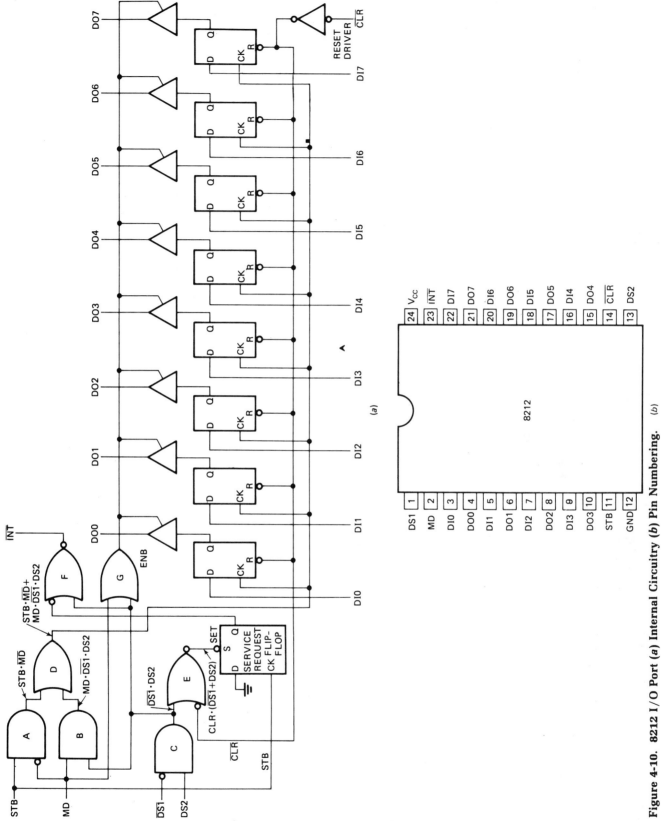

Figure 4-10. 8212 I/O Port (*a*) Internal Circuitry (*b*) Pin Numbering.

Table 4-1
8212 Signals

Signal	Description	Type*
DI0–DI7	Data	Input
DO0–DO7	Data	Three-state output
$\overline{DS1}$, DS2	Device select	Input
MD	Mode select	Input
STB	Data strobe	Input
$\overline{CLR}$	Device clear	Input
$\overline{INT}$	Interrupt request	Output

*Input and output are relative to the 8212.

Next we will analyze the 8212 operation. The 8212 I/O port is selected by setting $\overline{DS1}$ low and DS2 high. Each of the flip-flops will react to the D inputs only when the clock input (CK) is high. When the clock is low, the previous Q output will be held constant.

The mode input (MD) decides whether the IC will be in the output or the input mode. If the mode input is high (referred to as the output mode), the output of the buffer enable or gate (gate G) of Fig. 4-10 is high, allowing output data to pass through to the buffers. The D flip-flop input clock is also set high by the output of OR gate D (MD · $\overline{DS1}$ · DS2 is true), so the D flip-flops will react to new inputs. After the propagation delay, the new inputs will appear at the Q output terminal of each flip-flop.

When MD goes low (input mode), the three-state enable line (output of gate G) reacts to the output of gate C. Whenever the device select inputs are false (that is, $\overline{DS1}$ high or DS2 low), the output of gate G will go low, causing the buffer outputs to float. The clocking of the D flip-flops will then depend on the state of the strobe (STB) input. A high on STB causes clocking of the flip-flops regardless of the state of the device selection inputs. Figure 4-11 summarizes these input mode relationships in a timing diagram.

The D flip-flops can be reset at any time by making the $\overline{CLR}$ input low. For normal operation, $\overline{CLR}$ must be high. The interrupt request signal is used to inform the processor that the I/O port has new data to send. The processing of interrupts by the processor will be discussed in a later section. For the time being, only the method of setting the signal will be described.

Refer to the simplified diagrams in Fig. 4-12 to follow the sequence of events. In the input mode, STB goes high to clock data from DI0 through DI7 into the flip-flops. When STB falls to the low level, the service request (SR) flip-flop is clocked. With the D input grounded, the Q output must follow. The low Q_{SR} signal is inverted in NOR gate F producing a low $\overline{INT}$ signal to the MPU. (We are assuming the device is not selected so that $\overline{DS1}$ · DS2 is low.)

The MPU will respond to the interrupt request by setting $\overline{DS1}$ · DS2 true to select the device. The high output of gate C produces two actions: The service request flip-flop SET input goes low, forcing Q_{SR} high, and the new high input to NOR gate G will change the state of $\overline{INT}$ and hold it high.

AN 8212 INPUT PORT The 8212 is a versatile design, so it can be used in various ways. One of the simplest is shown in Fig. 4-13a. While this example shows

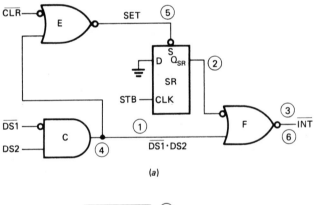

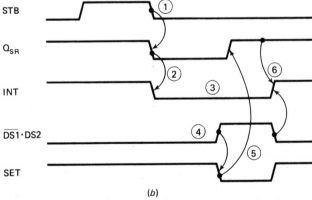

Figure 4-12. 8212 Interrupt Request (a) Simplified Schematic (b) Timing Diagrams.

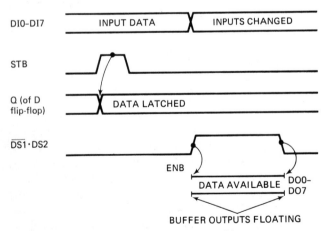

Figure 4-11. 8212 Input Mode Timing Diagram.

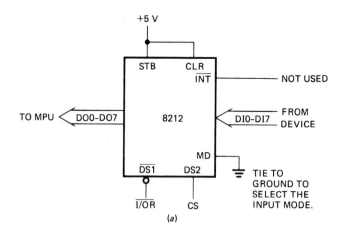

(a)

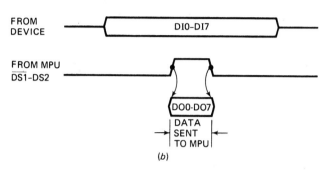

(b)

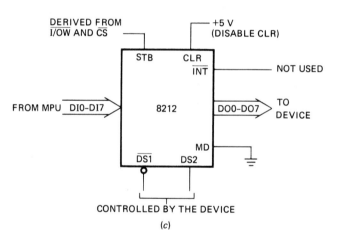

(c)

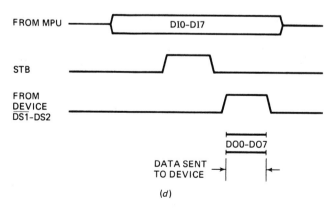

(d)

Figure 4-13. 8212 Port with Handshaking (a) Input-Port Wiring Diagram (b) Input-Timing Diagram (c) Output-Port Wiring Diagram (d) Output Timing Diagram.

the use as an input port, appropriate minor modifications would change it to an output port. Because STB is tied high, input data passes through the port continuously. The microprocessor can periodically sample the data lines to read the latest input. The output buffers are enabled by the device selection lines when the processor wants the next input.

AN 8212 OUTPUT PORT WITH HANDSHAKING A slightly more involved 8212 port is shown in Fig. 4-13c. This time the device is used for output, and control signals are exchanged between the processor and device before data transfer begins. Exchange of signals in this way is often called *handshaking*. With MD grounded, the MPU sets STB (after it has stabilized the output data on the bus) to clock the D flip-flops. In response to the high STB, the 8212 accepts the data. When the external device wants to read the data, it sets $\overline{DS1}$ · DS2 true, enabling the three-state output.

I/O Devices Review

1. Why is the fan-out of the 8080A important?

2. List two ways of accommodating the limited drive of the 8080A.

3. What should be done with output signal lines that are 16 in (40.6 cm) long?

4. Define "fully decoded address selection."

5. How does the 8095 buffer design provide for placing only one input on the data bus at any time?

6. Describe the operation of the 8212 in the output mode. In the input mode.

7. Why must the MD input be grounded in Fig. 4-12a?

8. What does setting the STB input high in Fig. 4-12c accomplish?

MEMORY-MAPPED I/O

Memory-mapped I/O treats external devices as memory locations, in contrast to accumulator I/O, which assigns them device codes. Because the devices are considered to be memory by the MPU, any of the memory transfer instructions such as MOV, STAX, LDAX, and ADD can be used. In fact, 2 bytes can be transferred using SHLD, for example. Furthermore, any of the general-purpose registers can be used as the source or destination for the data. Table 4-2 compares these two I/O techniques.

Table 4-2
Comparison of Accumulator I/O and Memory-Mapped I/O

	Accumulator I/O	Memory-mapped I/O	

Instructions	OUT
	IN
		MOV B, M
		MOV C, M
		MOV D, M
		MOV E, M
		MOV H, M
		MOV L, M
		MOV A, M
		STAX B
		STAX D
		LDAX B
		LDAX D
		ADD M
		ADC M
		SUB M
		SBB M
			MOV M, B
			MOV M, C
			MOV M, D
			MOV M, E
			MOV M, H
			MOV M, L
			MOV M, A
			ANA M
			XRA M
			ORA M
			CMP M
			INR M
			DCR M
			MVI M
			STA
			LDA
			SHLD
			LHLD

Control signals	$\overline{\text{I/OW}}$ $\overline{\text{I/OR}}$	$\overline{\text{MEMW}}$ $\overline{\text{MEMR}}$	
Data transfer	Between accumulator and the device	Between any general register (A, B, C, D, H, and L) and the device	
Device decoding	Device select pulse decoded from 8-bit device code (A0–A7 or A8–A15)	Device select pulse decoded from 16-bit address (A0–A15)	
Source of device address	From immediate data byte of the I/O instruction	From the address in an instruction or register pair	

There are several advantages to memory-mapped I/O. Being able to use any of the general-purpose registers, instead of just the accumulator, can shorten the program. By storing the 16-bit address for the peripheral device in the HL register pair and using register-addressed instructions, a memory-mapped I/O transfer can proceed faster than accumulator I/O because the device code need not be fetched from memory. More than 256 device codes are allowed (though more would probably never be required in a microcomputer). Two-byte data transfers are available, and input data can be directly used in arithmetic or logic instructions.

Among the disadvantages of memory-mapped I/O is the need to decode a 16-bit address, even if the device code is only 8 bits long. To clarify this statement, consider how the device with address $F3_{16}$ would distinguish between its address $00F3_{16}$ and $02F3_{16}$, $03F3_{16}$, and so on, unless the upper address byte were also decoded. Some memory addresses are sacrificed for device codes also. The loss may not be a serious problem in a processor that can address a 65K memory, like the 8080A.

Figure 4-14 shows the basic difference in control signal usage for memory-mapped and accumulator I/O. The memory and device codes available in each scheme are also indicated, assuming that addresses above 8000_{16} are reserved for devices in the memory-mapped case.

One way to assign the 16-bit address space in a memory-mapped system might be the following:

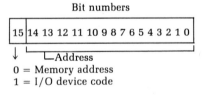

Bit numbers

0 = Memory address
1 = I/O device code

The same I/O devices that were used with accumulator I/O can be used with memory mapping. Essentially the only alteration that must be made in the circuits previously discussed is to change $\overline{\text{I/OR}}$ to $\overline{\text{MEMR}}$ and $\overline{\text{I/OW}}$ to $\overline{\text{MEMW}}$. As an illustration of how straightforward the conversion is, Fig. 4-15 shows the 8212 input port of Fig. 4-13a used in this way. Of course, the software must be changed

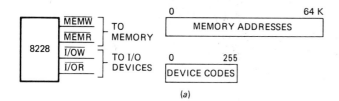

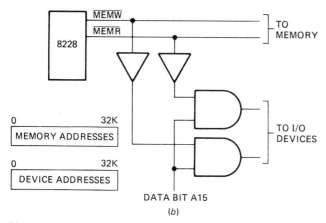

Figure 4-14. I/O Signal Comparison (*a*) Accumulator I/O (*b*) Memory-Mapped I/O.

to instructions which use the revised hardware configuration. Instead of the input (IN) instruction, MOV A, M or other memory data transfer instructions could be used.

Memory-Mapped I/O Review

1. What is the distinguishing characteristic of memory-mapped I/O?

2. True or false? A device with address 0314_{16} must use memory-mapped I/O.

3. List the instructions that can be used with memory-mapped I/O.

4. Discuss the advantages and disadvantages of memory-mapped I/O.

5. What change in the I/O port wiring of Fig. 4-13*b* must be made to convert it to memory-

mapped I/O? What software changes are necessary?

INTERRUPTS

An interrupt is a signal that arrives at any time and causes the processor to break out of its normal execution sequence and begin a special interrupt sequence instead. This section will describe the types of interrupts that a microprocessor may receive, the instructions available to process and control interrupts, timing and priority, and finally a thorough investigation of the 8259 priority interrupt control unit.

MPU Interrupt Configurations

When only a single line is available for input of interrupt signals to the MPU, the configuration is called a *single-interrupt* system. As Fig. 4-16*a* shows, many devices are ORed on one line. The processor must interrogate, or *poll,* the devices to find the particular one that has requested service.

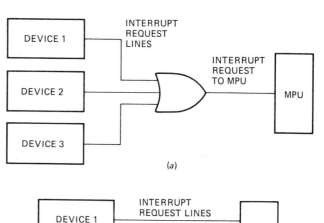

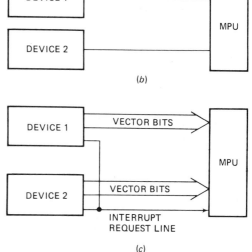

Figure 4-16. Interrupt Request Configurations (*a*) Single (*b*) Multiple (*c*) Vectored.

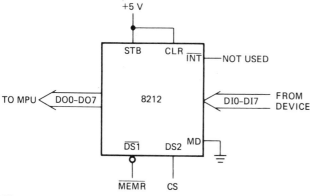

Figure 4-15. A Memory Mapped I/O Port.

A *multiple-interrupt* structured microprocessor furnishes several independent interrupt request lines. In this situation, the processor does not need to poll the devices because the one requesting service is uniquely identified. By adding the hardware for multiple interrupts, and thus eliminating polling, the programming burden has been reduced. The MC6800 is an example of a microprocessor with a multiple-interrupt arrangement. It has two interrupt lines.

Most sophisticated is the *vectored-interrupt* method supported by the 8080A microprocessor. In this architecture, each interrupting device provides a unique address which specifies the program which services its interrupt. Once again more complexity of hardware is traded off for simpler software in going to vectored interrupts. Not only must the processor be able to support the vectoring, but also the external devices must be able to supply the vector address in this arrangement.

Interrupt Handling Instructions

The 8080A supplies a substantial capability for accommodating vectored interrupts. When combined with supporting ICs, a powerful I/O handling capability can be constructed. There are two classes of instructions in the 8080A repertoire that relate to interrupts: control and vectoring.

CONTROL INSTRUCTIONS The 8080A contains an interrupt enable flip-flop that dictates whether or not interrupt requests will be honored. If the flip-flop is set, the MPU will recognize and respond to interrupts. When the flip-flop is reset, the processor ignores all interrupt requests. Interrupts are disabled by the RESET signal that starts the processor sequence, so the programmer must enable them. As you might expect, there is one instruction that sets the flip-flop, enable interrupts (EI), and another that clears it, disable interrupts (DI).

Operation code	FB	F3
Mnemonic	EI	DI
Addressing mode	None	
Status bits affected	None	
Clock periods	4	
Execution time	2 μs	

Format

Bit numbers

	7 6 5 4 3 2 1 0	7 6 5 4 3 2 1 0
Memory cell m	1 1 1 1 1 0 1 1	1 1 1 1 0 0 1 1

Examples of the use of these instructions will be presented in the following section.

VECTORED-INTERRUPT INSTRUCTIONS A vectored-interrupt instruction (called the RST instruction) is a special-purpose subroutine call. The instruction is supplied not from computer memory, but by the interrupting device. The device provides a 3-bit number, or *vector*, in the instruction. When one of these instructions is received, the processor enters a special interrupt state. (In all cases we will assume that interrupts are enabled, except when explicitly disabled.) Then the processor causes the program counter to be set to a vector address.

Format

Bit numbers

7	6	5	4		3	2	1	0
1	1	v	v		v	1	1	1

where vvv is the 3-bit vector

Vector	Address
000	0
001	1
010	2
011	3
100	4
101	5
110	6
111	7

In normal use, the vector is used with routines stored in the lower 64 bytes of memory. Each of these routines is 8 bytes long, as indicated by Fig. 4-17. Their length is dictated by the lower 3 bits of the vector address. These routines each service their respective interrupts. Table 4-3 lists the instructions, together with their vector addresses.

Addressing mode	None
Status bits affected	None
Clock periods	11
Execution time	5.5 μs

COMPREHENSIVE INTERRUPT EXAMPLE We will work a comprehensive example showing how the interrupting device causes a particular RST instruction to be executed, in turn forcing control to be transferred to the interrupt processing routine. We will see that the interrupt processing routine must execute a return (RET) instruction last to give control back to the main program.

Let the interrupting device be a floppy disk which generates an RST 3 instruction. Decoding the instruction shows that the interrupt vector is 3:

ADDRESS$_{16}$	ROUTINE
0000	VECTOR SERVICE ROUTINE 0
0008	VECTOR SERVICE ROUTINE 1
0010	VECTOR SERVICE ROUTINE 2
0018	VECTOR SERVICE ROUTINE 3
0020	VECTOR SERVICE ROUTINE 4
0028	VECTOR SERVICE ROUTINE 5
0030	VECTOR SERVICE ROUTINE 6
0038	VECTOR SERVICE ROUTINE 7

Figure 4-17. Address of Interrupt Servicing Routines.

$$RST\ 3 = DF_{16} = 11\underbrace{01\ 1}111_2$$
$$vvv = 3$$

When the processor recognizes the interrupt request (assuming interrupts are enabled) it automatically enters the interrupt state by:

1. Waiting until the current instruction is completed.

2. Clearing the interrupt enable flip-flop. (This action will prevent any other interrupts from disturbing the process.)

3. Taking the RST 3 instruction from the data lines instead of from memory.

4. Pushing the program counter on the stack (just as a normal call instruction would do). The address of the next sequential instruction in the main program is thus saved.

5. Forcing a jump to the 0018_{16} (vector address when vvv = 3).

Figure 4-18 diagrams this series of operations.

Once we are in this *interrupt servicing routine*, we must be very careful not to disturb the settings of registers or status bits. If we have to use any register, it must first be pushed on the stack. The stack is popped just prior to returning to the main program, so the register contents before and after the interrupt remain unchanged. Before exiting the interrupt servicing routine, there are two other tasks that must be completed. First, interrupts must be reenabled if we ever want to receive another (remember that in honoring the interrupt request the processor cleared the flip-flop.) Second, as mentioned above, we must execute a return instruction to cause the next address to be popped from the stack and placed in the program counter. Listed in Table 4-4 is a typical interrupt servicing routine. Figure 4-19 is a flowchart for the routine.

As you can see, there is not much memory space for processing. If more is needed, a jump to some other memory location can be made. Then all the memory needed is accessible.

Interrupt Process Timing

Having discussed the instructions available for interrupt handling and the general sequence of events, we will now look in more detail at the timing and control signals involved. Figure 4-20 shows the relationships between the signals from the microprocessor and the external device.

As explained earlier, the interrupt is initiated by the external device setting the interrupt request signal (INT) to the processor high. The processor will acknowledge the request, unless interrupts have been disabled by either a

1. Disable interrupt instruction

2. Reset condition

3. Previous processor acknowledgment clearing the flip-flop

External devices can tell when interrupts will be accepted because the 8080A holds the interrupt enabled (INTE) line high to indicate that the flip-flop is set. The INTE signal falls on the rising edge of Φ2 in T1 when the interrupt is acknowledged, as the 8080A automatically disables other interrupts to service the current one.

The external device receives an acknowledgment on the data bus during T1, with the data bits listed in Table 4-5 set to indicate status. The primary interrupt status indicator is INTA, which is converted

Table 4-3
RST Instruction

Operation code	Mnemonic	Vector	Vector address$_{16}$
C7	RST 0	0	0000
CF	RST 1	1	0008
D7	RST 2	2	0010
DF	RST 3	3	0018
E7	RST 4	4	0020
EF	RST 5	5	0028
F7	RST 6	6	0030
FF	RST 7	7	0038

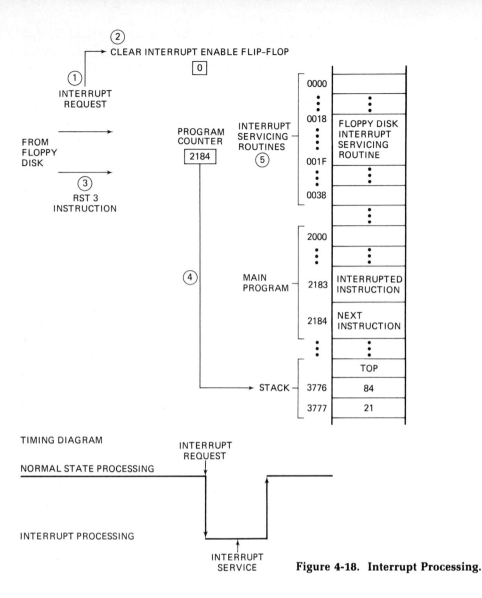

Figure 4-18. Interrupt Processing.

to a separate acknowledge signal if the 8228 system controller is used with the 8080A.

After acknowledging the interrupt request, the 8080A initiates the special interrupt instruction fetch sequence.

1. The program counter is not incremented.

2. The status bits on the data lines during T1 and T2 indicate interrupt acknowledge and no memory reference for instruction fetch. (Recall that memory read, MEMR, is set high on D7 in a normal instruction fetch.) This difference informs the device that the processor expects

Table 4-4
Interrupt Servicing Routine

Mnemonic	Address	Op code	Comments
PUSH A	0018	F5	Save accumulator and status bits
MVI A, 3	0019	3E	Store indicator of interrupt
	001A	03	vector in D register
MOV D, A	001B	57	
POP A	001C	F1	Restore accumulator and status bits
EI	001D	FB	Reenable interrupts
RET	001E	C9	Return
	001F	. . .	Not used

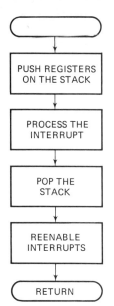

Figure 4-19. Interrupt Servicing Routine Flowchart.

the next instruction to be supplied externally and not from memory.

3. The processor fetches an instruction from the device that causes the program counter to be pushed on the stack and gives the starting address of the servicing routine (either CALL or RST.)

4. The processor references the appropriate interrupt service routine as a result of the CALL or RST.

The two instructions that can be supplied by the device require different hardware for implementation. An explanation of each approach is given below.

USING RST The external device senses the transition of INTA from low to high during T2. A circuit like the one shown in Fig. 4-21 then generates the RST instruction. The chip is enabled by INTA (data bus bit D0) going high during T1, when SYNC is also high. Inputs D0, D1, D2, D6, and D7 of the buffer are tied to V_{CC}. The bits selecting the vector are either grounded or tied to +5 V. For example, bits D5 and D3 would be high and D4 low for a vector value of 5.

SPECIAL 8228 FEATURE A simplified approach to generating the RST instruction can be taken if a single-interrupt configuration is suitable to the system. In this case, the 8228 is used and its INTA output is tied to the +12-V power supply through a 1-kilohm (kΩ) resistor. Then the external device does not supply the RST instruction. Instead, the 8228 inserts the op code for RST 7 in response to the microprocessor setting INTE true. Now all interrupts must be handled by the RST 7 subroutine at address 0038_{16}.

USING CALL There are two possible configurations to consider using when a CALL instruction is to

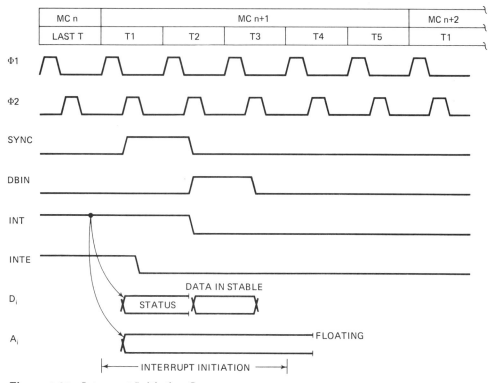

Figure 4-20. Interrupt Initiation Sequence.

Table 4-5
Interrupt Response Data Bit Settings

Bit	Meaning
D0	Interrupt acknowledge (INTA)
D1	Read/write control ($\overline{WO}$)
D5	Fetch cycle initiated (M1)

be generated by the device. If the system does not include the 8228, fairly complex logic is needed. The external device must first send the CALL op code (CD_{16}) to the 8080A when INTA is high. It must then suppress normal memory referring during the next two machine cycles and transmit the low and high address bytes for the subroutine entrance to the MPU. The 8259 priority interrupt control unit, described later in this chapter, can perform these functions.

If there is an 8228 in the microcomputer, the task of the external device is simplified. The 8228 generates a separate $\overline{INTA}$ signal. The external device responds to a true $\overline{INTA}$ with the op code of the CALL instruction. Then the 8228 automatically generates two more $\overline{INTA}$ low transitions during the next two machine cycles. The external logic can use these pulses to disable memory selection and respond with the address bytes.

NEC 8080A DIFFERENCE The NEC 8080A makes the issuing of a CALL instruction by external logic simpler. When the NEC 8080A receives a CALL instruction operation code in response to INTA true, it holds INTA true for the following two machine cycles as well. In effect, the 8080A signals replace those of the 8228 in this situation.

The Halt State and Interrupts

Recall that the halt instruction causes the processor to stop executing instructions. Once stopped, how

is the processor restarted? The halt state can be terminated by an interrupt request (INT high). In servicing the interrupt, the processor will reference the servicing routine, which will reinitiate operation.

If interrupts were inhibited when the processor halted, the interrupt request will not be acknowledged. What does the operator do then? The only way to leave the halt state, in that case, is to turn the power off and back on again.

Interrupt Review

1. Distinguish between single-, multiple-, and vectored-interrupt configurations. Which configuration requires polling?

2. What instructions control the interrupt enable flip-flop in the 8080A?

3. How can you determine the entrance address for the servicing routine of an RST instruction?

4. Why must the external device issue an instruction that causes the program counter to be pushed on the stack in response to an interrupt acknowledge?

5. What instructions should be included in every interrupt servicing routine?

6. Describe the timing of interrupt signals in the 8080A.

7. What is the responsibility of an external device that generates an RST instruction after the MPU acknowledges the interrupt? What if a CALL is used? How can the 8228 simplify each situation?

8. How are interrupts handled if the processor is in the halt state?

PRIORITY INTERRUPT CONTROL UNIT

The 8259 *priority interrupt control unit (PICU)* is an NMOS, 28-pin DIP designed to work with an 8080A. All 8259 outputs are TTL-compatible. An 8228 system controller is required in any system that uses an 8259. The 8259 can coordinate a maximum of eight external interrupts, or one device can act as the master for up to eight slave 8259s producing 64 levels of interrupt priority. Such a complex arrangement would not normally be used with a microprocessor, though.

8259 Signals

The pin assignments for the 8259 are shown in Fig. 4-22, and each of the signals is briefly described

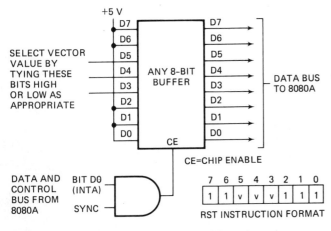

Figure 4-21. Circuit for Generating RST.

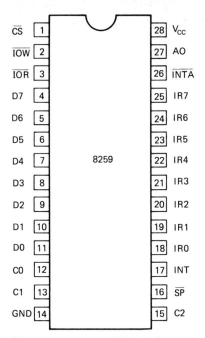

Figure 4-22. 8259 Pin Assignments.

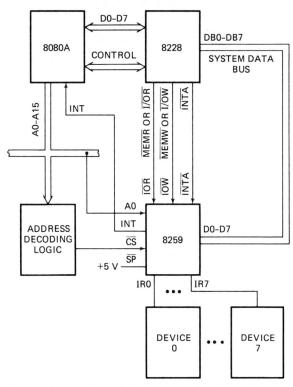

Figure 4-23. Single 8259 System Simplified Diagram.

in Table 4-6. The 8259 can be used in either a memory-mapped I/O or I/O port fashion. As Fig. 4-23 shows, bit A15 of the address bus is attached to the A0 input to the chip. You will also see that the 8259 is treated as a device with two addresses—a low address when the A0 input is zero and a high address when A0 is high.

A system with master-slave 8259s is shown in Fig. 4-24. An important feature to note is that the $\overline{SP}$ input is high for the master unit and grounded for the slave.

The master services devices 0 through 6 and the slave is connected to IR7 of the master and responds to the interrupts of devices 7 through 14.

8259 Functions

The 8259 not only manages the multiple interrupts, but also provides the object code for the CALL instruction and the 2 address bytes, as described in the previous section. The address in the last 2 bytes is the subroutine entrance of the interrupt handling software.

While the 8259 offers a great deal of flexibility in choosing these addresses, they are not entirely independent. The user has a choice of any starting

Table 4-6
8259 Signal Description

Name	Purpose	Type
$\overline{CS}$	Device select	Input
A0	I/O port identification	Input
D0–D7	Data bus	Bidirectional, three state
$\overline{IOR}$	Read control	Input
$\overline{IOW}$	Write control	Input
IR0–IR7	Interrupt requests from external devices	Input
INT	Interrupt request to 8080A	Output
$\overline{INTA}$	Interrupt acknowledge	Input
$\overline{SP}$	Master/slave identification (high for master, low for slaves)	Input
C0–C2	Cascade signals to select slaves in multiple 8259 systems	Output (from master)/input (to slaves)

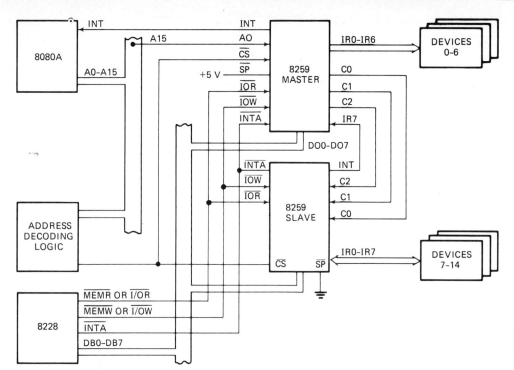

Figure 4-24. Master-Slave 8259 System Simplified Diagram.

address for the memory block that contains the interrupt handling routines. Within that block, the option of allowing either 4 or 8 bytes per routine is offered by the 8259. The memory map for each of these arrangements is shown in Fig. 4-25 (note that the illustration assumes a starting address of 1000_{16} was selected). Actually the four-cell option may be most useful, because a jump instruction would normally be placed in that location.

Each entrance cell is uniquely assigned to a given interrupt level. As Fig. 4-25 shows for the first option, cell 1000 is assigned to level 0, cell 1004 to level 2, and so on. The second option is similar, except that entrances are eight locations apart.

The 8259 also provides for *interrupt priority arbitration:* That is, it arbitrates between simultaneously occurring interrupts to decide which will be serviced first by the processor. This means that if devices 2 and 4 both send interrupts, the 8259 will choose the device with the higher priority and forward its interrupt to the 8080A. Such service is typical of any interrupt priority arbitration logic. The 8259, however, carries arbitration a step farther. Not only does it arbitrate at the time the interrupts occur, but it can also prevent a lower-level interrupt from interrupting the servicing routine of a higher level. This means that, once the service routine starts running, it can only be interrupted by a higher-level device. The 8259 offers quite a variety of priority assignment protocols. Each of them is described below. Because the 8259 is a programmable device, each mode must be selected by control signals from the 8080A.

FULLY NESTED MODE The fully nested mode is the default condition: Unless the 8259 is programmed to assume another mode of operation, it will take the fully nested mode. This mode establishes a fixed priority. The priority of a device depends on which IR pin it is connected to. Pin 0 has the highest priority and pin 7 the lowest.

Interrupt priorities never change in the fully nested mode. That means an interrupt on a lower-priority IR line will never be acknowledged as long as there exists one on a higher-priority line or while an interrupt service request for a higher-priority interrupt is executing.

For example, assume that interrupts are produced by the devices on IR3 and IR6 at the same time. As the timing diagram in Fig. 4-26 shows, the priority 6 interrupt does not get to the MPU, although interrupts may be enabled by the 8080A, until the priority 3 processing is complete. When a priority 2 interrupt occurs, however, the priority 3 processing is suspended and the servicing routine for the device on IR2 is run.

ROTATING PRIORITIES, MODE A The fixed-priorities scheme of the fully nested mode can result in a poor response to low-level interrupts. In some cases, the lowest priority may never get access to the processor. With mode A rotating priorities, every level is guaranteed a chance to interrupt the processor. After a given interrupt level has been serviced, it moves to the position of lowest priority. A few examples, shown in Table 4-7, will make it easier

Interrupt Level	Address		
0	1000	C3	← Jump Instruction
	1001	20 ⎤	← Address
		14 ⎦	
	1002		Not used
	1003		
1	1004	C3	
	1005	60	
	1006	14	
	1007		
2	1008	C3	
	1009	20	
	100A	25	
	100B		
3	100C	C3	
	100D	F0	
	100E	12	
	100F	12	
	.	.	
	.	.	
	.	.	

(a)

Interrupt Level	Address	
0	1000	C3
	1001	20
	1002	14
	1003	
	1004	
	1005	
	1006	
	1007	
1	1008	C3
	1009	60
	100A	14
	100B	
	100C	
	100D	
	100E	
	100F	
2	1010	C3
	.	.
	.	.
	.	.

(b)

Figure 4-25. Interrupt Address With the 8259 (a) Option 1–4 Cells Per Entrance (b) Option 2–8 Cells Per Entrance.

Table 4-7
Priority Level of Device Interrupt Request Lines

	Lowest							Highest
Initially	IR7	IR6	IR5	IR4	IR3	IR2	IR1	IR0
After an IR3 interrupt is acknowledged	IR3	IR7	IR6	IR5	IR4	IR2	IR1	IR0
After an IR6 interrupt is acknowledged	IR6	IR3	IR7	IR5	IR4	IR2	IR1	IR0

to visualize how the priority levels are rearranged. The effect of mode A is to offer equal service to all priorities levels. The priorities are rearranged when control codes from the MPU inform the 8259 that processing of the last interrupt has been completed.

ROTATING PRIORITES, MODE B In this mode, the processor can specify the lowest priority level at any time. The priorities of the other IR lines are then assigned sequentially, but the highest level can be freely chosen. Consider the examples in Table 4-8. As can be seen, the highest-priority IR line is always one greater than the one selected to have lowest priority. Where IR2 is the lowest level, IR3 has the highest and with IR5 lowest, IR6 is highest.

POLLED MODE The priority arbitration can be bypassed entirely by using the polled mode. Then the 8259 is referenced by the processor to find the status of I/O devices, but no interrupts are generated. When the MPU interrogates the 8259, a status word provides an indication of the highest-level IR line that is requesting an interrupt and an indication that an interrupt request is active. The format for that word is shown below.

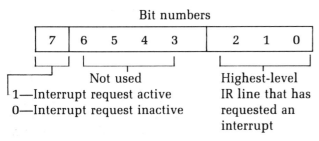

When polling is used in a master-slave configuration, the master is polled first. The slave with an active interrupt is shown in bits 0 to 2. Another polling request from the processor then goes to that slave. For example, the master unit provides a status word of

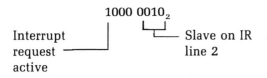

Then slave 2 is polled and responds with

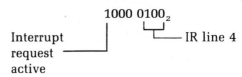

The microprocessor has found that the highest-priority interrupt request is from the device on IR line 4 of slave unit 2.

SIMPLE MASK MODE Masking permits enabling or disabling interrupts on an individual IR line level. There are two *mask modes* available in the 8259, either of which can be superimposed on the fully nested priority or rotating priority modes A or B. In the simple mask mode, the MPU outputs an 8-bit mask—each bit represents the respective IR line. Any bit that is set disables interrupts on the corresponding IR line:

Bit numbers and IR line numbers

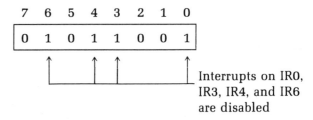

SPECIAL MASK MODE This mask allows the processor to allow interrupts from a lower-priority-level device to interrupt the service routine of a higher-priority mode. The 8-bit mask is interpreted to mean that 0s will allow that IR level to interrupt a service request for a higher level. 1s in the mask disable this feature.

Bit numbers and IR line numbers

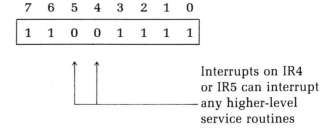

Table 4-8
Priority Level of Device Interrupt Request Lines

	Lowest							Highest
Initially	IR7	IR6	IR5	IR4	IR3	IR2	IR1	IR0
After the MPU specifies IR2 lowest-level priority	IR2	IR1	IR0	IR7	IR6	IR5	IR4	IR3
After MPU specifies IR5 lowest-level priority	IR5	IR4	IR3	IR2	IR1	IR0	IR7	IR6

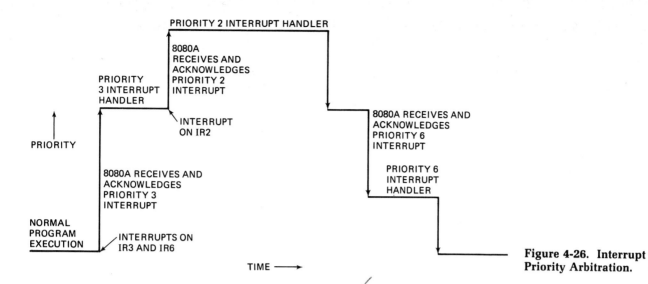

Figure 4-26. Interrupt Priority Arbitration.

8259 Architecture

An understanding of some of the internal registers of the 8259 is necessary, before looking into how to program it. As Fig. 4-27 shows, the 8259 has eight functional components. The data bus buffer temporarily holds data transiting between the internal bus and system data bus. The cascade comparator recognizes a slave unit's address. Read/write logic informs the control unit of the direction of data flow.

The interrupt request (IR) and interrupt status (IS) registers maintain the bookkeeping for the priority arbitration logic, as controlled by the processor-supplied mask (if used). The IR register latches all input from the external devices. Any device with a pending interrupt request sets the appropriate bit in the IR register to 1. Only the bit for the highest-level IR line will be set in the IS register. The IS register reflects the result of the arbitration logic. That bit remains set until the interrupt handling program in the processor clears it by issuing an "end of interrupt" command. Should a higher-level interrupt request come along while that routine is running, its bit is also set in the IS register. If the IS register contains

$$0100 \quad 1000_2$$
$$\uparrow \qquad \uparrow$$
$$\text{Level 6} \quad \text{Level 3}$$

we know that the interrupt handler for level 6 was interrupted by a request from IR3.

Because the interrupt request from the external device is not latched until the bit is set in the IS register, the device must hold the IR line high until

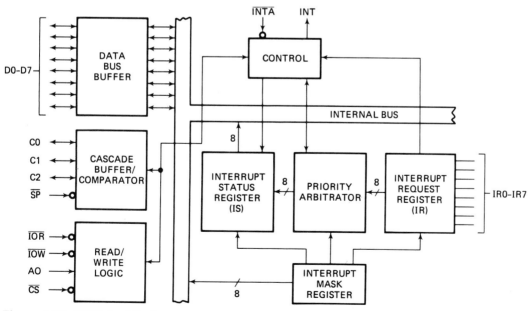

Figure 4-27. 8259 Architecture.

acknowledged. A mask from the processor can prevent bits in the IR and IS registers from being set.

Programming the 8259

The 8259 is programmed by the processor sending a series of initialization and operational control words. The processor addresses the 8259 as two I/O ports or memory locations. All address bits except one are the same for the ports. The final bit is used to set or clear the A0 input.

The initialization sequence of commands that must be sent is diagrammed in Fig. 4-28. Two initialization control words (ICW) are always used. In a master-slave system, a third initialization control word must be sent to the master, then sets of three words are passed to each slave. Finally, options and mask bits can be selected if desired.

Table 4-9 lists the control words for the 8259. After the initialization sequence has been sent, writing data in the high port (A0 = 1) will cause the 8259 to interpret the 8 bits as a mask, unless preceded by ICW1. The operational control words can be sent at any time after the initialization. A typical control word sequence for the configuration shown in Fig. 4-23 is given in Table 4-10.

Priority Interrupt Control Unit Review

1. What are the $\overline{IOR}$ and $\overline{IOW}$ inputs to the 8259 used for?

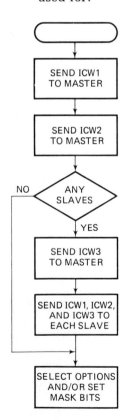

Figure 4-28. 8259 Initialization Sequence.

2. How is the $\overline{SP}$ input used to designate master and slave units?

3. Describe the two addressing options for the entrances to interrupt handling routines provided by the 8259.

4. How is the priority of an interrupt level established in the fully nested mode?

5. How does rotating priority mode A differ from mode B?

6. How does the processor locate pending interrupts in the polled mode?

7. How do the two types of masks influence the priority arbitration?

8. List the types of initialization control words that must be issued in a master-slave system with two slaves.

DIRECT MEMORY ACCESS (DMA)

At times the data transfer to peripheral equipment may be so rapid that interrupts will not provide an adequate data exchange rate. Furthermore, a large number of interrupts will severely reduce the processing speed of the mainline program. In such cases a special controller can be used to perform high-speed transfers between memory and external devices directly. Such a direct memory access controller uses the buses in a manner quite similar to that used by the processor.

In an 8080A system, the hold state is used for direct memory access. With other processors DMA may proceed after suspending the processor or by "stretching" clock pulses. Turning our interest to the 8080A, though, we will want to understand how the DMA controller emulates the MPU on the address, data, and control buses. To accomplish the emulation, each DMA channel must have a 16-bit address register and a counter for the number of bytes to transfer. A status register is usually provided as well. Because the processor and external devices cannot simultaneously access memory, one must wait for the other. This *memory cycle stealing* by the external device does slow the processor down, because it cannot execute instructions without accessing memory.

A simplified DMA system is shown in Fig. 4-29. The processor and DMA controller indicate to each other which of them is presently directing the system buses by means of the HOLD and hold acknowledge (HLDA) signals. The devices, in turn, request use of the data bus and are granted it by the control signals between each of the peripherals and the DMA controller. Although the DMA controller is connect-

Table 4-9
8259 Control Words

A0 setting	Control word	Bit number	Meaning
0	Initialization control word 1 (ICW1)	0	Not interpreted.
		1	Set, this is only a master 8259 system. Clear, this is a master-slave system.
		2	Set, address vector option 1 (four words between entrance cells). Clear, address vector option 2 (eight words between entrance cells).
		3	Not interpreted.
		4	Always set.
		5–7	Bits 5–7 of the constant portion of vector address (refer to Fig. 4-25). Bit 5 not interrupted if option 2 was selected.
1	Initialization control word 2 (ICW2)	0–7	Bits 8–15 of the constant portion of the vector address (refer to Fig. 4-25).
1	Initialization control word 3 (ICW3)	0–7	To a master unit: Any bit set means that a slave is attached to that IR line.
		0–2	To a slave unit: Identifies slave's IR lines number at the master unit.
		3–7	Not interpreted by slave.
0	Operational control word 2 (OCW2)	0–2	See bits 5–7 for explanation.
		3	Always 0.
		4	Always 0.
		5–7	Operation: 0—No operation. 1—End of interrupt (ignore bits 0–2). 2—No operation. 3—Special end of interrupt, reset the interrupt status (IS) register bit specified in bits 0–2. 4—No operation. 5—End of interrupt, start rotating priority mode A (ignore bits 0–2). 6—Start rotating priority mode B (bits 0–2 specify lowest level). 7—End of interrupt, start rotating priority mode B (bits 0–2 specify lowest level).
0	Operational control word 3 (OCW3)	0–1	Set status: 0—Illegal. 1—Illegal. 2—Select reading of the interrupt request (IR) register. 3—Select reading of the interrupt status (IS) register.
		2	Set, polled mode selected. Clear, other mode selected.

Table 4-9 *(continued)*
8259 Control Words

A0 setting	Control word	Bit number	Meaning
		3	Always 1.
		4	Always 0.
		5–6	Mask mode: 0—Illegal. 1—Illegal. 2—Cancel special mask mode. 3—Select special mask mode.
		7	Not interpreted

ed to the data bus, data from the external devices does not pass through the controller. Instead, once a device has been granted access to the data bus, data passes directly between the device and memory. The data bus is only used by the DMA controller to accept commands from the processor or to send status information to the processor.

Direct Memory Access Review

1. When is DMA the preferred method of I/O?

2. What state in the 8080A is used during direct memory access data transfers?

3. List the registers usually found in a DMA controller.

4. True or false? Data from the peripheral device to be written into memory passes through the DMA controller to the data bus.

THE 8257 DMA CONTROLLER

The 8257 DMA controller, used in 8080A systems, supports four DMA channels. Each channel can be assigned to a peripheral device. All signals to or from the MNOS DIP are TTL-compatible. A diagram of pin assignments for the chip is shown in Fig. 4-30. Each of the signals is briefly explained in Table 4-11.

For the 8257 to mimic the processor, it must duplicate all signals needed to control memory reading and writing. Table 4-12 compares the 8257 signals with those of the 8080A and the 8228. The table indicates that the 8257 multiplexes the upper 8 bits of the address of the data bus. For this reason, an 8212 I/O port (or its equivalent) must be used to demultiplex the data bus output pins from the 8257. A system consisting of the 8080A, with its support chips, 8212, and 8257 is shown in Fig. 4-31. Only signals involved with DMA transfers are in-

Table 4-10
Control Word Sequence

	A0	Output	Control word	Meaning
Initialize master in fully nested mode	0	02	ICW1	Master-slave system, eight words between vectors
	1	10	ICW2	Base address for master vector is 1000_{16}
	1	80	ICW3	Slave on IR7
Initialize slave	0	02	ICW1	Master-slave system
	1	18	ICW2	Base address for slave vector is 1800_{16}
	1	07	ICW3	Slave is on IR line 7
	0	A0	OCW2	Rotate priorities mode A with end of interrupt
	0	60	OCW3	Select special mask
	1	02	MASK	Allow level 1 to interrupt level 0 service routine

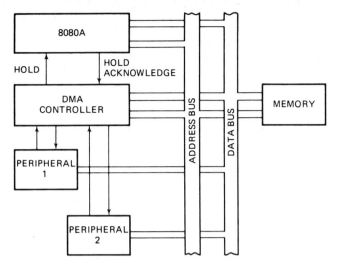

Figure 4-29. Simplified DMA Controller Block Diagram.

```
 I/OR   1          40  A7
 I/OW   2          39  A6
 MEMR   3          38  A5
 MEMW   4          37  A4
 MARK   5          36  TC
 READY  6          35  A3
 HLDA   7          34  A2
 ADDSTB 8          33  A1
 AEN    9          32  A0
 HRQ   10   8257   31  Vcc
 CS    11          30  DB0
 Φ2    12          29  DB1
 RESET 13          28  DB2
 DACK2 14          27  DB3
 DACK3 15          26  DB4
 DRQ3  16          25  DACK0
 DRQ2  17          24  DACK1
 DRQ1  18          23  DB5
 DRQ0  19          22  DB6
 GND   20          21  DB7
```

Figure 4-30. 8257 DMA Controller.

cluded in this illustration. Memory would be connected to the address and system data buses in the normal manner.

The diagram illustrates how the low-order address bits (A0 through A7) are derived directly from the 8257, but the high-order bits (A8 through A15) are furnished by the 8212 I/O port. It obtains their value by demultiplexing the data bus from the 8257 at the proper time.

8257 Registers

Every DMA channel of the 8257 has two registers. The 16-bit address registers contain the next memory

Table 4-11
8257 Signal Summary

Signal name	Meaning	Type
DB0–DB7	Data bus	Three state bidirectional
A0–A4	Low-order address bus	Three state, bidirectional
A5–A7	Remaining low-order address bus	Three state, output
I/OR	Processor input strobe	Three state, bidirectional
I/OW	Processor output strobe	Three state, bidirectional
MEMR	Memory read strobe	Three state, output
MEMW	Memory write strobe	Three state, output
MARK	128-byte count strobe	Output
TC	Terminal count strobe	Output
READY	Memory ready/not ready	Input
HRQ	Hold request to MPU	Output
HLDA	Hold acknowledge from MPU	Input
ADDSTB	Address on data bus strobe	Output
AEN	DMA bus enable/disable	Output
CS	Device select	Input
Φ2	Clock	Input
RESET	System reset	Input
DRQ0–DRQ3	Service request from external devices	Input
DACK0–DACK3	Service acknowledge to external devices	Output

Table 4-12
Comparison of MPU and DMA Signals

MPU Device	Signal	8257 Signal	Purpose
8080A	A0–A15	A0–A7, DB0–DB7	Address bus
8228	DB0–DB7	DB0–DB7	Data bus
8228	$\overline{\text{I/OR}}$, $\overline{\text{I/OW}}$	$\overline{\text{I/OR}}$, $\overline{\text{I/OW}}$	I/O read and write strobe
8228	$\overline{\text{MEMR}}$, $\overline{\text{MEMW}}$	$\overline{\text{MEMR}}$, $\overline{\text{MEMW}}$	Memory data strobes
8080A	READY	READY	Memory ready/not ready
8080A	RESET	RESET	System reset

location that will be written or read. The byte count and direction control satisfies two purposes: The lower 14 bits are the number of bytes that will be transferred, and bits 14 and 15 indicate the direction or transfer. A ninth register is used by the 8257 for commands and a tenth for status.

To transfer any block of data by DMA, the starting address, number of words, and direction must be loaded into these registers by the processor. As each word is transferred in the DMA operations, the register contents change:

1. The address register increments to the next memory address.

2. The count register decrements, meaning that 1 byte has been exchanged. (Because the last byte is exchanged on a 0 count, this register should be set to n − 1 to transfer n words.)

In order to minimize pin count on the 8257 package, the address lines are used for a double purpose. In addition to carrying the address information from the 8257, pins A0 through A4 also designate the register to receive data from the processor. Table 4-13 lists the meanings of these bit values. Because the address and byte count registers are 16 bits long, it takes two output operations to set the values in each. The first output byte goes

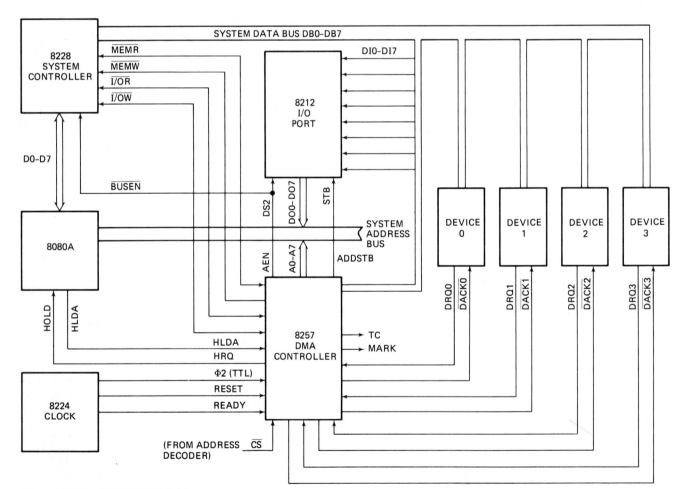

Figure 4-31. 8080A DMA System.

Table 4-13
8257 Register Addressing

Bits				
A3	A2	A1	A0	Destination/source of data
0	0	0	0	Channel 0 address register
0	0	0	1	Channel 0 byte count register
0	0	1	0	Channel 1 address register
0	0	1	1	Channel 1 byte count register
0	1	0	0	Channel 2 address register
0	1	0	1	Channel 2 byte count register
0	1	1	0	Channel 3 address register
0	1	1	1	Channel 3 byte count register
1	0	0	0	Command register on output, status register on input
9–15				Not used

to the low-order 8 bits and the second output goes to the high-order 8 bits of the designated register. The $\overline{CS}$ signal must be low before the MPU accesses the 8257. (To avoid problems during DMA operations, $\overline{CS}$ must be high. This signal is automatically raised by the 8257 during data transfer.)

Priority Arbitration

What happens if two or more devices attempt to access the 8257 simultaneously? A priority arbitrator, much like the one for interrupts in the last section, decides which device gets acknowledged first. The external devices request service by setting their DRQ signal line high. The acknowledge ($\overline{DACK}$) signal informs the device that its request is being honored.

The priority arbitration scheme to be used is selected by programming the 8257. In the *fixed priority mode* the device requests are always honored in the same order. The device on DRQ0 has highest priority and the one on DRQ3 the lowest.

The *round robin mode* guarantees equal service to every device. The low-priority device cannot be locked out by higher-priority ones in this scheme. Using round robin, the last channel that was serviced moves to the bottom of the priority list. Table 4-14 shows the channel priorities for every situation.

Table 4-14
Round Robin Channel Priority for 8257

Channel priority	Initialization	Last channel serviced 0	1	2	3
Highest	0	1	2	3	0
	1	2	3	0	1
	2	3	0	1	2
Lowest	3	0	1	2	3

DMA Options

The 8257 can transfer data in either a *byte-by-byte transfer* or *burst transfer* mode. The latter method provides the highest data throughput rate. The direction of transfer is specified by the program in the processor. The DMA controller will also allow the device to specify the direction, though this is rarely done.

TRANSFER MODES The external device can transfer its data a single byte at a time, under 8257 control. In this mode, the device raises the DRQ signal prior to each transfer. When the DMA controller responds with the $\overline{DACK}$ acknowledgment, the device drops DRQ. To transfer data in a burst mode, the device holds DRQ true until the entire block has been sent or received. Only then is that signal dropped.

TRANSFER DIRECTION The processor specifies the direction of data transfer by the settings of the upper 2 bits in the byte count register. Table 4-15 is a tabulation of those settings. Note the reversal of meanings of two values when using I/O port addressing instead of memory-mapped addressing. The following section on programming the 8257 provides more background on these addressing methods.

During a *read* cycle, the contents of a memory location, corresponding to the value in the 8257 address register, are transferred to the external device. The address register specifies the cell to receive data during a *write* cycle. The *verify* cycle effectively delays the data transfer, usually giving external devices that transfer data in blocks more time (possibly to compute a cyclic redundancy check for example). No data transfer occurs during the verify cycle.

DMA Timing

The timing to effect a DMA data transfer, Fig. 4-32, shows the sequence of events that occurs. First, the device raises the DRQ signal to request service. After the priority arbitration logic gives that device highest priority or if that is the only request, the 8257 sends

Table 4-15
Directional Bits

Bit numbers 15	14	8257 Acting as an I/O port	8257 Acting as a memory-mapped device
0	0	Verify cycle	Verify cycle
0	1	Write cycle	Read cycle
1	0	Read cycle	Write cycle
1	1	Not used	Not used

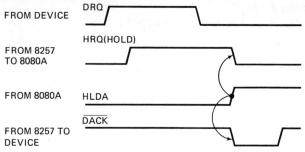
Figure 4-32. DMA Acknowledgment Timing Diagram.

a true HRQ signal to the 8080A. The 8080A recognizes the signal as a hold request (HOLD) and responds with hold acknowledge (HLDA); then the 8257 can drop HRQ and set $\overline{DACK}$ true (low), acknowledging the request from the device and giving it access to the data bus.

Before discussing how data is strobed onto the bus, a few other signals must be explained. The AEN line (Fig. 4-33) from the 8257 goes to two other DIPs. That signal is connected to the $\overline{BUSEN}$ input to the 8228 system controller. As long as $\overline{BUSEN}$ is high, the 8228 performs normally, but with $\overline{BUSEN}$ low the 8228 will float the data bus. With the 8228 effectively disconnected, the 8257 controller can provide bus access to the external devices. The AEN line also goes to the 8212 I/O port. Recall that the 8212 is selected by a low input on $\overline{DS1}$ and a high on DS2. The $\overline{DS1}$ input is grounded, so it is always true. Thus, at the same time AEN is disabling the 8228, it is also enabling the I/O port by making DS2 high.

The address strobe (ADDSTB) output identifies the interval when the high-order address byte is on the data lines for the 8212 to demultiplex it. When the address strobe is high, the high-order byte is routed to bits A8 to A15 of the address bus through the 8212.

The 8257 also provides two other signals which indicate the progress of the data transfer. The terminal count (TC) output becomes high when a byte counter reaches zero. The true TC signal means that the last byte for a given DMA channel is being sent. The MARK output goes true on every 128th byte

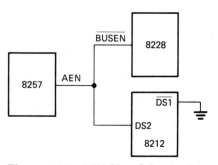
Figure 4-33. AEN Signal Connections.

exchanged. The signal is useful in floppy disks or tape cassettes which block data in 128- or 256-byte records.

The remainder of the DMA transfer timing diagram is shown in Fig. 4-34. Prior to acknowledging the device, the 8257 has set the proper address on bits A0 to A7 of the address bus and bits DB0 to DB7 of the data bus. The 8212 latches the latter onto bits A8 to A15 of the address bus. That data remains latched until the next high address strobe. The device receives the $\overline{DACK}$ signal and prepares either to receive or transmit. The data is actually transferred when the appropriate I/O or memory strobe signal goes low.

Programming the 8257

The 8257 appears as either 16 I/O ports or 16 memory locations (listed in Table 4-13) to the programmer. Figure 4-35a illustrates the 8257 used as an I/O port. A simple interchange of wires converts the DMA controller to a memory-mapped device, as shown in Fig. 4-35b. The programmer loads the command register with the command for the next DMA operation, after loading the address and byte count registers. Table 4-16 lists these commands.

☐ **EXAMPLE** An example of programming the 8257 is given here. The 8257 is used as an I/O port in this example. The addresses for the registers are

Address register, channel 0	10_{16}
Byte count register, channel 0	11_{16}
Command register	18_{16}

MVI	A, 00	Send the low byte to the
OUT	10	address register, channel 0
MVI	A, 10	Send the high byte to the
OUT	10	address register, channel 0
MVI	A, 00	Send the low byte to the count
OUT	11	register, channel 0
MVI	A, 41	Send the high byte to the
OUT	11	count register, channel 0
MVI	A, 11	Set control register to enable
OUT	18	channel 0 round robin priority

The starting address for the transfer will be 1000_{16}. There will be 256_{10} words written. (The byte count and direction register was set to 4100_{16}, which translates into 100_{16} words to transfer and a direction code for the write cycle.) Finally, the bits in the command register are set.

There are a few features in Table 4-16 that require further comment. Bit 5 allows the programmer to

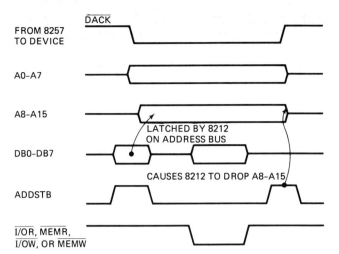

Figure 4-34. DMA Data Transfer Timing Diagram.

Table 4-16
Command Register Code Words *

Bit Number	Meaning
0	Set—enable, clear—disable channel 0
1	Set—enable, clear—disable channel 1
2	Set—enable, clear—disable channel 2
3	Set—enable, clear—disable channel 3
4	Clear—fixed priority, set—round robin priority
5	Clear—normal write pulse, set—extended write pulse
6	Set—for TC disable option
7	Set—autoload option

* Note: The command register is cleared by a system reset.

choose to extend write pulses. The write pulse can be advanced one clock cycle earlier than normal. This action will give a slow external device more time when sending data to memory.

Setting bit 6 in the command register disables the DMA channel involved when the TC signal goes high. Disabling the channel when the word count is exhausted ensures that the DMA operation stops properly. The channel is reenabled by the processor setting its bit in the command word again. In the autoload option (see below), bit 6 does not affect channel 2.

The autoload option is selected with bit 7. The purpose of the autoload is to allow DMA to proceed without reinitiating the address and byte count register prior to each record transfer. Autoload works only with DMA channel 2 and requires that channel 3 be reserved as a buffer. The program in the 8080A loads channel 3 with the address, count, and direction for the next channel 2 transfer. When the byte

count for channel 2 reaches zero, it is automatically reloaded with the values from channel 3.

Channel 3		*Channel 2*
Address register	→	Address register
Byte count register	→	Byte count register

The data exchange on channel 2 continues with the new units.

If the address and byte count registers of channel 2 (instead of channel 3) are loaded in the autoload mode, the information from the channel 2 registers is copied into channel 3. Thereafter the values of the address and count are refreshed in channel 2 from channel 3.

The condition of the 8257 can be read by executing an input from the same address as the command register (see Table 4-13); the status bits are listed in Table 4-17. If bits 0 through 3 are set, it means that a true terminal count signal has been issued on that channel. Bit 4 is used with the autoload option. In autoload, the value in the channel 3 registers must not change as they are being written into the channel 2 registers. As long as bit 4 is set, the data can be written in channel 3 registers, without disturbing the process. Every time the status register is read, all the bits, except bit 4, are cleared.

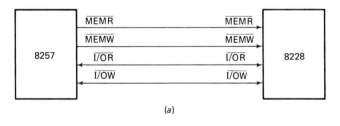

(a)

(b)

Figure 4-35. 8257 Addressing (a) I/O Port (b) Memory Mapped.

Table 4-17
8257 Status Registers

Bit number	Meaning
0	TC status on channel 0
1	TC status on channel 1
2	TC status on channel 2
3	TC status on channel 3
4	Update status
5–7	Not used

8257 DMA Controller Review

1. How many external devices can be connected to the 8257 in normal operations? With the autoload option selected?

2. What signals are used by devices to request service? Which signals are used by the 8257 to acknowledge the devices?

3. Why is the AEN output of the 8257 connected to the $\overline{\text{BUSEN}}$ input of the 8228 system controller and the DS2 input of the 8212 I/O port in Fig. 4-31?

4. List the ten 8257 registers. Describe how they are addressed.

5. Distinguish between the fixed and round robin priority arbitration schemes of the 8257.

6. How does an external device signal that it is using burst mode data transfers?

7. Describe the three transfer direction cycles used by the 8257.

8. Explain the purpose of the HRQ signal in Fig. 4-31.

9. Why is the 8257 permitted to drop the data lines representing bits A8 to A15 so early in the timing diagram of Fig. 4-34?

10. How is an 8257 controller addressed as an I/O port distinguished from one addressed by memory-mapped I/O?

11. Why are two outputs necessary to load an address register of the 8257?

12. Explain the result of setting bit 6 in the command register. What happens if bit 7 is also set?

CHAPTER SUMMARY

1. The moving of data between the peripheral devices and the microcomputer is the responsibility of the I/O circuitry and programs. Input and output are always relative to the processor; the computer receives input data and transmits output data.

2. Normally either accumulator I/O or memory-mapped I/O instructions are used in exchanging information. Accumulator I/O instructions require an I/O port, while memory-mapped commands treat the device as a memory address.

3. Interrupt signals allow the device to request service from the MPU. Direct memory access devices can read or write memory just like the processor.

4. An I/O port is a buffer between the system buses and the external device. The port is addressed with either the upper or lower eight lines of the address bus. The port address is called its device code.

5. A family of support chips simplifies the task of interfacing the 8080A to external equipment. If those devices are not used, low-power Schottky TTL integrated circuits are recommended for use in the interface logic. Outputs should be buffered and bus drivers, together with termination networks, should be used on long transmission paths.

6. Fully decoded address selection interprets every bit of the address or device code. Linear selection decodes only a few bits.

7. The 8095 three-state buffer is frequently used on 8080A input and output lines. The buffer is enabled by a device selection strobe from the address decoder logic and an input strobe from the computer.

8. The 8212 I/O port consists of eight D flip-flops used to latch data. Its output is compatible with the three-state system data bus.

9. Devices are addressed as memory locations in a memory-mapped I/O architecture. Memory transfer instructions are used to move data between the processors and the external equipment.

10. The microcomputer can use single, multiple, or vectored interrupts. The 8080A has special instructions in its repertoire to support vectored-interrupt processing and other instructions to control interrupts. A summary of the input/output instructions is provided in Table 4-18.

11. The interrupt device supplies the starting address of the servicing routine in an RST instruction. The processor enters the interrupt state by clearing the interrupt enable flip-flop, taking the next instruction from the data lines, and pushing the program counter on the stack. The servicing routine must reenable interrupts and exit with a return instruction to pop the stack and load the program counter with the address of the instruction following the interrupted one.

12. The external device can respond to an interrupt acknowledgment from the processor by supplying either a RST or CALL instruction.

13. The halt state can be terminated with an interrupt.

14. The 8259 priority interrupt control unit can coordinate up to eight external interrupts. In a master-slave system, even more interrupts can be handled. The 8259 provides arbitration of simultaneous interrupts. The 8259 is initialized and controlled by the microcomputer program.

15. The peripheral can bypass the processor in accessing memory by using direct memory access. The 8080A hold state is employed when DMA is used.

16. The 8257 DMA controller can provide four channels for direct memory access. The 8257 modes are selected by the program in the 8080A.

Table 4-18
Input/Output Instructions*

Instruction	Operation code	Number of bytes	Execution time, μs
DI	F3	1	2
EI	FB	1	2
IN	DB	2	5
OUT	D3	2	5
RST 0	C7	1	5.5
RST 1	CF	1	5.5
RST 2	D7	1	5.5
RST 3	DF	1	5.5
RST 4	E7	1	5.5
RST 5	EF	1	5.5
RST 6	F7	1	5.5
RST 7	FF	1	5.5

*Status bits are not affected by these instructions.

KEY TERMS AND CONCEPTS

Input/output (I/O)	Fully decoded address selection	8259 priority interrupt control unit (PICU)
Peripheral equipment	Linear selection	
Accumulator I/O	8095 buffer	Interrupt priority arbitration
Memory-mapped I/O	Jamming data	Fully nested mode
I/O port	8212 I/O port	Rotating priorites
Interrupt signals	Handshaking	Polled mode
Direct memory access (DMA)	Single interrupt	Mask modes
Device code (DC)	Polling	8257 DMA controller
Interfacing	Multiple interrupt	Fixed priority mode
Buffered signals	Vectored interrupt	Round robin mode
Bus drivers	Interrupt servicing routine	Byte-by-byte transfer
Termination networks	Halt state	Burst transfer

PROBLEMS

4-1 A 128-byte block of data is stored in sequential addresses starting at 1200_{16}. Write a routine to transfer this data to a floppy disk on I/O port 27_{16}. (A loop will be required.)

4-2 How many 74LS00 quad NAND gate ICs can be safely connected to an 8080A output?

4-3 If the 74LS30 NAND gate in Fig. 4-8 is to be used to fully decode the device address $D7_{16}$, which inputs require inverters?

4-4 Draw a diagram, similar to Fig. 4-9b, showing how two 8095 buffers can be used for output on the data bus.

4-5 Write a routine to receive a 256-word record from a memory-mapped cassette recorder. The device address is 8237_{16} and data is to be stored beginning at address 0210_{16}.

4-6 The recorder in Prob. 4-5 sends an interrupt whenever a CRC error is detected in the data being sent to the processor. An RST 3 instruction is provided by the device. Write an interrupt handling routine which will process the interrupt by executing the program of Prob. 4-5 again. Be sure also to reenable interrupts and take care of other normal interrupt servicing tasks.

4-7 An 8259 master-slave system consists of two slaves attached to IR6 and IR7 of the master. Devices 0 through 5 are attached to the master, 6 through 13 on the IR6 slave, and 14 through 21 on the IR7 slave. Prepare a table, similar to Table 4-10, with the proper output data to

1. Initialize the master. Use four words between vector addresses and a base address for the master of 4300_{16}.
2. Initialize each slave. Base address for the slave on IR6 is 5100_{16} and the one on IR7 is 5900_{16}.
3. Start rotating priorities mode B.
4. Allow interrupts from devices 4 and 5 to interrupt any other service request.
5. Return to the fully nested mode.
6. Cancel the mask of step 4.
7. Start the polling mode.

4-8 There is a simple mask of 51_{16} active in the 8259. Rotating priorities mode B is in effect and the current order of priority is

Lowest							Highest
IR5	IR4	IR3	IR2	IR1	IR0	IR7	IR6

The processor issues on OCW2 of $E3_{16}$. When the devices on IR lines 4 and 7 simultaneously request interrupts, which will be serviced first?

4-9 The address for the 8257 channel 2 address register is 50_{16}. Write a program to input 128_{10} words from the floppy disk by DMA transfer. Starting address for storing the data is 0500_{16}. Fixed priority with extended write pulses and the TC disable option are to be selected.

4-10 The CRT terminal is receiving DMA data in the burst mode controlled by channel 1 of the 8257. The floppy disk uses channel 0, also in burst mode. Round robin priority and the autoload option have been selected. After initialization, the following DMA transfers have occurred:

1. Terminal—read 200_{10} words
2. Floppy disk—verify cycle
3. Floppy disk—read 126_{10} words
4. Terminal—read 350_{10} words

Until this time, no conflicts have happened, but now the terminal and disk simultaneously request a DMA transfer. The disk wants to write 256_{10} words and the terminal read 100_{10} words. (*a*) Which one gets first access to the bus? (*b*) How may words are transferred? (*c*) Answer the same questions with fixed priority mode selected.

EXPERIMENT 3

PURPOSE: To investigate a parallel interface.

PARTS LIST:

Item	Quantity
8212	1
5082-7340 hexadecimal display	2
74LS00	1
74LS20	1
Single-pole single-throw switch	1

IC DIAGRAMS:

PROCEDURE: This circuit will be used again in the following experiment, so do not disassemble it until Experiment 4 is completed.

STEP 1. Following the schematic, construct the circuit given in Fig. 4-37. Connect $\overline{CS}$ to +5 V.

STEP 2. Connect the DI7 input to +5 V and ground DI0 through DI6. What values are shown on the displays?

STEP 3. Your answer should have been 80_{16}. If not, check your connections carefully.

STEP 4. Now wire the address selection logic gates from Fig. 4-38. Disconnect the +5 V and connect the address selection logic to the $\overline{CS}$ input. Connect the appropriate

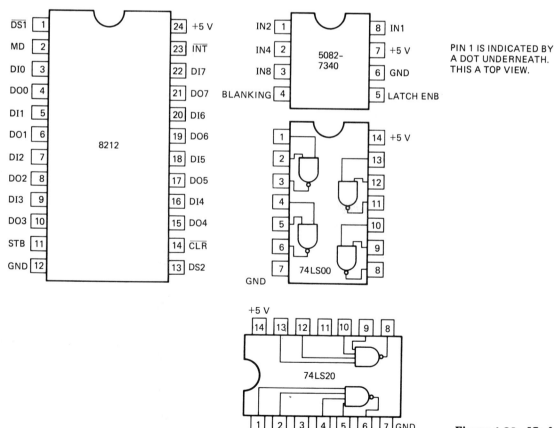

PIN 1 IS INDICATED BY A DOT UNDERNEATH. THIS A TOP VIEW.

Figure 4-36. ICs for Experiment 4

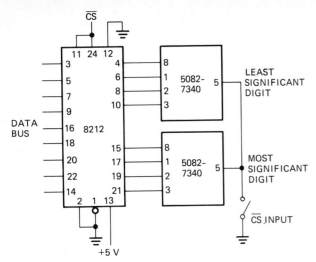

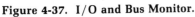

Figure 4-37. I/O and Bus Monitor.

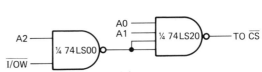

Figure 4-38. Address Decoding Logic.

lines of the address bus from the computer. Also connect the data bus lines of the microcomputer to the 8212. The device address is 07_{16}.

STEP 5. Write a program to output FF_{16} on output port 07_{16}.

STEP 6. Load and execute your program. What result did you obtain?

STEP 7. Modify your program to count from 00_{16} to FF_{16} at a regular rate that is slow enough to observe the numbers changing in the displays. (You may want to use the time-delay program from the last experiment.)

5

SERIAL INPUT/OUTPUT

For some applications, the parallel I/O techniques explained in the previous chapter are not suitable. In those cases, serial data transfer may be more useful. Serial communications is frequently employed when there are long distances between the transmitter and receiver. The most common example of serial data exchange is digital communications by means of telephone lines. Widely separated computers can pass data back and forth in almost no time by using the telephone network. Another example of serial communications is peripheral equipment that can only process data 1 bit at a time. Such devices as printers, CRT terminals, and cassette recorders may be limited to serial data exchange.

CHAPTER OBJECTIVES

Upon completion of this chapter, you should be able to:

1. Draw a simple block diagram of a telecommunications system
2. Describe the operating principles of serial data transmitter/receivers
3. Explain how serial bit boundaries are delineated by clock pulses
4. Distinguish between synchronous and asynchronous serial I/O protocols
5. List the control signals used with standard modems
6. Describe the operation of typical synchronous and asynchronous receiver/transmitters

SERIAL DATA EXCHANGE

The problem confronting us in dealing with serial data transfer from an 8-bit microprocessor is essentially one of *parallel-to-serial conversion:* converting parallel data to serial. As Fig. 5-1 shows, data can be converted by a series of shift register operations. By left shifting an 8-bit register, a serial bit stream is produced from a parallel word (Fig. 5-1a). The most significant bit is made available for transmission first, followed by bit 6, and so on. To assemble a parallel data word from a serial bit stream (*serial-to-parallel conversion*), the process is simply reversed, as Fig. 5-1b illustrates.

If the data is to be transmitted by telephone, a device that can convert numerical values to sound must be used, because 1s and 0s cannot be placed directly on the lines. A *modem* (modulator-demodulator) performs this function. The transmitted bit stream is changed to an audio signal that represents the binary pattern. On the receiving end, the modem changes the audio back to binary digits. Figure 5-2 is a block diagram of a two-way serial communications network. Both units can send or receive data. If the system is *half-duplex,* then one station transmits while the other receives. A *full-duplex* system permits simultaneous transmission and reception by both computers.

A serial peripheral is shown in Fig. 5-3. Here a serial-to-parallel converter is used to change the bit stream from the device into 8-bit words for the computer. For two-way communications, a parallel-to-serial converter is needed for data moving in the other direction.

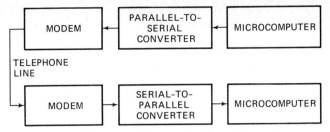

Figure 5-2. Telephone Communications Network.

Serial Data Representation

Serial data is transmitted as a series of pulses that are held at either a high or low voltage level for the proper time interval. The pulses must be synchronized with a series of clock pulses to indicate the bit boundaries. Figure 5-4a shows how the number 62_{16} would be transmitted in serial format. Here the data is stable on the trailing edge of the clock. Some communications systems require that the transitions between the 1 and the 0 level be correct on the leading edge of the clock. Of course the clock in the transmitter and receiver must use the same frequency (or some multiple of the same frequency).

Many times an additional time period is allowed for the signal settling. This delay is used for the signal to assume its new value before it is sampled. These extra time intervals are called *settling delays,* or *guard times.* Figure 5-4b shows how these delays affect transmission and Fig. 5-4c shows the impact on reception. Note that attempting to read the data during the settling interval could result in obtaining an erroneous value.

Serial Receiver/Transmitter

There are many integrated circuits available to assist with the exchange of serial information. Later in this chapter, we will look into two such devices in detail. At this time, let us consider a somewhat simplified receiver/transmitter to see what functions it must perform. Figure 5-5 is such a device. Parallel data from the processor is held in a register until it can move into the transmit buffer, which contains the information until it has been shifted onto the serial output line. *Double buffering* with two buffers is used so the processor can forward word $n + 1$

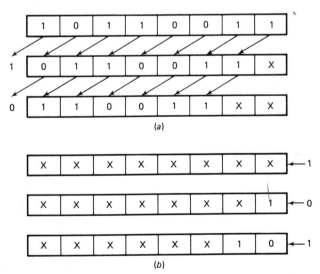

Figure 5-1. Parallel/Serial Conversion (a) Parallel-to-Serial Conversion by Shifting (b) Serial-to-Parallel Conversion by Shifting.

Figure 5-3. Serial Peripheral.

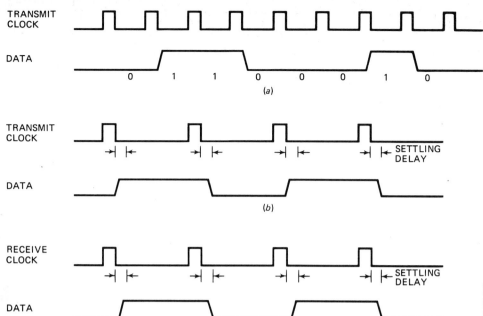

Figure 5-4. Serial Data Timing
(a) Serial Data Transmission
(b) Transmission Settling Delay
(c) Reception Settling Delay.

as word n is being transmitted, thus providing a faster data throughput rate.

Serial data being received is shifted into the receive buffer. After this buffer is filled with 8 bits, the parallel word is passed to the receive holding buffer. Double buffering again permits a faster data rate to be maintained. The data then moves to the data register and into the processor.

Control is exercised by means of coded orders sent to the receiver/transmitter. Under program control, the device can be enabled or disabled, change modes, or report status. In the latter case, the status condition codes are forwarded on their unique lines to the processor.

Baud Rate

The data rate of a serial channel is equal to the number of characters sent in 1 second (s). For a binary serial channel, the *baud rate* is the same as the number of bits sent per second (bits/s). Common baud rates are 300, 1200, 4800, and 9600.

As you may have deduced, the transmit and receive *clock rates* are related to the baud rate. Figure 5-6a shows an example of a clock that has the same frequency as the baud rate. Data transitions take place on each clock pulse. This clock is referred to as a ×1 clock signal. A ×4 clock signal is shown in the Fig. 5-6b. Now there are four clock pulses for

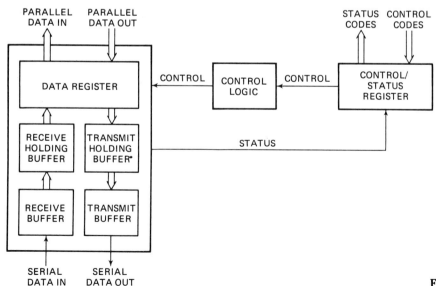

Figure 5-5. Serial Receiver/Transmitter.

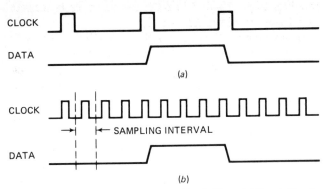

Figure 5-6. Clock Rates (a) ×1 Clock Signal (b) ×4 Clock Signal.

every bit transition. The faster clock rate makes it easier to sample the center portion of the data signal when the voltage level would be most stable. Clock rates of ×16 and ×64 are also frequently encountered.

Synchronization

The clocks in the sending and receiving devices may be running at the same frequency, but out of *synchronization.* Figure 5-7 shows the result of this problem. The receiver only sees the data stream; the transmitter clock is not sent over the channel. If there is a *clock skew,* that is, if the receiver clock is offset, or *skewed,* in time, it may cause data to be read too early or too late, as in receive clock pulse 3 which reads too soon. The receiver interprets the data as a 0 when, in fact, a 1 was transmitted during transmit clock pulse 3. This mistake is called a *framing error.*

A special *sync signal* can be sent prior to the

start of data, as Fig. 5-7b shows. Until the data was to be sent, the transmitter held the data line high. The high signal is called a *mark,* so the time until data starts is referred to as *marking.* Just before the start of data, the signal goes low for half the width of a normal bit period. If the receiver aligns the trailing edge of its clock with the sync signal, it will be properly phased to read the serial data.

Another synchronization method uses a special *sync character* or pattern. This character would never appear in a normal data stream. The receiver moves a "frame" along the incoming bit sequence until it can recognize the sync character. Figure 5-7c shows the use of a sync pattern. During the "search for sync," the time interval represented by the frame is, in effect, moved earlier or later.

When a ×16 or ×64 clock is used by the receiver, synchronization is not as critical. Even if the receive clock is off a cycle or two from the transmit clock, the skewing is usually not serious enough to miss the center section of the data pulse.

Serial Data Transfer Review

1. Describe the operation of a serial-to-parallel converter.

2. Define the term "modem."

3. Distinguish between half-duplex and full-duplex modes of serial communication.

4. How does a clock transition indicate the bit boundaries of serial data?

5. Why is a settling delay sometimes provided in serial data communications?

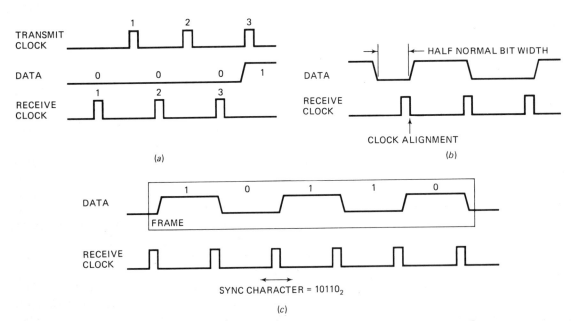

Figure 5-7. Synchronization (a) Out of Sync (b) Sync Signal (c) Sync Character or Pattern.

6. Explain the reason for two transmit and two receive buffers in a receiver/transmitter.

7. What is the baud rate of a serial binary telephone system that sends 1200 bits/s?

8. What is the value of running the receive clock at a higher frequency than the baud rate?

9. Name two methods of synchronization.

10. What does the term "marking" mean?

SYNCHRONOUS SERIAL PROTOCOL

There are several common rules, or *communication protocols,* in use for serial communications. One of these is the *synchronous serial protocol* characterized by having the transmitter supply data on every clock pulse. Synchronous serial transmission is most often used at data rates above 2000 baud.

Figure 5-8 shows how the receive clock is synchronized with the data. Even when no useful data is being sent over the channel, the transmitter must send data. In such cases the transmitter sends one or more sync characters. The sync character is also used to delineate word boundaries, as shown in the example below (16_{16} is used as the sync character), which uses two sync characters:

| 1110 0000 | 0001 0110 | 0001 0110 | 1110 1111 |

| Word 1 | Sync | Sync | Word 2 |
| | character 1 | character 2 | |

Synchronous serial receivers normal use a ×1 clock. The clock rate is simply the reciprocal of the baud rate. For example, if the baud rate is 2400, the clock period would be 416.7 μs.

Although the word length shown above (and the word length of most microprocessors) is 8-bits, synchronous serial communications can use any length from 5- to 8-bit words. In addition, a parity bit is frequently appended to the word.

Handshaking

To this point, the discussion has avoided the initialization of communications. Among the unanswered questions are: How does the transmitter tell the receiver to get ready? What if the receiver is turned off? How are errors handled?

In answering these and other questions, we will look at some of the features of a synchronous telephone protocol. Before data is sent, the transmitter and receiver exchange several control characters (*handshaking*). These characters establish the link. Table 5-1 lists a typical message sequence. ASCII control characters are used in this example.

First the transmitter asks if the receiver is ready (ENQ character). The receiver replies and transmission begins. The header consists of the start of text character, then the data block is sent. An end of block character is followed by two cyclic redundancy check (CRC) codes. The receiver acknowledges receipt of either an even or odd number of data blocks; for example, the first data block is odd, the second even, and so on. The process repeats until all data is sent. The end of transmission character completes the transfer.

Synchronous Serial Protocol Review

1. What is another word with the same meaning as protocol?

2. True or false? One would expect synchronous serial protocol to be used in a 4800-baud communications link.

3. True or false? A ×16 receiver clock is most often used with synchronous serial data transmission.

4. How are words delineated under the synchronous serial protocol?

5. How many bits can be sent in each synchronous serial word (excluding the parity bit)?

6. Define the term "handshaking."

ASYNCHRONOUS SERIAL PROTOCOL

The timing method of *asynchronous serial protocol* allows the transmitter to send only when there is data to transmit; in contrast to synchronous protocols, there is no need to send sync characters to fill periods when no data is ready to send. Asynchronous timing is most often used below 1800 baud. Because every data unit must be indicated by a synchronization indicator, the efficiency of asynchronous data transmission is lower than synchronous.

When the transmitter is not sending data, the data line is set to a mark. When a word is to be transmitted, it is always preceded by a *start bit* (a 0) and terminated

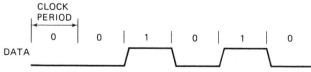

Figure 5-8. Synchronous Serial Data.

Table 5-1
Handshaking Protocol with a Telephone

Source	ASCII control character	Meaning
Transmitter	ENQ	Are you ready to receive?
Receiver	DC0	Yes (receiver must have been set up in advance).
Transmitter	STX DATA BLOCK ETB CRC CRC	Start of text. End of block. Cyclic redundancy check sent twice.
Receiver		Receiver has checked data with CRC. No errors have been detected.
		and
	DC1	An even number of data blocks has been received so far.
		or
	DC0	An odd number of data blocks has been received so far.
Transmitter	STX Data block ETB CRC CRC	Repeat until all data has been sent.
Transmitter	EOT	End of transmission.

42-43

by 1, 1½, or 2 *stop bits* (always 1s). The word can range in length from 5 to 8 bits and a parity bit can be appended.

For example, a standard teletype (TTY) serial character would be transmitted as

0 |X X X X X X X| P |1 1|
↑   ↑
Start   7 Data bits   Parity   Two stop bits
bit   bit

Each TTY character then consists of 11 bits. At the standard rate of 10 char/s, the TTY asynchronous serial data rate is 110 baud.

A reference was made above to 1½ stop bits. How can 1½ bits be represented? Remember that a bit in a serial data stream simply means that the signal is held constant for a certain time interval. To generate 1½ stop bits, the 1 level is just held for 1½ times the normal interval.

Because sync characters are not used in asynchronous timing, there is no framing to be done. Eliminating the framing operation also makes it impossible to encounter a framing error, though other types of errors may occur.

Asynchronous Serial Protocol Review

1. What signal is sent by an asynchronous serial transmitter when it has no data to send?

2. What bits precede a word in this type of timing? What bits follow the word?

3. Why is the standard TTY data rate 110 baud?

4. How can 1½ stop bits be transmitted?

5. True or false? Framing errors never occur when asynchronous data exchange is used.

Standard Modem Control Signals

A set of signals to initiate data communications between modems has been established. By use of four discrete control lines, a modem can establish that the I/O device, called a *data terminal,* is ready to communicate. Table 5-2 tabulates a typical signal sequence for data terminal transmission. Note that in the standard terminology a modem is called a *data set.*

Table 5-2
Control Signals

Step	Signal	Level	Set by	Meaning
1	$\overline{DTR}$	Low	Data terminal	Data terminal ready.
2	$\overline{DSR}$	Low	Modem	Data set (modem) ready to receive. Transmission cannot begin until this signal goes low.
3	. . .	. . .	. . .	Text is prepared
4	$\overline{RTS}$	Low	Data terminal	Request to send. The data terminal is ready to send to the modem. ($\overline{DSR}$ and $\overline{DTR}$ must remain low.)
5	$\overline{CTS}$	Low	Modem	Clear to send. The modem lowers this signal 2 µs after receipt of $\overline{RST}$, if ready to receive.
6	. . .	. . .	Data terminal	Data is transmitted.

First, both devices signal they are ready with low $\overline{DTR}$ and $\overline{DSR}$ lines. When the data terminal has composed the message, it lowers $\overline{RTS}$. After the modem responds with $\overline{CTS}$ true, the exchange begins.

If the modem is the transmitter and the data terminal the receiver, the order of $\overline{DTR}$ and $\overline{DSR}$ are reversed. The modem makes $\overline{RTS}$ true and the data terminal responds with $\overline{CTS}$.

Standard Modem Control Signals Review

1. What is the purpose of the $\overline{DTR}$ signal?

2. True or false? Upon receipt or an $\overline{RTS}$ true signal, the receiving unit sets $\overline{CTS}$ high to indicate that the data can be sent.

3. What is another name for a data set?

4. Name the two other signals that must remain low as long as $\overline{RTS}$ is low.

5. List the sequence of the standard modem signals for a situation in which the data set transmits.

THE SYNCHRONOUS RECEIVER/TRANSMITTER

There are two basic types of synchronous data transmission. The *character-oriented synchronous data* method is organized to exchange complete character codes. The IBM Bisync protocol is an example of character-oriented synchronous I/O. Table 5-1 gave an example of this communication protocol. Another means of synchronous I/O are the *bit-oriented synchronous data* protocols, such as SLDC and HDLC (see discussion below). The receiver/transmitters covered in this chapter use bit-oriented synchronous I/O.

SDLC and HDLC Protocols

Before investigating the actual ICs, we will first examine one family of widely used bit synchronous communication protocols. The *synchronous data link control (SDLC)* protocol is used in networks with a single primary and multiple secondary stations. (The quite similar HDLC protocol is often used in retail store systems.) Figure 5-9 shows SDLC/HDLC multipoint and point-to-point networks.

The *high-level data link control (HDLC)* is a standard protocol established by the International Standards Organization (ISO). The ISO X.25 packet switching system is implemented by means of the HDLC discipline. SDLC is an IBM protocol used in the system network architecture (SNA) communications.

Communications is only permitted between the primary and a secondary station; two secondary stations cannot talk directly to each other. An address field in every message identifies the secondary to receive it or the secondary that sent it. An acknowledgment for messages received correctly is periodically sent by the receiving station.

All messages are formatted into frames, as Fig. 5-10 shows. The first field in any frame is a start flag of $7E_{16}$. The address field identifies the sending or receiving station. The SDLC address field is always 8 bits long, but the HDLC address can be any length. The receiver can determine the length by examining

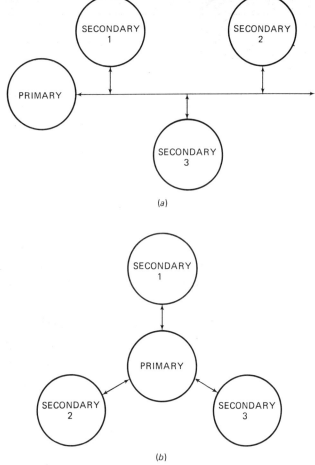

(a)

(b)

Figure 5-9. SDLC/HDLC Networks (a) Multipoint (b) Point-to-point.

the first bit in each byte of the address. If the first bit is 0, then another address byte follows. If the bit is 1, then the current address byte is the last.

The SDLC control field is always 8 bits. Either 8- or 16-bit control fields are used in HDLC. If the first bit of the field is 0, the field is 16 bits in length. A first bit value of 1 signals an 8-bit field.

The information field can consist of a bit stream of any length. No breaks in the information field are allowed. If the transmitter does not receive a continual data stream, it will abort the message. (The

abort signal is FF_{16} for SDLC and $7F_{16}$ for HDLC.) Control characters can be embedded in the data. For these protocols, control characters are six or more consecutive 1s. To prevent data from looking like control characters, the transmitter automatically inserts a 0 following five consecutive 1s in the data stream (zero bit insertion). The receiver automatically strips them off.

The frame check character is a means of error detection. The character is calculated using the bit pattern of the address, control, and information fields. The frame is terminated by a stop flag of $7E_{16}$. All fields are transmitted least significant bit first, though the user need not be concerned with this requirement. The synchronous I/O device takes care of it in the serial-to-parallel and parallel-to-serial conversions. Between frames, an idle pattern is transmitted. The idle pattern is a continuous high level on the data line.

The signal conventions to indicate the binary values may use either *nonreturn to zero (NRZ)* or *nonreturn to zero, inverted (NRZI),* conventions. With NRZ, a high level is interpreted as a 1 and a low as 0. A transition between the high and low levels (in either direction) represents a 0 in NRZI, and no transition a 1. Figure 5-11 illustrates the two conventions.

The Synchronous Receiver/Transmitter Review

1. Name two methods of synchronous data transmission.

2. Distinguish between SDLC and HDLC protocols.

3. True or false? The SDLC protocol permits direct communication between secondary stations.

4. List the fields in an SDLC frame.

5. How would the HDLC receiver be able to tell that the control field is 16 bits long?

6. How does the NRZ convention differ from NRZI?

7E	ADDRESS FIELD	CONTROL FIELD	INFORMATION FIELD	FRAME CHECK	7E
START FLAG	8-BITS	8-BITS	ANY LENGTH	16-BITS	STOP FLAG

(a)

7E	ADDRESS FIELD	CONTROL FIELD	INFORMATION FIELD	FRAME CHECK	7E
START FLAG	ANY LENGTH	8 OR 16-BITS	ANY LENGTH	16-BITS	STOP FLAG

(b)

Figure 5-10. SDLC/HDLC Frames (a) SDLC Frame (b) HDLC Frame.

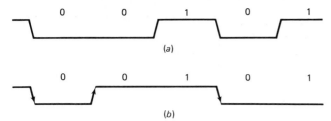

Figure 5-11. NRZ and NRZI Logic (a) NRZ (b) NRZI.

THE NEC µPD379 SYNCHRONOUS RECEIVER/TRANSMITTER

The NEC µPD379 is a typical synchronous I/O integrated circuit. The device communicates using either standard synchronous or SDLC protocols under program control. Both half- or full-duplex modes are supported. Other characteristics are listed in Table 5-3.

The chip configuration is shown in Fig. 5-12. Table 5-4 briefly describes the purpose of each signal. Note that the chip requires three power-supply voltages: +5, −5, and +12 V.

Mode Select

The µPD379 can operate in either the standard synchronous I/O or SDLC modes, as was mentioned above. In switching between the two modes, the user must first change to the idle or closed mode. Once in the closed mode, the device can then enter either of the two operational modes. The mode-changing signals (MS1 and MS2) are latched on the rising edge of the mode select strobe (MRL) signal.

The mode selection control signals are as shown below:

Mode	MS1	MS2
Closed (idle)	0	X
Standard synchronous	1	0
SDLC	1	1

Note: X = don't care.

Closed-Mode Functions

The closed mode is always used to initialize the device. The sequence for starting communications is listed in Table 5-5. After power is applied, the device is selected and MRL is set low. MS1 is lowered to enter the closed mode. Next, the operating mode selection is made. If in the synchronous mode, the type of sync character to be used must be programmed first.

Table 5-3
NEC µPD379 Characteristics

Bits per character	8
Errors detected	Overrun, underrun
Number of sync characters	1
Baud rate	DC to 800 K baud
Clock rate	×1

Either the ASCII SYN code (16_{16}) or a programmed sync character can be used. To select the standard character, SYNC/$\overline{\text{ZIP}}$ is set high when the closed mode is selected. Any other character is programmed by setting SYNC/$\overline{\text{ZIP}}$ low when entering the closed mode and strobing in the character on TD0–TD7 with $\overline{\text{TCBL}}$. Timing diagrams for both sync character selections are shown in Fig. 5-13.

Clock pulses are then applied to the transmitter and receiver clock inputs, TC and RC. After setting MRL high, the mode is entered when MS1 is raised.

Standard Synchronous Protocol

After the previous series of operations, communications can begin. To transmit once in the standard

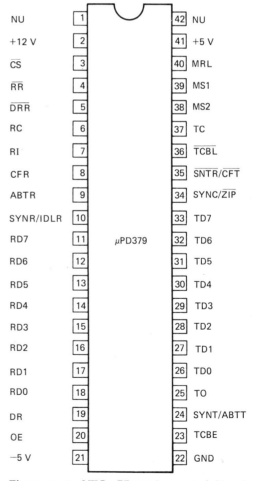

Figure 5-12. NEC µPD379 Integrated Circuit.

Table 5-4
μPD379 Signals

| Signal | Purpose | | Type |
	Standard synchronous	SDLC	
RD0–RD7	Data bus	Data bus	Output
TD0–TD7	Data bus	Data bus	Input
$\overline{RR}$	Receive logic select	Receive logic select	Input
$\overline{CS}$	Device select	Device select	Input
MS1, MS2	Mode select	Mode select	Input
MRL	Mode select strobe	Mode select strobe	Input
TO	Serial data	Serial data	Output
TC	Transmitter clock	Transmitter clock	Input
TCBE	Transmit character buffer empty	Transmit character buffer empty	Output
SYNT/ABTT	Sync character	Abort pattern	Output
$\overline{SNTR/CFT}$	Reset SYNT	Reset TCBE and transmit stop flag	Input
TCBL	Strobe for TD0–TD7	Strobe for TD0–TD7	Input
RI	Serial data	Serial data	Input
RC	Receiver clock	Receiver clock	Input
DR	Receiver character buffer full	Receiver character buffer full	Output
$\overline{DRR}$	Reset DR	Reset DR	Input
CFR	· · ·	Stop flag received	Output
ABTR	· · ·	Abort pattern received	Output
SYNR/IDLR	Sync character received	Idle pattern received	Output
OE	Overrun error	Overrun error	Output
SYNC/$\overline{ZIP}$	Sync character input on TD0–TD7	Prohibit zero insertion pattern	Input

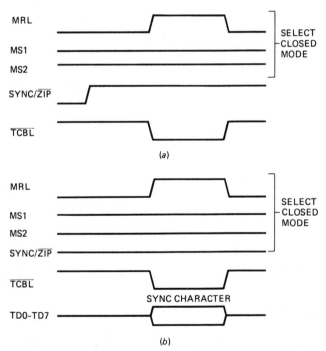

Figure 5-13. Sync Character Selection (a) ASCII Sync Character (b) Programmed Sync Character.

mode, the data is simply strobed onto TD0 through TD7 by $\overline{TCBL}$. The device requests each byte by raising the transmit character buffer empty signal (TCBE). This signal is used as an output strobe by the processor. If the processor does not supply valid data in time, the μPD379 will insert a sync character. Figure 5-14 is a timing diagram of the transmission sequence.

Receiving data, Fig. 5-15, begins with a low $\overline{RR}$ signal. When the first sync character is recognized, SYNR is raised. This signal remains high until the first character, which is not sync, is recognized. The DR line indicates when each character has been received. This signal can be used to strobe in the received data. The DR signal is reset by the processor sending a true $\overline{DRR}$.

If the processor does not read data before the next byte is ready, an *overrun* error has occurred. The device will signify the event by holding DR high and raising OE when the next byte is sent to the received data buffer. The previous byte is lost, in this case.

Table 5-5
μPD379 Initialization

1. Set $\overline{CS}$ and MRL low.

2. Enter closed mode by setting MS1 low and MRL high.

3. Reset MRL.

4. Set MS2 low for synchronous I/O, high for SDLC.

5. If in the synchronous mode, select the sync character.
   a. Set SYNC/$\overline{ZIP}$ high for standard character.
   b. Set SYNC/$\overline{ZIP}$ low to program a character on TD0–TD7.

6. Set TCBL low.

7. Apply clock pulses to TC and RC inputs.

8. Set MRL high. Enter the chosen mode by setting MS1 high.

SDLC Protocol

The μPD379 uses NRZ logic, as explained in an earlier section of this chapter. NRZ logic represents a 1 with a high voltage level. A low level is a 0.

The μPD379 will insert 0s in the data stream automatically if five consecutive 1s appear in a byte. For example, if the character is $7C_{16}$:

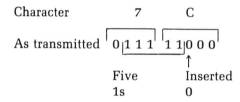

The receiving device removes the unnecessary 0s. This feature can be suppressed when the SDLC mode is selected by setting $\overline{ZIP}$ low.

Recall that the SDLC protocol requires a constant data output stream. If the processor does not have data ready when required by the μPD379, an underflow error occurs. The device sends an abort signal (FF_{16}) until the next character is available from the processor. Between frames, the device transmits an idle pattern of $7FFF_{16}$.

Figure 5-16 shows the timing for entering the SDLC mode. The processor is notified when to transmit each character by the TCBE signal. At that time, the MPU places the data on the lines and lowers $\overline{TCBL}$ to reset TCBE.

Receiving SDLC data, Fig. 5-17, begins by selecting $\overline{RR}$ (low). This signal causes the μPD379 to search for a $7E_{16}$ flag pattern. Once found, the data is forwarded to the processor in a similar manner to that used with the standard synchronous protocol. If the processor fails to accept the data before the next byte is received, an overrun error signal is generated. If the receiver detects 15 consecutive 1s, the IDLR line goes high. An abort pattern (FF_{16}) causes the receiver to set ABTR true.

A simplified block diagram of a memory-mapped μPD379 connection to the processor is shown in Fig. 5-18. The three least significant address bits are used for the MS1, MS2, and SYNC/$\overline{ZIP}$ signals.

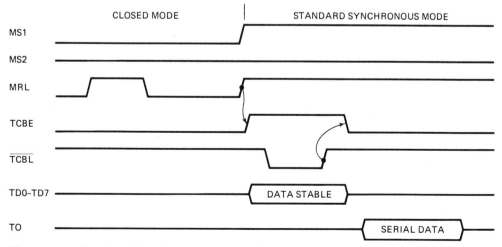

Figure 5-14. Standard Synchronous Protocol Transmit Timing.

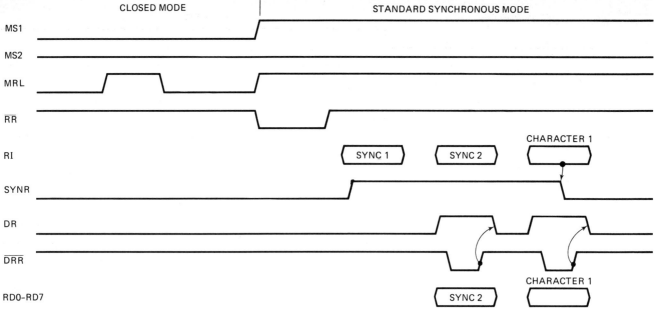

Figure 5-15. Standard Synchronous Protocol Receive Timing.

The address decoder produces the low $\overline{CS}$ signal to enable the device. In this example, a device address of 1 1000 0000 0000$_2$, in bits 3 through 15, will be used. Table 5-6 explains the meanings of the various addresses.

μPD379 Review

1. What errors can this device detect?

2. What mode must the μPD379 be in before other selections can be made?

3. How can the sync character be changed under program control?

4. List the normal sequence of receive control

signals between the microprocessor and the receiver/transmitter.

5. How would the character 3E$_{16}$ be transmitted?

6. In the memory-mapped I/O example, why does address C006 select the closed mode?

THE NEC μPD369 UNIVERSAL ASYNCHRONOUS RECEIVER/TRANSMITTER

The NEC μPD369 *universal asynchronous receiver/transmitter (UART)* is similar to most other UARTs, except that the μPD369 uses the 8080A power-supply voltages ($+5$, -5, and $+12$ V). Features

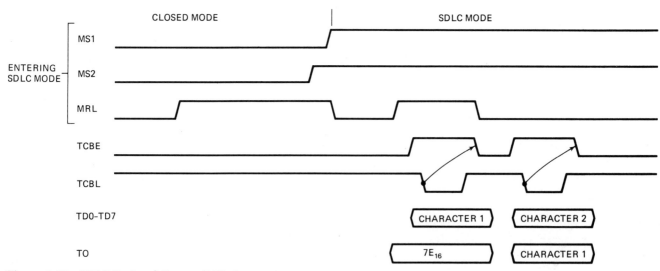

Figure 5-16. SDLC Protocol Transmit Timing.

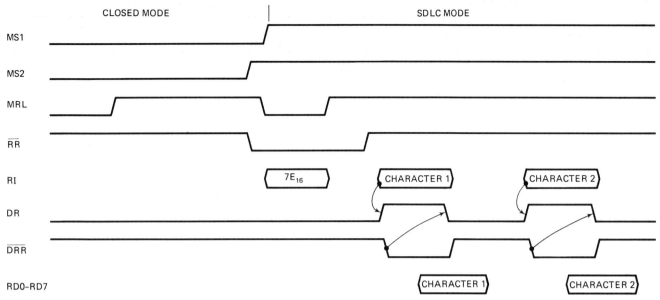

Figure 5-17. SDLC Protocol Receive Timing.

of the device include half- or full-duplex operation. Each character may consist of 5, 6, 7, or 8 bits. There are options for 1, 1½ (with 5 data bits only), or 2 stop bits. The μPD369 has baud rates that range from DC to 50K baud and a clock rate of ×16. Parity, overrun, and framing errors can be detected. A diagram of the pin configuration is shown in Fig. 5-19, and Table 5-7 describes each of the signals.

Some of the signals require further amplification. When RRD is low, the parallel input lines (RR0 through RR7) are connected to the receive register. A low $\overline{\text{THRL}}$ data write strobe loads TR0 through TR7 into the transmit holding register. The control input strobe, CRL, cause the control signals to be sampled. When MR is pulsed for 500 ns or longer, the transmit and receive buffers are cleared and all error status lines and $\overline{\text{DRR}}$ are reset; TRO, THRE, and TRE are set.

Transmission

Transmission and reception processes are both double-buffered in the μPD369. One of these buffers is a holding buffer and the other the data buffer.

Figure 5-20 shows the double buffering for transmission. The device signals the status of each buffer to the MPU. TRE is high when the transmit buffer is empty and stays high until new data is moved into the transmit holding buffer. When the transmit holding buffer is empty, THRE goes high and remains high until new data on TR0 through TR7 is strobed in by $\overline{\text{THRL}}$.

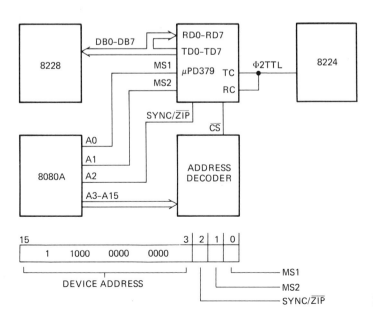

Figure 5-18. Memory Mapped μPD379.

Table 5-6
Addresses and Meanings

Address$_{16}$	Mode	Other selections
C000	Closed	Sync character is being transmitted on TR0–TR7.
C001	Standard	Data may be sent or received.
C002	Closed	Sync character is being transmitted on TR0–TR7.
C003	SDLC	Zero insertion is suppressed. Data may be sent or received.
C004	Closed	Standard sync character.
C005	Standard	Data may be sent or received.
C006	Closed	Standard sync character.
C007	SDLC	Zero insertion is enabled. Data may be sent or received.

Table 5-7
μPD369 Signals

Signal	Description	Type
RR0–RR7	Parallel received data	Output
TR0–TR7	Parallel transmit data	Input
TRO	Serial data	Output
RI	Serial data	Input
MR	Master reset	Input
TRC	Transmit clock	Input
RRC	Receive clock	Input
PI	Parity inhibit	Input
SBS	Stop bits select	Input
WLS1, WLS2	Word length select	Input
EPE	Even/odd parity select	Input
CRL	Control load	Input
TRE	Transmit register empty	Output
THRE	Transmit holding register empty	Output
THRL	Transmit holding register load	Input
PE	Parity error	Output
FE	Framing error	Output
OE	Overrun error	Output
SFD	Status flag disconnect	Input
DR	Data received	Output
DRR	Data received reset	Input
RRD	Parallel data read strobe	Input

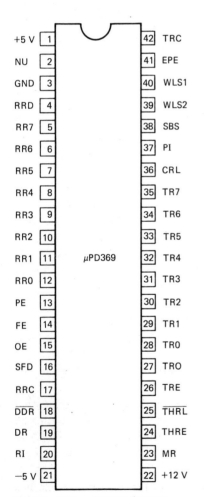

Figure 5-19. μPD369 UART.

Mode Selection

Before communications begin, several mode selections must be made. The PI control line allows the user to specify whether a parity bit is to be appended to the data or not. If PI is high when CRL is raised, no parity bit will be used. If PI is low, a parity bit will be inserted. (In all the control signals discussed below, CRL must go high before the device will interpret them.) The EPE chooses the type of parity used when PI is low. A low EPE level means odd parity; a high level even parity. The number of stop bits depends on the SBS signal. If it is low, 1 stop bit is selected. When high, stop bits are designated, unless the word length is 5 bits. In that

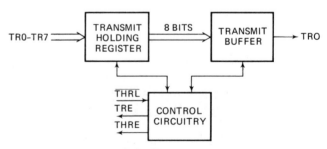

Figure 5-20. Transmit Buffers.

Table 5-8
Word Length Selection

WLS1	WLS2	Length
Low	Low	5 bits
High	Low	6
Low	High	7
High	High	8

case, 1½ stop bits are used instead. Word length selections depend on the settings of WLS1 and WLS2, as shown in Table 5-8.

Reception

The receive buffering is shown in Fig. 5-21. After a complete word is assembled in the receive buffer from the serial input on RI, the data is loaded into the holding buffer and DR set high. The data can be sampled on RR0 through RR7 when RRD is low. After sampling, the processor lowers $\overline{DDR}$ to reset the RRD strobe.

In case of error, the μPD369 will set one of the status lines. To enable reading them, SFO must be pulsed low. When a parity error is detected, PE is raised. A high FE signal is caused by a framing error (That is, valid stop bits were not detected at the end of a character). In case of overrun when the processor does not read the data from the holding buffer before the receive buffer is full, the OE signal goes high. Should this signal become true, the first data word is lost.

μPD369 Review

1. How does the μPD369 differ from most other UARTs?

2. What is the control signal sequence between processor and UART for output data?

3. How would even parity be specified to the μPD369?

4. What does a high level on the OE line signify?

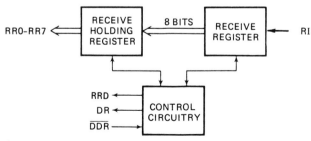

Figure 5-21. Receiver Buffers.

CHAPTER SUMMARY

1. Data can be converted between serial and parallel forms by means of a shift register.

2. A modem is used to change binary values to an audio signal for transmission. When receiving, the modem reverses the process.

3. Half-duplex communications systems allow one station to transmit and the other to receive at any time. Full duplex provides simultaneous transmission and reception.

4. Serial data is a stream of pulses held at high or low levels for the proper time interval. The pulses are synchronized with a clock.

5. Settling delay periods are allowed to assure that the signal reaches a steady state after transitions.

6. A serial receiver/transmitter accepts parallel data from the processor and buffers it onto the serial output line. As data comes in on the serial line, it is converted to parallel then passed to the microprocessor. All modes of the device can be controlled by the program.

7. The baud rate equals the number of bits sent per second in a serial channel. Both the transmitter and receiver clocks must be a multiple of the baud rate.

8. The receiver must synchronize its clock with the transmitter. If the clocks are badly skewed, a framing error will result. Sync signals are used by the receiver to locate the correct time for clock transitions. Alternatively, sync characters may be used to identify frame boundaries.

9. Synchronous serial transmission is best suited for faster data rates; asynchronous serial transmission is used in slower communications.

10. In a synchronous systems, data is always transmitted. When no useful information is available, the transmitter sends sync characters. Word lengths in these systems can be 5 to 8 bits.

11. Handshaking between stations is required before communications can begin. Control characters exchanged between the transmitter and receiver are employed to initialize the devices.

12. The asynchronous protocol requires the transmitter to send only when there is information furnished by the microcomputer. No sync characters are used. Words are bracketed by start and stop bits.

13. A standard set of modem control signals has been established. These signals allow the de-

vices to initiate data exchanges in either direction.

14. Synchronous communications can be either character- or bit-oriented. Among the most popular bit-oriented protocols are SDLC and HDLC.

15. NRZ and NRZI conventions are used in SDLC and HDLC protocols.

16. Integrated circuit synchronous and asynchronous receiver/transmitters that perform all communications functions are readily available.

KEY TERMS AND CONCEPTS

Parallel-to-serial conversion

Serial-to-parallel conversion

Modem

Half-duplex system

Full-duplex system

Settling delays

Guard times

Double buffering

Baud rate

Clock rates

Synchronization

Clock skew

Framing error

Sync signal

Mark

Sync character

Communication protocols

Synchronous serial protocol

Handshaking

Asynchronous serial protocol

Start bit

Stop bits

Data terminal

Data set

Character-oriented
synchronous data

Bit-oriented synchronous data

Synchronous data
link control (SDLC)

High-level data link
control (HDLC)

Zero bit insertion

Nonreturn to zero (NRZ)

Nonreturn to zero,
inverted (NRZI)

Universal asynchronous
receiver/transmitter (UART)

PROBLEMS

5-1 Draw the corresponding NRZ and NRZI waveforms to transmit the number 74_{16}. (Remember that the least significant bit is transmitted first.)

5-2 Draw a simplified block diagram, similar to Fig. 5-18, showing a memory-mapped μPD369 UART.

5-3 Show the parallel-to-serial conversion of the first 3 bits of $B7_{16}$. (Refer to Fig. 5-1.)

5-4 In an analogous manner to Prob. 5-3, show the serial-to-parallel conversion of the first 3 bits in the bit stream

$$0101 \quad 1101$$

5-5 Draw a serial data waveform representing the data stream $6E_{16}$ sent with a ×1 clock; with a ×4 clock.

5-6 How would the serial data in the words below

be transmitted, if two sync characters are used to delineate word boundaries? Word 1: 03_{16}; word 2: $C2_{16}$.

5-7 A synchronous serial receiver has a baud rate of 4800. What is its clock frequency?

5-8 An asynchronous serial transmitter sends characters of 8 data bits. Parity and 2 stop bits are used in the system. If 100 characters are sent per second, what is the baud rate?

5-9 Show the format for an SDLC frame if the fields are as listed below:

Frame check	$21E2_{16}$
Information	$46CB09_{16}$
Control field	76_{16}
Address	$F4_{16}$

5-10 How would the control field appear in an HDLC frame if the control information is $6C4E_{16}$?

EXPERIMENT 4

PURPOSE: To investigate parallel-to-serial conversion.

PROCEDURE: This experiment uses the circuit from Experiment 3.

STEP 1. Write a program to output the accumulator, then shift it left 1 bit. Delay 1 s. If all 8 bits have not been sent, repeat the shift. When all bits have been transmitted stop.

STEP 2. Disconnect all wires between the 8212 and the displays except for the least significant bit. (Pin 4 of the 8212 and pin 8 of the 5082-7340.) Set the accumulator to 55_{16}. Run the program and record the results on a table like the one below.

Bit	Display
7	
6	
5	
4	
3	
2	
1	
0	

6

TELETYPE CURRENT LOOPS

Asynchronous serial data transmission is frequently used between micropro-cessors and teletype (TTY) printers and keyboards. Data from the processor is printed on the paper and can also be punched in paper tape. To send to the MPU, a key is depressed and the coded character is forwarded. Because the teletype may be located a good distance from the microcomputer, a reliable and inexpensive communications channel is desirable. By using serial com-munications, a simple two-wire cable can be used. This cable is much more economical than an 8-bit parallel line. Low-impedance *current loops* are used as the transmission channel because they are resistant to errors that noise can introduce. Digital signals can be transmitted for distances up to 5000 ft (1500 m) over current loops without degrading.

CHAPTER OBJECTIVES

Upon completion of this chapter, you should be able to:

1. Describe the data format used in teletype communications
2. Explain the mechanical mechanism of the teletype printer/keyboard and relate it to the data input
3. Decode 7- and 8-bit teletype characters
4. List the logic levels for 20-mA current loops
5. Draw a block diagram of a typical teletype current loop
6. Explain why opto-isolators are required in current loops used with microprocessors
7. Explain the input and output circuits used in current loops by means of a schematic diagram
8. Write programs which interface a microprocessor to a teletype printer and keyboard

TELETYPE CHARACTERISTICS

The serial communication with a teletype is usually run at 110, 150, or 300 baud rates. The transmission from either end of the loop is asynchronous. Figure 6-1 shows a teletype connected to a microprocessor by means of a twisted-pair transmission line. Often the transmission line is shielded to avoid picking up noise. A UART like the one we studied in Chap. 5 is used as an interface between the parallel I/O of the microprocessor and the serial channel.

The Model 33 Teletype is a good example of the type of peripheral we have been discussing. It can send or receive 10 char/s. Each teletype character sent requires 11 bits. Recall from the last chapter that 1 *start bit,* 8 data bits, and 2 *stop bits* comprise each character. Figure 6-2 shows the character format and timing. Because each character consists of 11 bits and 10 characters are sent per second, the data rate is 110 baud. Later in this chapter we will see how the microprocessor converts the 8 parallel bits in a computer word to the 11 serial bits.

Mechanical Characteristics

Although a teletype appears to be a single piece of equipment, it is actually two separate devices from the microcomputer's point of view. The receiving device is the *printer* that converts the digital signals to letters. The sending component is the *keyboard* that generates a bit pattern when a key is pressed. An optional item is the paper tape reader/punch. If the punch is on when the printer is printing a character, the print bars will also punch through the tape. In an analogous manner, the reader parallels the keyboard operations, allowing data to be transmitted at a faster rate than the operator can type.

PRINTER. The printer begins operation after a start bit is detected. The start bit will cause the clutch to engage the mechanical linkages and also enable the selector-magnets for decoding. When the 8 data bits arrive (requiring 8 bits $\times$ 9.09 ms/bit = 72.72 ms), they trip the selector-magnet which catches eight spinning, notched wheels. These wheels raise or lower the print bars, selecting the character to be printed. Once the character is in position, the print hammer strikes the head against the ribbon and paper. The stop bits give the printer time to

terminate the print operation and prepare for the next start bit.

KEYBOARD. The keyboard operations depend on a distributor to produce signals, as shown in Fig. 6-3. Depressing any key causes the keyboard encoder to open or close switches in series with each data bit. The distributor generates the 11 bits by use of a commutator that rotates counterclockwise. The commutator first connects the start contact to the output line. After rotating to the first bit position, the state of the keyboard encoder switch decides whether an open or short circuit is sensed on the output lines. The commutator continues to rotate through each of the other data bit contacts. It finally passes the stop 1 and stop 2 contacts and then waits until the next key is pressed. A synchronous motor turns the commutator and provides the precise 9.09 ms timing. This motor must be well maintained or else sync errors will develop.

CHARACTER SET. There are several character sets in use by various pieces of teletype equipment. Most commonly used are 7- or 8-bit ASCII characters. The 7-bit characters will either use bit number 7 as a parity bit or always leave it in the zero state. The *8-bit characters,* as listed in Table 6-1, always set that bit to a 1. The choice of character set does not affect the hardware interface because 8 data bits must be sent regardless of coding. The software that processes the characters must, however, be programmed to use the appropriate character set.

Teletype Characteristics Review

1. Why are teletype current loops used?

2. How many bits are needed for each teletype character? How are they used?

3. What delimits the start and stop of each bit in a character?

4. Explain how the keyboard distributor encodes each character.

CURRENT LOOPS

Data signals from the processor move through the UART, which converts them to serial, and through

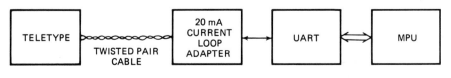

Figure 6-1. Teletype Communications Channel.

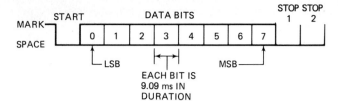

Figure 6-2. Teletype Data Format.

the current loop converter, which changes them from TTL levels to currents. Instead of using high and low voltage levels, current loops represent the two data states by the presence or absence of current flow. A logic 1 is indicated by a 20-mA current, logic 0 by no current.

The current loop in Fig. 6-4 shows the important features for the circuit.

The current flows from the converter to the negative terminal of the printer (pin 6). The printer positive terminal is connected to the negative terminal of the keyboard (pin 3). From the keyboard, the circuit leads to the ground terminal of the current regulator, which produces the current flowing in the loop with the aid of a +15-V power supply. Finally, the circuit is completed at the negative terminal of the converter.

20-mA Converter

The *20-mA converter* used in this circuit provides the necessary voltage isolation between the microprocessor and current loop. By employing an *opto-isolator* (also called an "optical isolator"), voltage isolation of several thousand volts can be achieved, though such high voltages would never appear in the circuit. The opto-isolator works much

Table 6-1
8-Bit Teletype Characters

Character	Code	Character	Code
0	B0	O	CF
1	B1	P	D0
2	B2	Q	D1
3	B3	R	D2
4	B4	S	D3
5	B5	T	D4
6	B6	U	D5
7	B7	V	D6
8	B8	W	D7
9	B9	X	D8
A	C1	Y	D9
B	C2	Z	DA
C	C3		
D	C4	.	AE
E	C5	,	AC
F	C6	?	BF
G	C7	=	BD
H	C8	*	AA
I	C9	$	A4
J	CA	%	A5
K	CB	!	A1
L	CC	,	A7
M	CD	SP	A0
N	CE	LF	8A
		CR	8D

like a relay. The infrared light-emitting diode (LED) converts the incoming signal to light. The light is sensed by a light-sensitive semiconductor, such as a photoresistive detector or phototransistor. That component, in turn, acts as a switch and produces the correct output conditions.

The converter is a discrete component circuit which has seven inputs or outputs, as shown in Fig. 6-5a. Two leads are for the TTL input and output. The 20-mA input and output connections are made at the appropriate positive and negative terminal pairs. Another input is the common 20-mA current sink termination. A +5-V power supply is required, and the remaining pin is usually attached to ground.

Three separate circuits are actually used in the converter. The current-to-TTL conversion is performed by the circuit shown in Fig. 6-5b. Diode

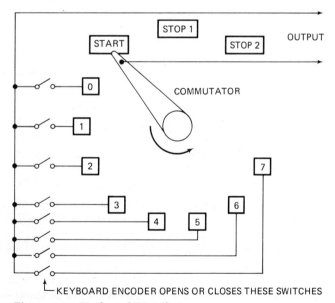

Figure 6-3. Keyboard Distributor.

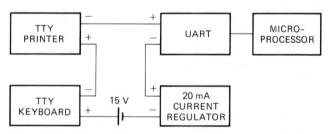

Figure 6-4. Current Loop.

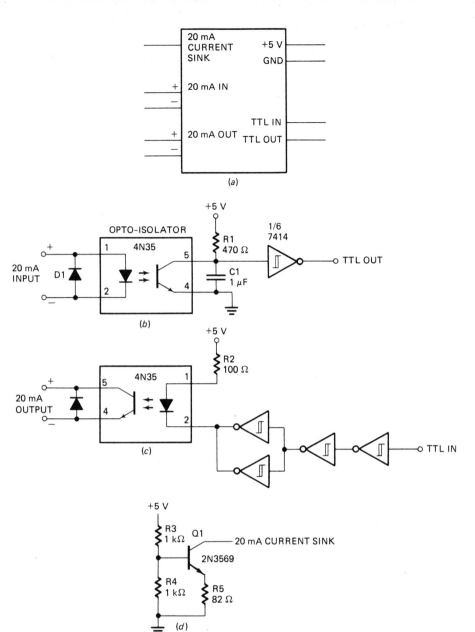

Figure 6-5. 20mA Current Loop
Converter (a) Pin Configuration
(b) Current-to-TTL Converter
(c) TTL-to-Current Converter
(d) Current Sink.

D1 is just used to prevent damage in case the loop is connected with reverse polarity. An opto-isolator, such as the 4N35, provides the isolation, as was explained above. When current flows in the loop, the LED in the 4N35 is forward-biased, causing it to emit light. Light striking the phototransistor causes it to saturate with a V_{CE} of about 0.3 V. This low voltage applied to the Schmitt trigger inverter (one of the six inverters in a 7414) produces a high at the TTL output. If no current flows in the loop, the LED does not emit and the phototransistor is off. Then +5 V appears at the inverter input and the TTL output is low. The data rate is controlled by the value of C1. With the 1 microfarad (μF) value shown, a data rate in the range of DC to 300 bps can be maintained. Selecting a smaller capacitor will

increase the data rate; a value of 0.01 μF will allow the converter to run at up to 40K bps. As the data rate increases, however, so does the noise.

TTL-to-current conversion is the purpose of the circuit in Fig. 6-5c. The TTL input is applied to the opto-isolator through a network of Schmitt trigger inverters. The output transistor of the optical isolator acts as a switch in the current loop. A low TTL input passing through the three inverter stages appears as a +5-V level on pin 2 of the opto-isolator. This voltage reverse-biases the LED, causing the phototransistor to remain off. With the transistor off, no current can flow in the loop. On the other hand, a high at the TTL input produces a low voltage at the cathode of the LED. The LED is forward-biased, so it emits, saturating the transistor. Now current can flow in the loop. (See Prob. 6-8.) D2 protects this circuit in the same way as D1 in the previous case.

The current sink is a simple one-transistor circuit. Q1 is normally held on by the power supply. The transistor provides a low-impedance path to ground.

The converter can drive up to 10 TTL gates (fanout = 10), but can only accept a single input. A current less than 3 mA in the loop will be recognized as a logic 0; current more than 15 mA is a logic 1.

Current Loops Review

1. How is a logic 1 represented in a current loop? A logic 0?

2. Why is an opto-isolator used in the 20-mA converter? Explain briefly how the opto-isolator works.

3. What effect does current flowing into the circuit shown in Fig. 6-5*b* have? What current is produced when the TTL input shown in Fig. 6-5*c* is low?

4. How does changing the value of C1 in Fig. 6-5*b* from 1 to 0.01 μF effect the baud rate?

SYSTEM OPERATION

The teletype circuit can be used in either *half-* or *full-duplex* modes. Figure 6-6 shows the half-duplex configuration. In a half-duplex system, either the teletype or processor can transmit, but not at the same time. Basically the loop is a series circuit. The 20-mA input runs to the printer and through the keyboard and the power supply to ground. The circuit is completed through the sink and the 20-mA

output. In this case, we are using the μPD369 UART that was studied in Chap. 5.

Full-duplex operation (Fig. 6-7) calls for two current loops and two power supplies. Now the microcomputer and teletype can both transmit simultaneously. The keyboard loop terminates at the 20-mA input and the printer loop at the 20-mA output. Serial data passes in both directions between the UART and TTL input and output terminals.

System Operation Review

1. How are the connections of the teletype and 20-mA converter changed in going from half duplex to full duplex?

2. Why are two power supplies needed in the full-duplex mode?

3. Describe the purpose of each loop in the full-duplex configuration.

SOFTWARE INTERFACING TO TELETYPES

Many of the tasks required to interface a processor can be done by either hardware or software. For example, the appending and checking of the parity bit can be a function of either the μPD369 UART or the microprocessor program. Another one of these tasks is controlling the timing to send the serial bits of a character at 9.09 ms.

In this section we will see how the program can provide the timing accuracy required and also how the 8-bit character stored in memory can be used to generate the 11 bits needed for the teletype character.

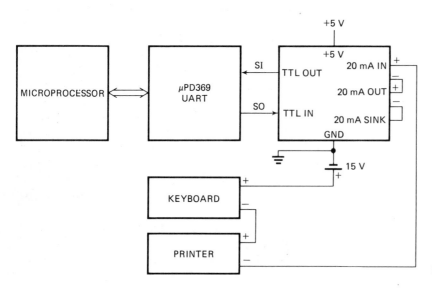

Figure 6-6. Half-Duplex Teletype System.

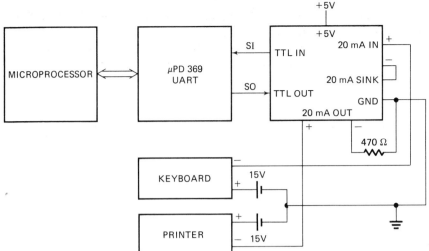

Figure 6-7. Full-Duplex Teletype System.

Output

A flowchart for the teletype output routine is shown in Fig. 6-8. In the first step a counter is set to 11 to maintain a count of the number of bits sent. Each bit is transmitted with a 9.09-ms delay between them. After each bit has been sent, the counter is decremented. If the counter is not zero, the loop is reentered to send the next character. When the counter reaches zero, the routine terminates.

The program is listed in Table 6-2. There is a main program and the delay subroutine in the table. Considering first the main program, the character to be sent must be in the E register before entering the routine. A series of rotate accumulator instructions will be used to shift the bits out one by one. Only the least significant bit of I/O port $0F_{16}$ is used, so the UART need only deal with a single bit, as Fig. 6-9 shows. Because of the simple interface, an AND gate can be used instead of a UART. (Although not in the program listing, the stack pointer must be properly initialized so that the subroutine call works correctly.)

After the counter has been initialized and the character placed in the accumulator (address 1002_{16}), the A register is ORed with itself. This operation does not change the accumulator, but it does clear the carry bit. The RAL instruction on the next line moves the carry bit (which was zero) to the LSB of the accumulator and shifts the MSB of the accumulator to the carry bit position. See Fig. 6-10*a*.

The output instruction places the accumulator contents on the data lines. Only data bit 0 is passed to the teletype, and that is a 0 for the start bit. The delay subroutine, which we will examine later, introduces the proper delay and the accumulator is rotated right, returning the MSB to bit 7 of the accumulator, as Fig. 6-10*b* shows.

Next, the carry bit is set, so the next right shift will bring a 1 into the MSB of the A register to act as one of the stop bits (Fig. 6-10*c*). Because 11 bits have not been transmitted, the loop is repeated. When the RAR instruction is reached again, the set carry bit moves into the accumulator (Fig. 6-10*d*). The same process repeats until all data bits and 2 stop bits have been sent. By use of the carry status, we were able to insert the stop and start bits to convert the 8 data bits into a complete teletype character.

Now we will see how the delay was created. If our 8080A has a 2-MHz clock, then we can use the execution rate of two instructions to cause the

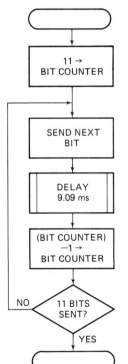

Figure 6-8. Teletype Output Routine.

Table 6-2
Teletype Output Routine

Label	Mnemonic	Address	Op code	Comment
	MVI D, 11	1000	16	Set bit counter to 11.
		1001	0B	
	MOV A, E	1002	7B	Place data in accumulator.
	ORA A	1003	B7	Clear carry bit.
	RAL	1004	17	Carry A bit 0 of accumulator to act as start bit.
LOOP	OUT 0F	1005	D3	Send data on port $0F_{16}$.
		1006	0F	
	CALL DELAY	1007	CD	9.1-ms delay subroutine.
		1008	50	
		1009	10	
	RAR	100A	1F	
	STC	100B	37	Set carry for stop bits.
	DCR D	100C	15	Decrement bit counter.
	JNZ LOOP	100D	C2	Is counter 0? If not, go to send next character.
		100E	05	
		100F	10	
	HLT	1010	76	Stop.
DELAY	MVI B, 6	1050	06	Load outer loop counter to perform outer loop six
		1051	06	times.
OUTLOOP	MVI C, 202	1052	0E	Load inner loop counter
		1053	CA	to perform inner loop 202 times.
INLOOP	DCR C	1054	0D	Decrement inner counter.
	JNZ INLOOP	1055	C2	If not zero, go to decrement again.
		1056	54	
		1057	10	
	DCR B	1058	05	Decrement outer counter.
	JNZ OUTLOOP	1059	C2	If not zero go to decrement again.
		105A	52	
		105B	10	
	RET	105C	C9	Return.

delay. We will use the DCR and JNZ instructions, which have execution times of

DCR	2.5 μs
JNZ	5.0 μs
TOTAL	7.5 μs

To create a delay of approximately 9.1 ms, we have to divide by the instruction delay:

$$9.1 \text{ ms}/7.5 \text{ μs} = 1213 \qquad (6\text{-}1)$$

Because the largest number we can use in a DCR instruction is FF_{16} (255_{10}), we must perform the decrementing loop several times. As the program shows, we can use an outer loop that repeats an inner loop six times. By setting the inner counter to 202_{10} we have

$$6 \times 202 = 1212$$

which is close enough to the value in Eq. (6-1). It is worthwhile emphasizing that this technique is an approximation and assumes that no wait states or interrupts occur. In reality it may be necessary to adjust the count in cell 1053 up or down slightly to create the desired delay.

Input

When the processor is receiving, the teletype provides the data with correct timing. The processor just waits for the bits to arrive. One method which could be used would be to attach the data received (DR) pin from the μPD369 UART to bit 7 of the

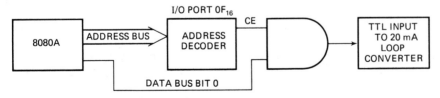

Figure 6-9. Simplified Teletype Output Circuit.

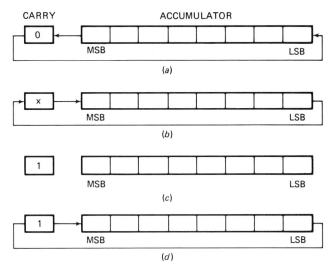

Figure 6-10. Shift Patterns (a) Bring a Zero Into the LSB Position (b) Restore MSB (c) Setting Carry to Act As Stop Bits (d) Moving Stop Bit Into Accumulator.

data bus. (Bit 0 will be used to receive the serial input.) The processor would stay in a loop of the three following instructions:

```
REPEAT  IN    0F      Input from port 0F
        ORA           Set status bits
        JP    REPEAT  Input again if not
                      negative
```

When the DR line goes high, it will set the sign bit. Sensing a negative value means that a new bit has been sent by the teletype.

After recognizing the start bit, the processor receives the serial data bits and packs them into a byte. After all 8 data bits arrive, the 2 stop bits are accepted, and the procedure is complete.

Software Interfacing to Teletypes Review

1. Name two tasks required in a teletype interface that either hardware or software can perform.

2. How does the output software produce the 11 teletype character bits from a data byte?

3. What technique was used by the output program to convert parallel data to serial?

4. Which data bit is sent to the teletype first in the output routine?

5. Why is a simple AND gate adequate for the output circuit shown in Fig. 6-9?

6. How does the software produce a 9.1-ms delay between bits?

7. True or false? The teletype input routine must contain a 9.09-ms delay loop.

CHAPTER SUMMARY

1. Current loops are used in teletype communications channels. Baud rates of 110, 150, or 300 are commonly used by these asynchronous serial channels. A UART interfaces between the processor and the current loop.

2. Each character is sent by 11 bits: 1 start bit, 8 data bits, and 2 stop bits. Each bit level is held for 9.09 ms.

3. The selector-magnet of the printer is controlled by the data bits, which cause the magnet to engage notches on eight notched wheels that raise or lower the print bars, thus selecting the character to be printed. Once the character is set on the print bars, a hammer strikes the head against the paper.

4. The keyboard distributor converts the key depressed to outgoing signals. The encoder opens or closes switches that control current flow as the commutator rotates.

5. Several character sets are used by various teletypes. The 7- and 8-bit ASCII codes are frequently encountered.

6. A 20-mA converter changes transmitted TTL levels to currents and received currents back to TTL levels. A logic 1 in a current loop is shown by current flow of 20 mA. No current means a logic 0 is being sent.

7. Voltage isolation in the converter is the reason for including an opto-isolator in the circuit.

8. Current loops permit teletypes to operate in either half- or full-duplex modes.

9. Software can take over many of the jobs necessary in interfacing. By adding more to the program, the hardware can be simplified a great deal, but the processor and memory are then dedicated to the interfacing task part of the time.

KEY TERMS AND CONCEPTS

Current loops	Stop bits	Keyboard	20-mA converter
Start bit	Printer	8-bit characters	Opto-isolator

6-1 The 8-bit ASCII character for the letter I is to be transmitted. Show the carry status bit and the accumulator values for the first 3 bits sent using the output routine.

6-2 What character does CC_{16} represent in 8-bit ASCII code? What is the purpose of the MSB if this were a 7-bit ASCII code which used parity?

6-3 How should the output routine be changed if we want to have 12-ms delays between character bits for an experimental teletype?

6-4 Write the code needed by the input routine to store the 8 data bits in memory cell 0200_{16}. (Remember that the LSB is received first and bit 7 is used by the DR line to signal when the bit has been received.)

6-5 Draw a block diagram of a teletype output circuit that replaces the AND gate shown in Fig. 6-9 with the μPD369 UART.

6-6 Repeat Prob. 6-5 for the input circuit.

6-7 If the teletype is sending the 7-bit ASCII character M (without parity) what would the state of the encoder switches shown in Fig. 6-3 be?

6-8 Assume that the LED shown in Fig. 6-5c drops 1.8 V and the resistance of the output stages of the inverters is zero. The maximum current that each inverter can sink in the low-output state is 16 mA. Explain why two inverters must be paralleled in this circuit.

6-9 V_{CE} of the phototransistor shown in Fig. 6-5b is 0.3 V. Assume that the only resistance in the circuit is R1 of 470 Ω. How long after the phototransistor is cut off does the input to the inverter reach 5 V?

6-10 What is the voltage on the base of Q1 in Fig. 6-5d. When current flows into the circuit, what is the emitter voltage if V_{CE} is 0.2 V and the transistor has negligible internal resistance in comparison to R5?

EXPERIMENT 5 _____

PURPOSE: To investigate teletype current loops.

PARTS LIST:

Item	Quantity
Diode	2
4N35 opto-isolator	2
82-Ω resistor	1
100-Ω resistor	1
470-Ω resistor	1
1-kΩ resistor	2
1-μF capacitor	1
74LS14	1
2N3569 transistor	1

Figure 6-11. 74LS14.

IC DIAGRAM:

PROCEDURE:

STEP 1. Using Fig. 6-5c as a guide, construct a TTL-to-current loop converter, a current loop-to-TTL converter, and a current sink.

STEP 2. Wire these components circuits as shown in Fig. 6-12.

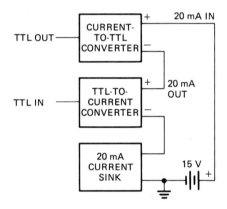

Figure 6-12. Test Circuit.

STEP 3. Attach an ammeter to the TTL output terminal. Connect +5 V to the TTL input terminal. Next disconnect the +5 V and ground the input. Explain your results.

STEP 4. Apply a pulser signal to the TTL input. What do you observe on the logic probe ammeter?

Steps 5 to 7 are optional

STEP 5. If you have a 20-mA teletype terminal available to you, it can be used with this circuit to print the characters as the program transmits them. Wire the 8212 as shown in Fig. 4-37 and the address selection as shown in Fig. 4-38. Use only the least significant bit of the data bus from the 8080A. (Only pin 3 of the 8212 need be connected.) Connect pin 4 of the 8212 to the TTL input of the TTL-to-current converter.

STEP 6. Wire the other circuit components as shown in Fig. 6-6.

STEP 7. The teletype output routine listed in Table 6-2 (with a device code of 07) is to be used to transmit each character. Before calling this routine, the ASCII code for the character must be loaded into the E register.

7

EIA STANDARD RS-232C INTERFACE

The most widely used serial communications interface is the *RS-232C interface*. This interface is defined in an Electronic Industries Association (EIA) standard which specifies the interconnection of the *data terminal equipment (DTE)* and *data communications equipment (DCE)*. When the interface is used between a microcomputer and peripheral, the computer is usually the DCE and the peripheral the DTE. This chapter describes the RS-232C circuits and then shows how they can be used in various configurations. Circuits which can convert between TTL or 20-mA current loops and RS-232C are also discussed.

CHAPTER OBJECTIVES

Upon completion of this chapter, you should be able to:

1. List the basic capabilities of the RS-232C interface.
2. Describe the four types of lines specified in the standard.
3. List the voltage levels used for logic and control signals.
4. Distinguish between primary and secondary channels.
5. Define the purpose of each signal in the RS-232C specification.
6. Group the signals by category.
7. Draw a timing diagram for a typical RS-232C handshaking situation.
8. Explain the electrical and mechanical characteristics of the standard.
9. Use a circuit diagram to explain how RS-232C signals can be converted to either TTL or 20-mA current loop levels.

RS-232C CAPABILITIES

This interface specification is quite general in its application. While it assigns the serial signals to specific pins on the connector, it does not restrict the type of data that can be sent. Any character length, bit code, and bit sequence can be used. Either synchronous or asynchronous communications may be employed. The interface is intended for fairly short cables, about 50 ft (15 m), between the computer and peripheral.

Data rates of up to 20K baud can be supported. The most frequently encountered rates are listed in Table 7-1. The reference for the interface is EIA Standard RS-232C, "Interface between Data Terminal Equipment and Data Communication Equipment Employing Serial Binary Data Interchange."

Four types of lines are presented in the specification:

> *Data signals*
> *Control signals*
> *Timing signals*
> *Signal grounds (returns)*

The data signals represent a logic 1 with a voltage between -3 and -25 V. A logic 0 is a voltage greater than $+3$ V and less than $+25$ V. Any voltage in the range of -3 to $+3$ V is an undefined level. Control signals are on if the voltage is $+3$ to $+25$ V and off between -3 and -25 V.

There are two kinds of channels that may possibly be included in an RS-232C interface. *Primary channels* run at the higher signal rate and are intended to transfer data. *Secondary channels* run at a slower rate and provide control information. Secondary channels are further subdivided into *auxiliary channels* whose data direction is independent of the primary and are controlled by a set of secondary control circuits and *backward channels* that always transmit in a direction opposite to the primary channel.

RS-232C Capabilities Review

1. True or false? RS-232C channels are ideally suited for communicating between a microcomputer and a CRT display that is 300 ft away.
2. What is the highest data rate recommended for RS-232C signals?
3. List the types of lines specified by the EIA standard.
4. Describe the RS-232C logic and control voltage levels.
5. Distinquish between a primary and secondary channel.

SIGNAL DESCRIPTION

There are a maximum of 25 signal lines, or circuits, in the RS-232C connector. Of these, two are grounds, four data signals, twelve control signals, and three timing signals. The remaining lines are either reserved or unassigned. Table 7-2 lists all of the signals by pin number and gives the circuit nomenclature and common abbreviation. Table 7-3 groups the signals by category.

Data Signals

The *transmitted data signal* (circuit BA) is generated by the data terminal equipment. The data terminal must hold this signal in the 1 state during the interval between characters or words and when no data is being transmitted. The data terminal cannot send this signal until all of the following control signals (if implemented) are 1: *request to send* (CA circuit), *clear to send* (CB circuit), *data set ready* (CC circuit), and *data terminal ready* (CD circuit). As already noted and as shown in Table 7-2, the common designator for the "transmitted data" signal is TXD.

Received data (circuit BB) is sent by the data communications equipment. The signal must be held at the logic 1 level whenever the *received line signal detector* (CF circuit) is off. In a half-duplex system this signal is held at logic 1 when *request to send* (circuit CA) is on and for a brief interval following the on-to-off transition of CA to allow for completion of transmission and the delay of line reflections. As noted, the "received data signal" is commonly abbreviated RXD.

The secondary channel has data signals equivalent to the two above. The *secondary transmitted data*

Table 7-1
RS-232C Baud Rates

Rate (baud)	Common use
50	
75	
110	
150	Teletype
300	
600	
1,200	
2,400	CRT terminal
4,800	
9.600	
19,200	

Table 7-2
RS-232C Signals

Pin number	Circuit	Common abbreviation	Description
1	AA	· · ·	Protective ground
2	BA	TXD	Transmitted data
3	BB	RXD	Received data
4	CA	RTS	Request to send
5	CB	CTS	Clear to send
6	CC	DSR	Data set ready
7	AB	· · ·	Signal ground (common return)
8	CF	DCD	Received line signal detector
9	· · ·	· · ·	Reserved for data set testing
10	· · ·	· · ·	Reserved for data set testing
11	· · ·	· · ·	Unassigned
12	SCF	· · ·	Secondary received line signal detector
13	SCB	· · ·	Secondary clear to send
14	SBA	· · ·	Secondary transmitted data
15	DB	· · ·	Transmission signal element timing (DCE source)
16	SBB	· · ·	Secondary received data
17	DD	· · ·	Receiver signal element timing (DCE source)
18	· · ·	· · ·	Unassigned
19	SCA	· · ·	Secondary request to send
20	CD	DTR	Data terminal ready
21	CG	· · ·	Signal quality detector
22	CE	· · ·	Ring indicator
23*	CH/CI	· · ·	Data signal rate selector (DTE/DCE source)
24	DA	· · ·	Transmit signal element timing (DTE source)
25	· · ·	· · ·	Unassigned

*Only one of these two signals is tied to pin 23.

(SBA circuit) is equivalent to transmitted data and *secondary received data* (SBB circuit) is an analog to received data.

Control Signals

The first control signal is *request to send* (circuit CA), which is originated by the data terminal equipment. For one-way or duplex channels, an on condition holds the data communication equipment in the transmit mode. In half-duplex channels, on maintains the equipment in transmit and inhibits receive; when off, the signal enables the receive mode. Once request to send has been turned off, it cannot be turned on again until *clear to send* (CB circuit) has been turned off by the data communication equipment. The common abbreviation for *request to send* is RTS.

The data communication equipment transmits *clear to send* (CB circuit) in response to an on condition on *data set ready* (CC) and *request to send* (CA) control lines. No data should be sent when this control is off. The abbreviation for this signal is CTS.

The status of the data communication equipment is presented by *data set ready* (CC circuit). The signal is on when the equipment is connected to the channel; is not in test, talk, or dial mode; and has completed timing functions and answer tones (if applicable). The on condition does not mean that the communications circuit has been established, only that the local equipment is ready. The abbreviation is DSR.

When the data terminal set is ready, it connects the data communication equipment to the channel with the *data terminal ready* (CD circuit) control. When the signal goes off, the data communication equipment is removed from the channel after completing any in-progress transmission. This control is abbreviated DTR.

Table 7-3
RS-232C Signals by Category

Circuit	CCITT equivalent	Ground	Data		Control		Timing	
			From DCE	To DCE	From DCE	To DCE	From DCE	To DCE
AA	101	X						
AB	102	X						
BA	103			X				
BB	104		X					
CA	105					X		
CB	106				X			
CC	107				X			
CD	108.2					X		
CE	125				X			
CF	109				X			
CG	110				X			
CH	111					X		
CI	112				X			
DA	113							X
DB	114						X	
DD	115						X	
SBA	118			X				
SBB	119		X					
SCA	120					X		
SCB	121				X			
SCF	122				X			

The on state of the *ring indicator* (CE circuit) from the data communications equipment means that a ringing signal is being received. When the data communication equipment is receiving a signal which meets its suitability criteria, the *received line signal detector* (circuit CF) is transmitted in the on state. This signal goes off when no signal or an unsuitable signal is received. This signal is also called "data carrier detected," which is why it is abbreviated DCD.

The *signal quality detector* (CG circuit) from the data communication equipment is on when there is no reason to believe a data error has occurred and off when there is a high probability of an error. The data communication equipment uses the *data signal rate selector* (CH or CI circuits) to designate which of two data signaling rates, in the case of dual-rate data sets, will be used. An on condition selects the faster rate. The source of this signal can be either data terminal set or communications equipment, but not both.

The *secondary request to send* (SCA circuit) is equivalent to "request to send" as described above, except this control applies to the secondary channel. In a similar manner, the *secondary clear to send* (SCB circuit) corresponds to "clear to send." Finally, the *secondary received line signal detector* (SCF circuit) provides the same operations on the secondary channel as the received line signal detector."

Timing Signals

The *transmitter signal element timing (DTE source)* (DA circuit) is sent by the data terminal to indicate the center of each bit on the transmitted data line. A corresponding signal from the data communication equipment, *transmitter signal element timing (DCE source)* (DB circuit), is used by the data terminal to change the data on the transmitted data line when the DB signal makes a transition from off to on. The *receiver signal element timing* (DD circuit) is sent by the data communication equipment to indicate the center of each bit on the received data line. A transition of on to off marks this time.

Grounds

The *protective ground* (AA circuit) connects to the equipment frame and may be connected to external grounds. The *signal ground* or *common return* (AB circuit) establishes a common ground reference potential for all RS-232C signals (except the protective ground). This circuit must be brought to one point and may be connected to the AA ground by an internal wire strap.

Selection

Not all of the signals provided need be implemented by a piece of equipment. In fact most communications systems do not. A very minimal system with only three signals is shown in Fig. 7-1a. Figure 7-1b is a more typical eight-signal channel system. Tables 7-4 and 7-5 list other options.

Handshaking

The initialization of communications on an RS-232C channel requires exchange of a series of control signals. Figure 7-2 is an example of how the data terminal and communication equipment can start the interchange. The request to send is raised by the terminal. When the data communications equipment responds with clear to send, the terminal responds with data terminal ready, which stays high as long as data is transmitted. (The request to send line can be reset after clear to send drops.)

Signal Description Review

1. Which two signals are used to transmit or receive data on the primary channel?

2. Can data transmission begin with the control signal states: RTS on, CTS on, DCD off? (These are the only control signals implemented.)

3. What is another name frequently used for the received line signal detector.

4. Which timing signal may be used to indicate the center of each bit transmitted by the data terminal?

5. Distinguish between the purpose of the protective ground (AA circuit) and the signal ground (AB circuit)

6. True or false? Every RS-232C interface must provide 25 lines in the cable.

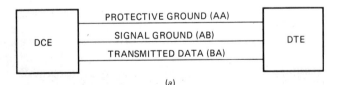

Figure 7-1A. RS-232C Communication Channels (a) Minimal System.

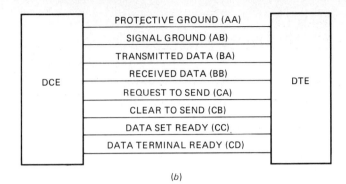

(b)

Figure 7-1B. RS-232C Communication Channels (b) Typical System.

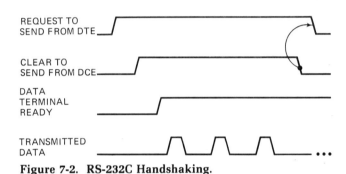

Figure 7-2. RS-232C Handshaking.

Table 7-4
RS-232C Interfaces

Configuration	Interface*
Transmit only	A
Transmit only†	B
Receive only	C
Half duplex	D
Full duplex†	D
Full duplex	E
Primary channel transmit only†/ secondary channel receive only	F
Primary channel transmit only/ secondary channel receive only	H
Primary channel receive only/ secondary channel transmit only†	G
Primary channel receive only/ secondary channel transmit only	I
Primary channel transmit only†/ half-duplex secondary channel	J
Primary channel receive only/half-duplex secondary channel	K
Half-duplex primary channel/half-duplex secondary channel	L
Full-duplex secondary channel†/ full-duplex secondary channel	L
Full-duplex primary channel/full-duplex secondary channel	M
Special	Z

*See Table 7-5.
†The CA signal (request to send) is included in the selection.

Table 7-5
RS-232C Data Communications Channels

	Interface From Table 7-4													
Circuit	A	B	C	D	E	F	G	H	I	J	K	L	M	Z
AA	*	*	*	*	*	*	*	*	*	*	*	*	*	*
AB	X	X	X	X	X	X	X	X	X	X	X	X	X	X
BA	X	X		X	X	X		X		X		X	X	S
BB			X	X	X		X		X		X	X	X	S
CA		X		X		X				X		X		S
CB	X	X		X	X	X		X		X		X	X	S
CC	X	X	X	X	X	X	X	X	X	X	X	X	X	S
CD	Y	Y	Y	Y	Y	Y	Y	Y	Y	Y	Y	Y	Y	S
CE	Y	Y	Y	Y	Y	Y	Y	Y	Y	Y	Y	Y	Y	S
CF		X	X	X		X		X			X	X	X	S
CG														S
CH/CI														S
DA/DB	Z	Z		Z	Z	Z		Z		Z	Z	Z	Z	S
DD			Z	Z	Z		Z		Z		Z	Z	Z	S
SBA							X		X	X	X	X	X	S
SBB						X		X		X	X	X	X	S
SCA							X		X	X	X			S
SCB							X		X	X	X	X	X	S
SCF						X		X		X	X	X	X	S

X—must be included
Y—switched service circuits only
Z—synchronous channel circuits only
*—optional
S—as specified by supplier.

ELECTRICAL CHARACTERISTICS

In regard to *electrical characteristics,* the equivalent circuit for all RS-232C line drivers and receivers is shown in Fig. 7-3. The same circuit is used for all signal lines regardless of their being used for data, control, or timing.

Each line driver must be able to withstand an open circuit or a short circuit between that signal line and any other conductor in that cable without sustaining damage to itself or damaging any associated equipment. Furthermore, any passive, noninductive load between the signal line and any other line (including the signal ground) must not damage the driver. All line receivers must be able to withstand a ±25-V input.

The load resistance of the receiver (R_R) must be between 3000 and 7000 Ω when measured with a voltage of less than 25 V. The total effective capacitance of the receiver (C_R) must be equal to or less than 2.5 nanofarads (nF). The reactive component of the load must not be inductive. This restriction means that relays cannot be used.

When implemented, the ready to send, data set ready, data terminal ready, and secondary request to send shall be used to detect either a power off condition or a disconnect in the channel cable.

The power off source impedance of the driver must be greater than 300 Ω. The driver voltage must, of course, be within the range of -25 to $+25$ V. The driver internal resistance (R_D) and effective capacitance (C_D) are not specified, but a short between any two conductors in the interconnecting cable must not produce a current in excess of 0.5 A.

When the receiver is as specified, the voltage at the interface point V_I shall be within ±5 to ±15 V. All signals must pass through the region without reversal in direction. No signal can exceed a rate of change of more than 30 V/μs.

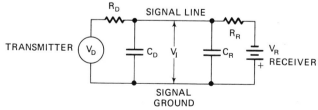

Figure 7-3. Line Driver and Receiver Equivalent Circuit.

Electrical Characteristics Review

1. Explain the meaning of each component of the equivalent circuit shown in Fig. 7-3.

2. What are the limits of the receiver DC load resistance?

3. True or false? A receiver effective capacitance of 1000 picofarads (pF) is acceptable in an RS-232C interface.

4. What maximum current is allowed if the transmitted data line is accidently allowed to contact the signal ground?

MECHANICAL CHARACTERISTICS

There is a great deal of flexibility in the *mechanical characteristics* and structure of the connector. The connector must be in the form of a plug, and the female end is associated with the data communications equipment. Extension cables are permitted if the load capacitance C_L at the interface point is less than 2.5 nF.

Any 25-pin connector may be used, but most manufacturers select one in the DB-25 series that is a subminiature, rectangular connector. Some part numbers are DB-25P or DB-25S of the TRW Cinch and ITT Cannon line of connectors and the AMP 17-81250-0 or 17-91250-0 connectors.

CONVERTING RS-232C LEVELS

We will be using the RS-232C interface with a microcomputer, so there is a requirement to convert between TTL and RS-232C voltages. There is also a requirement to invert the logic levels because a 1 is positive in TTL and negative in the RS-232C channel. There are many ways available to perform the level changing, including integrated circuits.

Several circuits for converting TTL to RS-232C levels are shown in Fig. 7-4. The first one uses an operational amplifier, such as a 741. The biasing on the noninverting input is selected half-way between the minimum value for a high TTL input and the maximum value of a low TTL output.

TTL high-output min	2.4 V
TTL low-output max	−0.4 V
Difference	2.0 V

Half of difference = 1.0 V

TTL low-output max + half difference
= 0.4 + 1.0 = 1.4 V

The TTL input is applied at the inverting input of the op amp. A high signal input will produce an output of about −8 V and a low input an output of +8 V.

The transistor circuit in Fig. 7-4*b* uses an inverter to reverse the logic level states. A TTL high is applied

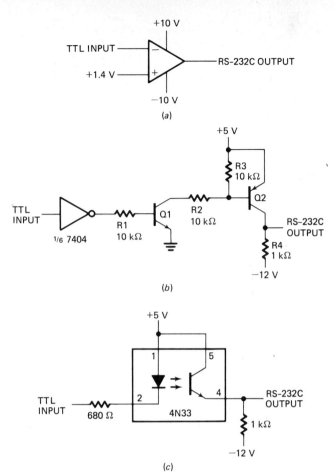

Figure 7-4. TTL–to–RS-232C Converters (*a*) Op Amp (*b*) Transistor (*c*) Opto-isolator.

to the base of Q1, turning both it and Q2 off. Because no current flows, the output is −12 V. A low input to the inverter turns both transistors on. The output will be about +4 V.

An opto-isolator can be used to perform the conversion, as shown in Fig. 7-4*c*. A low TTL input will forward-bias the LED. The light striking the phototransistor will cause it to conduct, pulling the output up to almost +5 V. When the TTL input is high, the LED is reverse-biased and the transistor off. A voltage of −12 V appears at the output.

Conversion from RS-232C to TTL is readily accomplished by the circuit shown in Fig. 7-5. When a negative input (logic on) is applied to the base

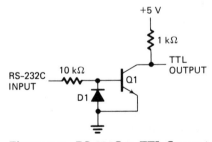

Figure 7-5. RS-232C-to-TTL Converter.

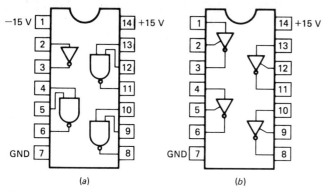

Figure 7-6. Integrated Circuit Converters (a) 1488 (b) 1489.

of Q1 turning it off, the power supply voltage of +5 V is seen as the TTL output. A positive RS-232C signal will, on the other hand, saturate the transistor, pulling the output to almost ground potential.

The integrated circuits shown in Fig. 7-6 also perform these level changes. The 1488 IC converts TTL levels to RS-232C. This DIP also acts as an RS-232C driver. There are three NAND gates and one inverter on the chip. The 1489 reverses the process of changing RS-232C levels back to TTL. This integrated circuit can be used as an RS-232C receiver. The additional inputs to the inverters (pins 2, 5, 9, and 12) are controlling signals enabling each of them independently.

It is also possible to convert between RS-232C voltages and teletype loop currents. Figure 7-7a illustrates a current loop–to–RS-232C conversion circuit. When current is flowing, the LED lights and turns on the transistor. That action produces a negative voltage on the output. No current flow causes the transistor to switch off, thus connecting the +12 V to the output. The voltages applied to the opto-isolator need not be +12 and −12 V. Any convenient values in the 3- to 15-V range will do.

The RS-232C–to–current loop converter shown in Fig. 7-7b uses two 7404 inverters to drive the LED. The diodes limit the input voltage of the first inverter

to a range of 0 to +5 V. As the input goes positive, the LED is reversed-biased and the transistor opens the loop. A negative input puts a low on the cathode of the LED, causing it to emit light. This action makes the transistor conduct and close the loop.

Converting RS-232C Levels Review

1. Why must RS-232C voltages be inverted to interface with TTL circuits?

2. Why is the diode D1 required on the input shown in Fig. 7-5?

3. What is the reason for the control inputs to the inverters of the 1489 IC?

4. Why are two series inverters used on the RS-232C input shown in Fig. 7-7b?

CHAPTER SUMMARY

1. The RS-232C standard specifies the purpose for each of 25 lines in a cable, but it does not place limits on the type of data, character length, bit code, or bit sequence. Serial synchronous or asynchronous communication with data rates up to 20K baud can be supported by the signal lines.

2. The specification provides for grounds, data signals, control signals, and timing signals. Data levels use −3 to −25 V for a 1 and +3 to +25 V for a 0. Voltages from −3 to +3 V are undefined; control signals are on if the voltage is +3 to +25 V and off if the voltage is −3 to −25 V.

3. Primary channels are higher speed than secondary channels and are used to transfer data. Secondary channels, intended for control, may be either auxiliary or backward channels.

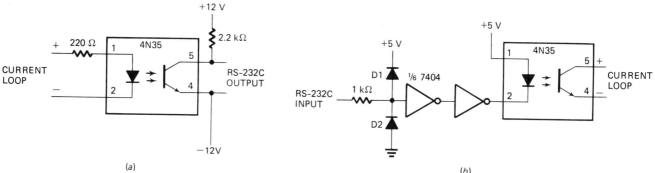

Figure 7-7. RS-232C and Current Loop Converters (a) Current Loop to RS-232C Converter (b) RS-232C to Current Loop Converter.

4. There are four data signals, twelve control signals, three timing signals, and two grounds provided by RS-232C channels.

5. Electrical specifications for the RS-232C interface include transmitter and receiver voltages, resistance, and capacitance. All loads must be noninductive. Provision to prevent damage in case of shorts must be built into the driver and receiver.

6. Mechanically, the builder of an RS-232C interface is given plenty of latitude. The type of connector is not specified and an extension cable is permitted.

7. Discrete component and integrated circuits can be used to shift levels between RS-232C and TTL voltages. The RS-232C signals can also be converted to 20-mA loop currents.

KEY TERMS AND CONCEPTS

RS-232C interface

Data terminal equipment (DTE)

Data communications equipment (DCE)

Data signals

Control signals

Timing signals

Signal grounds

Primary channels

Secondary channels

Auxiliary channels

Backward channels

Transmitted data (TXD)

Received data (RXD)

Request to send (RTS)

Clear to send (CTS)

Data set ready (DSR)

Data terminal ready (DTR)

Received line signal detector (DCD)

Protective ground

Signal ground or common return

Electrical characteristics

Mechanical characteristics

PROBLEMS

7-1 Draw a handshaking timing diagram for the initialization of an RS-232C communications sequence for the system shown in Fig. 7-1b.

7-2 The RS-232C interface is being repaired by a technician. At the time when RTS is on (+15 V) and DSR is off (−15 V), the technician accidently shorts the two pins with a screwdriver. What current flows between the lines?

7-3 The data communication equipment detected a parity error in the last 8 bits of data transmitted. Draw a timing diagram of the situation if the following lines are implemented:

AA   CB
AB   CC
BA   CD
BB   CG
CA

7-4 If the DC load resistance of an RS-232C interface is 5 kΩ and the receiver capacitance the maximum allowable value, what is the RC time constant of the load?

7-5 An RS-232C system uses +25 V for a logic 0 and −25 V for a logic 1. Assuming that the time constant of the load is the only factor determining the rise time from the 1 to 0 state, would the following receiver values provide acceptable operation?

$$R_R = 3 \text{ k}\Omega$$
$$C_R = 50 \text{ pF}$$
$$V_R = 0 \text{ V}$$

7-6 What biasing voltage would you select for the op amp TTL–to–RS-232C converter if the TTL integrated circuit you were using had a minimum high output of 2.8 V and a maximum low of 0.3 V?

7-7 Assume that $V_{CE,SAT}$ of Q1 and Q2 shown in Fig. 7-4*b* is 0.3 V. The voltage levels from the 7404 inverter are

> High: 3.0 V
> Low: 0 V

Find the current in each resistor when the TTL input is low. (The voltage drop between the base and emitter of Q1 and emitter to base of Q2 in saturation is 0.7 V.)

7-8 If the Q1 in Fig. 7-5 has the same parameters as those in Prob. 7-7 and the forward-bias voltage drop of D1 is 0.7 V, find the currents in the circuit when the input equals −4 V. When the input equals +5 V.

7-9 The diodes of the RS-232C–to–current loop converter drop 0.6 V when forward-biased. What is the voltage at the cathode of D2 when the input is −10 V? When it is +10 V?

7-10 What is the current through the 1-kΩ resistor for each input in Prob. 7-9?

EXPERIMENT 6 _____

PURPOSE: To construct and analyze an RS-232C interface.

PARTS LIST:

Item	Quantity
8212	1
74LS00	1
74LS20	1
4N33	1
1-kΩ resistor	1
680-Ω resistor	1
Computer terminal*	1

*An RS-232C terminal is an optional piece of equipment for this experiment.

PROCEDURE:

STEP 1. Construct the parallel interface shown in Figs. 4-37 and 4-38. Only the LSB of the bus and output data pins (3 and 4) of the 8212 need be connected.

STEP 2. Connect the TTL–to–RS-232C converter shown in Fig. 7-4c. Test it by applying the pulser to the input and check the results with a logic probe. (As an option, you may use any of the other circuits shown in Fig. 7-4 instead.)

STEP 3. Connect the RS-232C output to the received data pin of the computer terminal. Tie the signal ground and protective ground pins of the terminal to the microcomputer ground.

STEP 4. Refer to the operator's manual for your terminal. Using the character set for the terminal, output a series of characters by a program like that listed in Table 6-2. (You will probably want to change the instructions in cells 1003, 1004, and 1008 to NOP instructions. Use device code 07. Also, the count in cell 1001 should probably be changed to 8.) Some experimentation will be necessary to tailor the program to your particular terminal.

STEP 5 (OPTIONAL). If you do not have a terminal, the output can be monitored using a logic probe connected to the RS-232C output. Each bit will appear in sequence as the serial data is sent. To observe the pattern, change the period of the delay loop program to 1 s or so.

8

IEEE-488
GENERAL-PURPOSE
INTERFACE BUS

The *general-purpose interface bus (GPIB)* supports a wide latitude of functions. Originally conceived for programmable instrumentation, the bus is also suited for data transfer between the microcomputer and its peripheral equipment. The bus is specified in the IEEE standard 488-1978. This standard calls out functional requirements for the bus, as well as its electrical and mechanical characteristics. The operational use, however, is device-dependent and is left up to the equipment designer.

CHAPTER OBJECTIVES

Upon completion of this chapter, you should be able to:

1. List the capabilities of the IEEE-488 bus.
2. Describe the signal lines used by the bus.
3. Explain the functional partitioning of the bus interface.
4. Discuss the commands in the bus repertoire.
5. Show how messages are coded.
6. Distinguish between local and remote messages.
7. Describe the electrical and mechanical characteristics of the IEEE-488 bus.
8. Explain some typical operational bus transactions and give examples of both hardware and software interface processing.

IEEE-488 BUS OVERVIEW

The GPIB uses parallel data transfer, in contrast to the serial transmission used by the RS-232C interface. The basic data unit is 1 byte, which is sent from one system component to another. Members of the bus can be programmable or not.

In many ways the bus can be thought of as a party line. It uses a *handshaking* sequence to carry on communications. Three signals are used to perform the handshaking. This process is patented by Hewlett Packard, but they license it to other developers of GPIB hardware.

As this standard has evolved, it has been known by a variety of names. The IEEE-488 bus is also known as the "HPIB," "IEC BUS," "Plus Bus," and "ANSI MC 1.1 Bus." A maximum of 15 devices can be attached to the bus at any one time. The total transmission length must be less than 60 ft (20 m) with no more than 6 ft (2 m) between any two units.

The original IEEE-488 standard of 1975 was updated in 1978. The update was largely editorial, with few technical changes. One of the modifications allowed the standard low voltage for drivers to increase from 0.4 to 0.5 V to accommodate Schottky devices introduced since the original standard was issued. Another change recommends coded markings on the instruments. These identifiers would define the I/O capability, so the operator would not have to refer to the user's manual to find this information.

BUS STRUCTURE

The GPIB is a transparent communications channel, allowing equipment of various manufacturers to be interconnected in a single network. Regardless of their simplicity or complexity, all of the devices talk or listen in the same way.

The data is transferred point to point and does not require relay through a controller. Devices can be *listeners* (receiver), *talkers* (sender), *controllers* or any combination. Each device has a unique address. There are 31 primary addresses to select from and 961 secondary (2-byte) addresses possible.

Bus Signals

There are three sets of bus signals which comprise the 16 lines in the cable. The bidirectional *data bus* contains the eight lines used to transfer each data byte, as shown in Fig. 8-1. Control of the data is exercised by the three-wire *handshaking bus.* Other control signals are transmitted on the *general interface management bus.* The latter consists of five lines.

As you can see, there can be a diverse mix of communications abilities among the bus units. The most complex, such as a microprocessor, can talk, listen, and control the bus. Simpler devices, like a digital multimeter, can talk and listen. Simplest of all are the one-way equipments, a listen-only signal generator or a talk-only counter, for example.

The individual lines are listed in Table 8-1. The data input/output lines are numbered DIO1 through DIO8. These lines, of course, carry the message bits.

The next set of signals, used in the handshaking cycle, execute an *interlocked sequence* of control and status information exchanges. By "interlocked," we mean that one event in the sequence must occur before the next one can begin. The first of these signals is DAV, which indicates that information is available and valid on the DIO lines. A device signals its readiness to accept data by the state of the NRFD signal. The third line, NDAC, shows when data has been accepted by the device.

The ATN general-management signal tells how to interpret the DIO lines and which device should respond. A quiescent state, usually necessary at startup, can be established with the IFC signal. When a device needs service on the bus, it can signal with SRQ and request a break in the current sequence of events. The REN signal can lock out control of a device from its front panel switches. The EOF signal is used for two purposes: It can either indicate the end of a multibyte data transfer or, used with ATN, it means that a *polling* sequence is to be

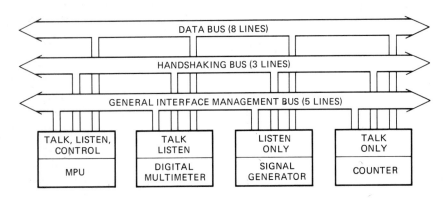

Figure 8-1. GPIB Bus Signals.

Table 8-1
GPIB Data and Control Buses

Bus	Line	Signal
Data bus	DIO1	Data input output 1
	DIO2	Data input output 2
	DIO3	Data input output 3
	DIO4	Data input output 4
	DIO5	Data input output 5
	DIO6	Data input output 6
	DIO7	Data input output 7
	DIO8	Data input output 8
Data byte transfer control (handshaking)	DAV	Data valid
	NDAC	No data accepted
	NRFD	Not ready for data
General interface management	ATN	Attention
	IFC	Interface clear
	SRQ	Service request
	REN	Remote enable
	EOI	End or identify

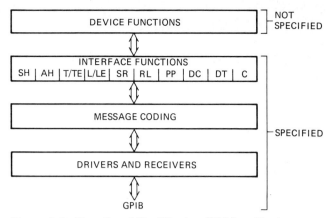

Figure 8-2. Functional Partitioning Within a Device.

executed (the polling will be explained later in this chapter).

Functional Partitioning

The IEEE-488 specification divides an equipment item into several component areas (*functional partitioning*). The immediate connection to the bus is made through drivers and receivers, as Fig. 8-2 shows. The drivers and receivers exchange data by means of the message coding section, which is transferring its signals to the device through a collection of interface functions. These functions will be fully described in the next section.

Briefly, the interface functions regulate the state of the bus control circuitry. The functions are mutually independent, so only one state is active at a time. A repertoire of the functions is specified by means of state diagrams. Even so, the functions do not necessarily have to be implemented by flip-flops.

On the other side of the interface functions are the device functions. Here the type of measurement the instrument can make, modes of operation, capabilities, and precision are controlled. Note that the specification for the GPIB covers all portions of the device, except for this last one.

Bus Structure Review

1. List the three sets of signal buses which comprise the 16 lines.

2. Define the term "interlocked sequence."

3. How does the IEEE-488 standard partition a device which is capable of communication on the bus?

4. What is the signal normally used to establish a quiescent state at initiation?

5. What is the purpose of the DAV signal?

FUNCTIONAL REPERTOIRE

The entire *functional repertoire* that the interface can perform is listed in Table 8-2. Keep in mind that these are only possibilities. Any particular device may be capable of only a few of them, or it may implement the entire repertoire. A description of each function is provided in the discussion that follows. Each function uses one or more of the bus lines to carry out the action.

The "source handshake" controls the talking device and allows it to transfer a data message. All transfer between source and acceptor handshaking devices originate with this function. The "acceptor handshake" is returned by the listening device(s). If more than one listener is involved, the slowest one determines the return rate.

Device-dependent data is sent by means of the "talker" or "extended talker." The talker is only

Table 8-2
Functional Repertoire

Interface function	Symbol
Source handshake	SH
Acceptor handshake	AH
Talker or extended talker	T/TE
Listener or extended listener	L/LE
Service request	SR
Remote local	RL
Parallel poll	PP
Device clear	DC
Device trigger	DT
Controller	C

active when addressed by a single byte. The extended talker requires a 2-byte address. The corresponding lister function receives device-dependent data with a single-byte address (listener) or 2-byte address (extended listener).

A device can obtain the notice of the controller with a "service request." The SR signal is sent as a single-bit reply in the status byte during a serial poll.

The remaining functions all have to do with controller operations. The "remote local" allows the front panel (manual) controls on the instrument to be enabled or disabled. The "parallel polling" mode allows eight devices to each send a status bit on the DIO lines. The device, or a group of devices, can be cleared and initialized by the "device clear" sequence, then operation can be remotely started with the "device trigger." The "controller" function can initiate device addresses, send universal commands, and transmit addressed commands. There can be more than one controller on the bus, but only one can be actively issuing commands. All others must be in the controller idle state.

Messages

Messages can be categorized as either local or remote. Local messages are those sent between the device and the interface functional logic. Remote messages are those sent between the device and the bus.

As was indicated earlier, remote messages will cause a state transition in some interface functions. Alternatively, remote messages can be device-dependent for internal control, and any type of remote message can be used. Specific examples of remote messages are provided in the operational section to follow.

Messages must be encoded and decoded. The coding section shown in Fig. 8-2 translates the remote messages to or from interface signal line voltages. Because this translation is part of the specification, only a certain set of remote messages is allowed.

In normal operations, two devices may transmit remote messages simultaneously. A result may be that the two messages come into conflict and the conflict must be resolved. The resolution is based on the fact that there are two types of transfers: active and passive. The active value always overrides the passive in the event of conflict.

Functional Repertoire Review

1. What function is used to originate all data transfers between a talker and listener?

2. What is the purpose of the SR function? When is this signal sent?

3. Explain the difference between local and remote messages.

4. Which section of the device (Fig. 8-2) translates remote messages to or from signal line voltages?

ELECTRICAL CHARACTERISTICS

In regard to *electrical characteristics*, the IEEE-488 bus uses TTL levels for all signals. Specifications cover drivers and receivers, load termination and capacitance, grounding, and cables. A logic 0 is defined as a high state and logic 1 a low state.

Open collector drivers can be used for all signals, as indicated by Table 8-3. For higher speed, three-state devices are allowed, with the exception of SRQ, NRFD, and NDAC signals. When parallel polling is used, the DIO lines must also be open collector.

The driver low-voltage level must be 0.5 V or less, with a minimum of 0 V. In the low state, the driver must be able to sink +48 mA without damage. A high output is defined as equal to or greater than 2.4 V at −5.2 mA. Maximum voltage is limited to 5.0 V. All electrical measurements are to be made at the device connector between the signal and logic ground.

Receiver input voltage in the low state will be between −0.6 and 0.8 V. A high input will range from 2.0 to 5.5 V. All receivers must limit negative excursions. Most often a diode clamp is used.

Every signal line is to be terminated in a resistive load. These loads serve to establish a steady-state voltage when all three-state drivers on a particular line are in the high-impedance state. The capacitive load limit is 100 pF within each device.

The 24-conductor bus should be constructed to minimize crosstalk between the signal lines and susceptibility to external noise. The resistance of each line must be no more than 0.14 Ω/m, but the common logic ground cannot exceed 0.085 Ω/m. The overall shield resistance is limited to 0.0085 Ω. The shield on the cable is grounded.

Table 8-3
Driver Output Stages

Output	Signals
Open collector only	SRQ, NRFD, and NDAC
Open collector or three state	DAV, IFC, ATN, REN, EOI, and DIO (except when parallel polling is used)

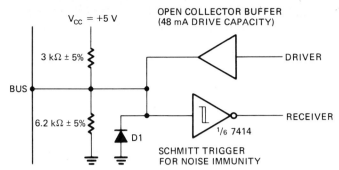

Figure 8-3. **Recommended I/O Circuit.**

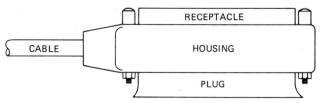

Figure 8-4. **Connector Housing.**

Transceiver Circuit

The recommended I/O circuit for the GPIB is shown in Fig. 8-3. The driver uses an open collector buffer with a 48-mA drive capacity. The Schmitt trigger buffer in the receiver offers good noise immunity. There are integrated circuits available to provide the interface. Typical circuits include the MC3440P or MC3441P quad receivers and the 8291, described in a following section.

Electrical Characteristics Review

1. List the voltage levels for high and low voltages on the IEEE-488 bus.

2. True or false? Use of three-state drivers for higher speed is permitted on all signal lines.

3. What is the ground reference for all electrical measurements?

4. Why are signal lines terminated in a resistive load?

5. Explain the purpose of the Schmitt trigger in the recommended transceiver circuit.

MECHANICAL CHARACTERISTICS

The connecter specified for the bus is a rack and panel type. Each cable is terminated with both a plug and receptacle, as shown in Fig. 8-4. This configuration makes it easy to daisy chain from one instrument to another.

The connector voltage rating is 200 V DC and current rating is 5 A per contact. Contact resistance must be less than 10 megohms. The contact material is to be gold over copper. Insulation resistance must exceed 10 gigohms.

There are 24 contacts arranged in two rows of 12 connectors. The surfaces must be self-wiping. Pin assignments are listed in Table 8-4. In addition to signal lines, there is an earth ground for the shield and grounds or returns for control signals. The grounds form a twisted pair with their respective signal lines.

BUS OPERATIONS

Flowcharts of *bus operations* which show corresponding actions for the talker and the listeners on the bus are shown in Fig. 8-5. The talker sets DAV high to respond to the collective NDAC low signal from all listeners and to indicate data is being changed. Upon sensing the high DAV signal, each listener will raise NRFD. Until all listeners respond, the talker waits.

After this condition is satisfied, the talker drops DAV to signify that the data is valid. As each listener inputs the data, it pulls NDAC low and allows NRFD

Table 8-4
Connector Pin Assignments

Pin	Signal
1	DIO1
2	DIO2
3	DIO3
4	DIO4
5	EOI
6	DAV
7	NRFD
8	NDAC
9	IFC
10	SRQ
11	ATN
12	SHIELD (earth ground)
13	DIO5
14	DIO6
15	DIO7
16	DIO8
17	REN
18	DAV ground
19	NRFD ground
20	NDAC ground
21	IFC ground
22	SRQ ground
23	ATN ground
24	LOGIC ground

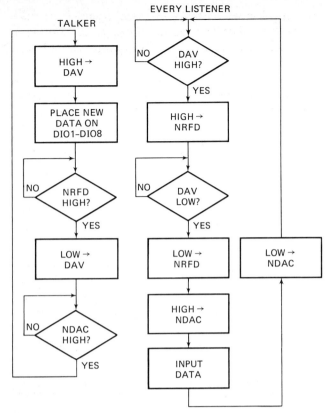

Figure 8-5. Flowcharts of Bus Operations.

pulling NDAC low, which allows the resistive load to pull NDAC up to 3.3 V (Fig. 8-3).

Controller Communications

Communication between a controller and the listeners is quite similar to that used by the talker. In this case, ATN is used to distinguish between commands (ATN true) and data (ATN false). The instruments listening must respond to ATN signals within 200 ns.

Thus, in a minimal interface, only the data lines (DIO1 through DIO8), DAV, NRFD, and NDAC are needed. If a controller is used, then IFC and ATN are added.

Other Signals

A talker labels the last byte in a data transfer with a monitor bit. When EOI is set to 1, the listeners know that the transfer has been completed.

A controller can disable the front panel controls of an instrument with the REN signal. As long as this line is held true (low), remote control is in effect. Only when REN is allowed to rise does the instrument revert to manual control. The switching between remote and local control is quite rapid—within 100 μs. Upon initiation, both ATN and REN are set true.

Service can be requested by an instrument sending a true SRQ signal to the controller. This input acts as an interrupt. Control then proceeds by a preselected rule, parallel polling, or serial polling. These control words are recommended in the appendix of the standard, but not considered to be a formal part of it.

Parallel Polling

A controller can poll, or ask the instruments for data, in a parallel fashion. A maximum of eight instruments can be polled, because each is assigned a unique bit on the data bus. To enter this state,

to go high. Sensing that NDAC is low from all listeners, the talker repeats the cycle for the next data word.

Figure 8-6 shows a timing diagram for the communications exchange. Notice that only the last listener raising or lowering NRFD or NDAC actually produces a change in the signal level.

Now the reason for the previously mentioned three handshaking signals becomes more obvious. They permit more than one listener on the bus. The open collector buffer outputs let all listeners signal one talker or controller. The collective change in signal levels lets them independently sample data, yet provides a way of denoting completion of all inputs. For example, as each listener accepts data it stops

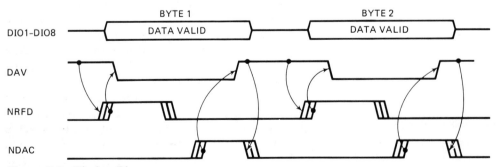

Figure 8-6. Timing Diagram.

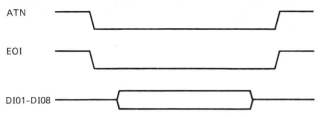

Figure 8-7. Parallel Polling Sequence.

the controller simultaneously drops EOI and ATN. Each instrument responds by transmitting 1 bit of status information. The meaning of each 1 or 0 status signal depends on the type of instrument involved. For example, a low could be an OK status reply. Figure 8-7 depicts the parallel polling timing.

A Typical Message Sequence

A list of remote messages is provided in Table 8-5. Each message is a unique combination of data and control signals. In the case of the first message, ACG, bits 5 through 7 of the data bus must be 0 and all others are "don't care" settings. To understand

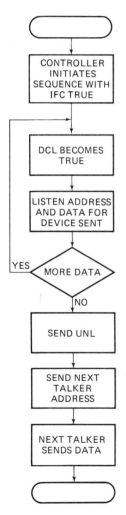

Figure 8-8. Message Sequence.

the application of some of these signals, consider a multimember bus. A microprocessor acts as a controller and talker on a bus with listeners and other talkers.

Figure 8-8 is a flowchart of the initial series of events. First, the processor sends the IFC message (sets bit true) to clear all interface logic. Next, the DCL message causes each device to enter a start state. Assume that next the processor wants to signal the first instrument. The MPU sends the listen address of that instrument followed by the programmable commands to the device.

The processor then sends a stop listening message (UNL) followed by the address and data for the next instrument. This procedure is repeated until all devices have been addressed.

Then the MPU sends the talk address for the first talker. The other talker, in turn, sends data to the addressed listener. The data codes sent to the device by either the controller or talker can use ASCII, or the 7-bit ISO codes listed in Table 8-6.

In most cases, Table 8-6 is just a repeat of the messages in Table 8-5 in a somewhat different form. Consider GTL, for example. In both tables, the code for "go to local" is 01_{16}. In other cases, a range of addresses is provided. The listen (MLA) address is shown to range from 02_{16} to $3E_{16}$ in Table 8-6. This range corresponds to the LLLLL field of Table 8-5.

IC Interfaces

A number of integrated circuit interfacing chips are now available. The Intel 8291 talker/listener chip shown in Fig. 8-9 is typical. It is controlled by a microprocessor to perform all the functions of a talker or listener. The 8291 can provide the complete handshaking sequence for either a source or accepting instrument and also handles all addressing modes.

Two of the registers in the IC are for data transfer to the microprocessor, while the 14 others support the control, status, and addressing required by the bus interface standard.

The 8291 can also request service, parallel poll, and send device clear, trigger, and local/remote commands. The IC recognizes primary or secondary addresses. The 8291 can read or write memory data without direct MPU action if an optional DMA controller chip is supplied.

Figure 8-10 shows a bus interface system that uses DMA. The 8292 in the diagram supplements the 8291 by doing the controller actions. The 8292 initializes the bus with the IFC signal. It can then follow with the commands as shown in Fig. 8-8, for example.

Table 8-5
Remote Message List

Mnemonic	Name	Type	Class	DIO 8	7	6	5	4	3	2	1	DAV	NRFD	NDAC	ATN	EOI	SRQ	IFC	REN
ACG	Address command group	M	C	X	0	0	0	X	X	X	X	X	X	X	X	X	X	X	X
ATN	Attention	U	U	X	X	X	X	X	X	X	X	X	X	X	1	X	X	X	X
DAB	Data byte	M	D	D	D	D	D	D	D	D	D	X	X	X	X	X	X	X	X
DAC	Data accepted	U	H	X	X	X	X	X	X	X	X	X	X	0	X	X	X	X	X
DAV	Data valid	U	H	X	X	X	X	X	X	X	X	1	X	X	X	X	X	X	X
DCL	Device clear	M	U	X	0	0	1	0	1	0	0	X	X	X	X	X	X	X	X
END	End	U	S	X	X	X	X	X	X	X	X	X	X	X	X	1	X	X	X
EOS	End of string	M	D	E	E	E	E	E	E	E	E	X	X	X	X	X	X	X	X
GET	Group execute trigger	M	C	X	0	0	0	1	0	0	0	X	X	X	X	X	X	X	X
GTL	Go to local	M	C	X	0	0	0	0	0	0	1	X	X	X	X	X	X	X	X
IDY	Identify	U	U	X	X	X	X	X	X	X	X	X	X	X	X	1	X	X	X
IFC	Interface clear	U	U	X	X	X	X	X	X	X	X	X	X	X	X	X	X	1	X
LAG	Listen address group	M	A	X	0	1	X	X	X	X	X	X	X	X	X	X	X	X	X
LLO	Local lock out	M	U	X	0	0	1	0	0	0	1	X	X	X	X	X	X	X	X
MLA	My listen address	M	A	X	0	1	L	L	L	L	L	X	X	X	X	X	X	X	X
MTA	My talk address	M	A	X	1	0	T	T	T	T	T	X	X	X	X	X	X	X	X
MSA	My secondary address	M	2	X	1	1	S	S	S	S	S	X	X	X	X	X	X	X	X
NUL	Null byte	M	D	0	0	0	0	0	0	0	0	X	X	X	X	X	X	X	X
OSA	Other secondary address	M	2	(OSA = SCG and $\overline{\text{MSA}}$)															
OTA	Other talk address	M	A	(OTA = TAG and $\overline{\text{MTA}}$)															
PCG	Primary command group	M	...	(PCC = ACG or UCG and LAG and TAG)															
PPC	Parallel poll configure	M	C	X	0	0	0	0	1	0	1	X	X	X	X	X	X	X	X
PPE	Parallel poll enable	M	2	X	1	1	0	Y	P	P	P	X	X	X	X	X	X	X	X
PPD	Parallel poll disable	M	2	X	1	1	1	D	D	D	D	X	X	X	X	X	X	X	X
PPR 1	Parallel poll response 1	U	S	X	X	X	X	X	X	X	1	X	X	X	X	X	X	X	X
PPR 2	Parallel poll response 2	U	S	X	X	X	X	X	X	1	X	X	X	X	X	X	X	X	X
PPR 3	Parallel poll response 3	U	S	X	X	X	X	X	1	X	X	X	X	X	X	X	X	X	X
PPR 4	Parallel poll response 4	U	S	X	X	X	X	1	X	X	X	X	X	X	X	X	X	X	X
PPR 5	Parallel poll response 5	U	S	X	X	X	1	X	X	X	X	X	X	X	X	X	X	X	X
PPR 6	Parallel poll response 6	U	S	X	X	1	X	X	X	X	X	X	X	X	X	X	X	X	X
PPR 7	Parallel poll response 7	U	S	X	1	X	X	X	X	X	X	X	X	X	X	X	X	X	X
PPR 8	Parallel poll response 8	U	S	1	X	X	X	X	X	X	X	X	X	X	X	X	X	X	X
PPU	Parallel poll unconfigure	M	U	X	0	0	1	0	1	0	1	X	X	X	X	X	X	X	X
REN	Remote enable	U	U	X	X	X	X	X	X	X	X	X	X	X	X	X	X	X	1
RFD	Ready for data	U	H	X	X	X	X	X	X	X	X	X	0	X	X	X	X	X	X
RQS	Request for service	U	S	X	1	X	X	X	X	X	X	X	X	X	X	X	X	X	X
SCG	Secondary command group	M	2	X	1	1	X	X	X	X	X	X	X	X	X	X	X	X	X
SDC	Selected device clear	M	C	X	0	0	0	0	1	0	0	X	X	X	X	X	X	X	X
SPD	Serial poll disable	M	U	X	0	0	1	1	0	0	1	X	X	X	X	X	X	X	X
SPE	Serial poll enable	M	U	X	0	0	1	1	0	0	0	X	X	X	X	X	X	X	X
SRQ	Service request	U	S	X	X	X	X	X	X	X	X	X	X	X	X	X	1	X	X
STB	Status byte	M	S	R	X	R	R	R	R	R	R	X	X	X	X	X	X	X	X
TCT	Take control	M	C	X	0	0	0	1	0	0	1	X	X	X	X	X	X	X	X
TAG	Talk address group	M	A	X	1	0	X	X	X	X	X	X	X	X	X	X	X	X	X
UCG	Universal command group	M	U	X	0	0	1	X	X	X	X	X	X	X	X	X	X	X	X
UNL	Unlisten	M	A	X	0	1	1	1	1	1	1	X	X	X	X	X	X	X	X
UNT	Untalk	M	A	X	1	0	1	1	1	1	1	X	X	X	X	X	X	X	X

Table 8-5 *(Continued)*

Notes:

Type:
  M—multiline
  U—single (uniline) message

Class:
  C—addressed command
  A—address (talk or listen)
  D—device dependent
  H—handshake
  U—universal command
  2—secondary
  S—status

Signals:
  0—high-level state
  1—low-level state
  D—device-dependent bits
  E—device-dependent code in EOS message
  L—device-dependent listen address
  T—device-dependent talk address
  S—device-dependent secondary address
  X—don't care
  P—specify the PPR message to be sent when parallel poll is executed
  Y—sense of PPR (either 0 or 1)
  R—device-dependent status

Table 8-6
ISO 7-Bit Code

DIO1–DIO4 (hexadecimal)	DIO5–DIO8 (hexadecimal)							
	0	1	2	3	4	5	6	7
0								
1	GTL	LLO						
2								
3								
4	SDC	DCL						
5	PPC	PPU	MLA assigned to device	MLA assigned to device	MTA assigned to device	MTA assigned to device	Defined by PCG code	Defined by PCG code
6								
7								
8	GET	SPE						
9	TCT	SPD						
A								
B								
C								
D								
E								
F				UNL		UNT		
	Address command group	Universal command group	Listen address group		Talk address group		Secondary command group	
	Primary command group							

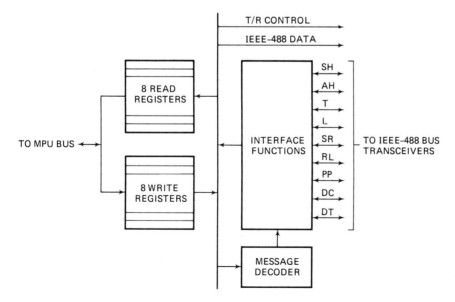

Figure 8-9. 8291 Talker/Listener.

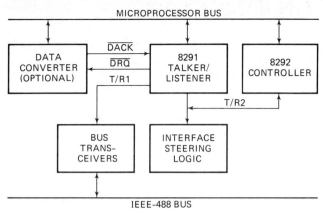

Figure 8-10. IEEE-488 Interface.

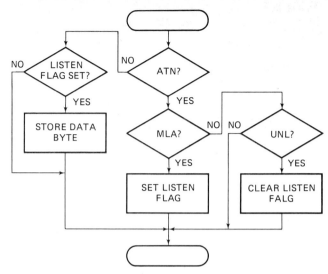

Figure 8-11. IEEE-488 Listener Program.

Bus Operations Review

1. How is the talker able to determine that all listeners have received the last data word and that the data lines can be changed?

2. Explain how it is possible to have multiple listeners on the bus. (Use the timing diagram given in Fig. 8-6.)

3. How can a listener tell the difference between commands and data from a controller?

4. What label is placed on the last byte in a sequence from a talker?

5. Describe the parallel polling process.

6. What are the levels of all lines on the bus for the unlisten remote message?

7. How are the remote messages (Table 8-5) related to the ISO 7-bit codes (Table 8-6)?

SOFTWARE INTERFACE

Instead of using integrated circuits to recognize and process the bus signals, a program in the microprocessor could be substituted. A flowchart for a program to complete the listener functions is shown in Fig. 8-11. This program is initiated by an interrupt which signifies that data has been received. The program first checks to see if the input is an attention message. If so, it then checks for its address in the data bits. If the address matches its own, it sets an indicator for the listening. If the data is not a match for its own address, the program asks if this could be an UNL message. If so, it clears the listen indicator which had been set by a previous message. If the ATN signal is not true, the program verifies that it is in the listen state and accepts the data

byte as a unique command. Note that if none of these conditions are satisfied the program exits without doing any processing.

Software Interfaces Review

1. What event initiates the software listening program?

2. What remote messages must be received before any data will be accepted?

3. What is the result of receiving a UNL message?

A TYPICAL GPIB INSTRUMENT

Programming a device on the bus is straightforward to an operator. As an example, we will consider a function generator that can be controlled by the bus. The generator works basically the same on the bus as when it is controlled manually.

The programming process requires first that all operations to be performed be defined. Then the program is designed. Afterwards the description is converted to the program codes that the instrument uses. Finally the program is written in the language that the controller requires. We will assume that our function generator only responds to the unique data commands listed in Table 8-7, and the controller uses ASCII coded commands. The listen addresses for the device is 34_{16}.

A command to address the function generator to listen and provide a 10-kHz sine wave with an amplitude of 5 V rms could be

Table 8-7
Instrument Unique Data Commands

Command	ASCII Code
Function	FU
Sine wave	1
Square wave	2
Triangle wave	3
Frequency	FR
Hz	HZ
kHz	KHZ
MHz	MHZ
Amplitude	AM
Volts peak to peak	VP
Volts rms	VR

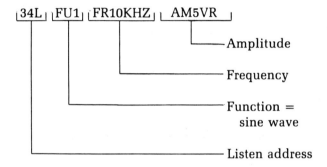

A 60-Hz square wave with 2.5 V peak-to-peak excursion could be provided by the command

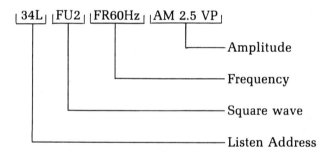

Most instruments would have a much larger repertoire of commands. Especially lacking in this case is the ability to report status. To perform that function, the generator would require a talk address.

The controller gains control of the instrument by forcing it to the remote mode. This state change is effected by setting ATN and REN true and sending the listen address of 34 for that device. Then any string of data messages can be addressed to the generator.

As each command is received, the generator processes it and responds. The listener function must also respond to the general commands listed in Table 8-5. In this manner, the generator can be programmed to initialize (DCL), respond to a serial poll (SPE), unlisten (UNL), untalk (UNT), and so on.

A PRACTICAL NOTE

Although the IEEE-488 bus specification standardizes a great number of the mechanical, electrical, and logical interfaces, others are optional or not defined. The result may be that two instruments may not be able to communicate directly over the bus. Unfortunately this problem has even been observed in two instruments from the same manufacturer.

The reason for this incompatibility stems from device-dependent program codes, output data formats, and data coding. For example, one instrument may use binary while another uses BCD.

To prevent such problems, be sure to note these conflicts in the equipment manuals. Do not assume that a claim of IEEE-488 compatibility necessarily implies that two devices can communicate on the bus.

CHAPTER SUMMARY

1. The IEEE-488 bus transfers data bytes in parallel. Three signals accomplish the handshaking necessary to communicate.

2. Devices performing any combination of talkers, listeners, or controllers can communicate on the bus. Each will have a unique address.

3. Three sets of signals comprise the GPIB: data, handshaking, and general interface management.

3. An interlocked sequence of control and status exchanges runs the bus.

5. Any IEEE-488-compatible equipment item is subdivided into the driver and receiver, message coding, interface functions, and device functions partitions. All partitions, except the device-dependent functions, are specified.

6. Ten functions that the GPIB can support are listed in the repertoire. These functions include those required for handshaking, talking, listening, requesting service, remote controlling, polling, clearing, and triggering.

7. The electrical and mechanical characteristics constrain the designer to certain types of drivers, terminations, receivers, and connectors.

8. In operation, a specific series of signals exchanged between a talker and listener synchronizes the time when data is valid and when data can change. Parallel polling is used to

obtain status from up to eight instruments at one time.

9. The bus logic can be implemented in either hardware or software.

KEY TERMS AND CONCEPTS

General-purpose interface bus (GPIB)

Listeners

Talkers

Controllers

Data bus

Handshaking bus

General interface management bus

Interlocked sequence

Functional partitioning

Functional repertoire

Electrical characteristics

Mechanical characteristics

Bus operations

Parallel polling

IC interfaces

Software interface

PROBLEMS

8-1 Assume that the voltage on the bus line is -0.4 V. What current is flowing through the two resistors shown in Fig. 8-3?

8-2 A high voltage is placed on the bus line in Fig. 8-3. If the voltage is 5.2 V, what is the input voltage to the receiver amplifier? What current flows in the 3-kΩ resistor?

8-3 Because of a malfunction, -2.0 V appears on the bus line of Fig. 8-3. What are the voltages across the resistors if D1 requires a forward bias of 0.7 V to conduct? Assuming all current flows into the driver, how much current will it sink?

8-4 Draw a timing diagram similar to that shown in Fig. 8-6 for a bus system consisting of two listeners and one talker. Assume that DAV is low for 0.5 μs and high for 1 μs. Listener 1 always responds 0.1 μs before listener 2.

Note: Use the remote message list in Table 8-5 to answer Prob. 8-5 through 8-9.

8-5 What would be the state of the data bus and other signals for a DCL command?

8-6 How would device 13_{10} send its listen address in the MLA message?

8-7 Assume that to disable a parallel polling sequence a device requires a data code of 11_{10}. Show the data content of the PPD message required.

8-8 A controller commands talker 26_{10} to take control with the appropriate remote message. What are the settings of the data bus and REN line?

8-9 A programmable calculator receives a command of BF_{16}. How would this remote message be interpreted?

8-10 What instruction would be used to command the function generator, discussed in this chapter, to produce the signal shown in Fig. 8-12?

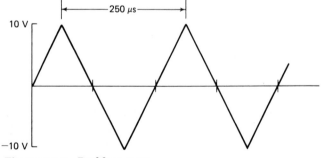

Figure 8-12. Problem 8-10.

EXPERIMENT 7 _____

PURPOSE: To investigate an IEEE-488 instrument.

PARTS LIST:

Item	Quantity
Any IEEE-488 bus instrument	1
Operation manual	1

PROCEDURE:

STEP 1. Is your instrument a talker, listener, controller, or a combination?

STEP 2. List the remote messages that can be sent or received by the instrument.

STEP 3. Briefly describe how to program the instrument for bus operations.

STEP 4. What device-dependent messages does the equipment receive or transmit?

STEP 5. If the instrument sends a status byte, explain the settings of each bit.

9

MICROCOMPUTER
BUSES

This chapter investigates bus standards that make it possible to construct a customized microcomputer by simply plugging in the proper selection of printed circuit cards. These buses are used within the computer to interconnect modules such as the processor, ROM, and RAM. In contrast to an external bus between equipment, such as the IEEE-488 bus, the microcomputer bus is within the computer cabinet. Although more components are used in a microcomputer built with one of these buses, overall costs can be reduced by their application. Cost reduction results from the existing support documentation, maintenance aids, standard enclosures, power supplies, and printed circuit cards. A large family of plug-compatible modules can be developed if the bus is mass-produced. Microcomputers that use a bus are very adaptable to change. An obsolete board can be removed and a new design substituted. Maintenance is also simplified by the module-swapping approach.

CHAPTER OBJECTIVES

Upon completion of this chapter, you should be able to:

1. Distinguish between unidirectional and bidirectional computer buses.
2. Explain the purpose of bus drivers and receivers.
3. Describe the general capabilities of two widely used buses.
4. Explain the use of the various signal lines of the bus.
5. Show how a collection of modules can be integrated into a complete microcomputer.

MULTIPLEXED BUSES

A microcomputer bus is a collection of wires that serve as a standard communication path between the modules which comprise the computer. The bus is multiplexed so that any member on it can originate or receive messages. Communication paths provided by the bus include the address, data, control, and power lines.

Bus connections are made to the long edge of a rectangular printed circuit (PC) board. The PC card serves to interconnect and support the electronic components. The card height is measured from the bus connector to the opposite side. The width is the distance between the sides perpendicular to the connector.

The cards slide into a cage which supports them and which also provides the *motherboard* or backplane holding receptacles for the card plugs. The guides on the holder must support the cards with precise spacing. This precision means that the width dimension of the PC board is critical in avoiding a loose fit.

The tops of the cards stick up above the cage. Frequently test points, displays, and switches are mounted on the top for maintenance operations. These features allow the technician to check the card without removing it from the cage. Extender boards are available to assist the technician. The extender connects to the PC board, increasing its height, so the card is outside the cage frame. The extended card remains connected to the bus at the same time the circuit is accessible for signal tracing.

Figure 9-1a shows a *daisy chain multiplexed bus.* A loop is formed interconnecting every module in the system. Each module acts as a source and acceptor for signals not addressed to it. The addressed acceptor recognizes that the data is intended for it, and does not pass the data on. A daisy chain forms a unidirectional bus. This limitation prevents the daisy chain from being used for data transfer, but daisy chains are used in addressing on some buses.

The *party line bus* offers direct access between any modules on the bus. There is only one source and one acceptor for each message. The party line is bidirectional, so it is often used for data exchange.

Bus Signals

The type of information being sent and the receiving module must be specified for every message transmitted. Control signals supply this necessary coordination. Another important control function is *bus arbitration.* Arbitration avoids the problem of having two transmitters using the bus at once. A priority auction is used by the arbitration circuitry to decide which of two transmitters simultaneously requesting the bus will be granted access.

With *synchronous bus control,* only one member (usually the microprocessor) originates all control and timing signals. Other bus members synchronize their operations to those signals when transmitting or receiving. If control and timing are generated jointly by the source and acceptor, *asynchronous bus control* is being used. Handshaking is frequently associated with asynchronous bus control. An example of a handshaking signal sequence is listed in Table 9-1.

Drivers

Special circuits called *drivers* are employed to connect or disconnect sources placing signals on the bus. The drivers assure electrical compatibility among all bus members. The drivers also offer a higher current drive for the signals than the output circuits of the processor are capable of, so the signals are more likely to reach their destination without error.

A driver is designed to drive one standard TTL load. A key attribute of the bus is its capacitive loading. The stray bus capacitance limits its bandwidth and, therefore, its maximum operating speed. A microcomputer with a 2-μs cycle time requires a bus with a capacitive load of less than 100 pF in each line.

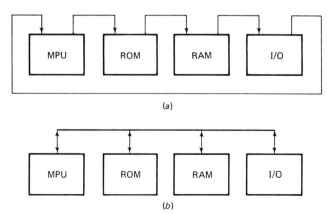

Figure 9-1. Multiplexed Buses (a) Daisy Chain (b) Party Line.

Table 9-1
Handshaking Signals

Source	Acceptor
Prepare to receive	Ready to receive
Places data on bus	
Data ready	Data accepted
Data lines dropped	

Several types of drivers are shown in Fig. 9-2. The logical OR driver includes a digital multiplexer that selects the source for the signal to be put on the bus. (These examples show single-bit operation only. Parallel circuits can be added to make the bus as wide as necessary.) The logical OR driver can only be used on a unidirectional bus because one of the sources is always connected to the bus. It is not a good choice for modules that are widely separated. Also once this type of driver is constructed, adding more sources is difficult.

A wired-OR driver uses open-collector gates directly wired to the bus. Recall that the transistor in the output stage of an open-collector gate will determine the logic level on the bus. The output transistor of all the gates that are not selected will be off, so only the selected gate controls the level. If the output transistor in that gate is on, the bus is pulled low. Otherwise the bus is high. Because the wired-OR driver permits the condition of no source being selected, this driver can be used on a bidirectional bus.

The three-state driver offers three output conditions: high, low, and high impedance. When any gate is enabled, its input appears at the output terminal. If the gate is disabled, the output is in the high-impedance state. We say that the output lines are floating. The three-state driver can be either a source or a sink on a bidirectional bus.

Receivers

The proper type of receiver can be quite effective in reducing the capacitive loading, and thus offer higher-speed operation. The loading on the bus increases with the number of receivers that are simultaneously enabled. If an enable line is provided

for the receiver, it can be set to a high-impedance state when there is no incoming message.

A simple receiver is illustrated in Fig. 9-3. The bus signal is passed only through the gate that is selected. By placing the address on the selection line, the one receiver to accept the message is designated.

Bus Circuits

A practical bus *transceiver* is shown in Fig. 9-4a. A transceiver is a combined driver and receiver. These circuits find frequent use when I/O devices are to be connected to the bus. A bidirectional data path is offered and a number of transceivers can be placed on the bus because they are three-state devices.

The circuit shown in Fig. 9-4b is a *bidirectional driver.* Four of these drivers are usually packaged in a single IC. The quad driver can source or sink 4 bits on the bus. The amplifier acts as a buffer which boosts the driver capacity. This latter attribute is particularly effective on heavily loaded buses. Table 9-2 summarizes three widely used microcomputer buses.

Multiplexed Buses Review

1. Define the term "bus."

2. If the PC card for a bus module is 5 × 10 in (12.7 × 25.4 cm), what is its width?

3. Distinguish between daisy chain and party line buses.

4. True or false? Most bidirectional buses use daisy chain loops.

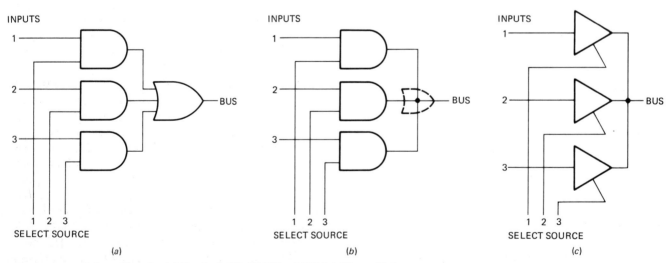

Figure 9-2. Driver Circuits (*a*) Logical OR (*b*) Wired OR (*c*) Three-State.

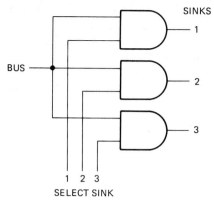

Figure 9-3. Receiver Circuit.

5. Explain the purpose of bus arbitration.

6. Why are drivers used for bus communication?

7. Explain why wired OR drivers can be used on a bidirectional bus and logical OR drivers cannot.

THE S-100 BUS

The *S-100 bus* is a parallel bus widely used in personal computers. Sometimes called the "hobby bus," the S-100 was invented by MITS for the 8080-based Altair 8800 microcomputer. The name originated from the 100 lines that make up the bus. After its introduction, the bus was used by IMSAI, Polymorphic, Processor Technology, and others in their equipment. Today there are more than 700 boards or modules for the bus produced by over 100 manufacturers. So you can see there are a lot

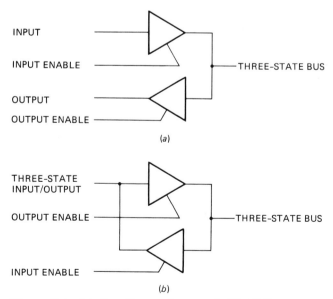

Figure 9-4. (a) Bus Transceiver and (b) Bidirectional Driver.

Table 9-2
Typical Buses

Characteristics	S-100	Multibus*	LSI-11†
Originator	MITS	Intel	DEC
Lines	100	86	72
Address	16	16	18
Data	16‡	16	16
Control	38	15	18
Interrupts	8	8	1
Grounds	2	8	8
Power	4	16	9
Spare	16	7	18
Number of supply voltages	3	5	3

*Multibus is a trademark of Intel Corporation.
†LSI-11 is a trademark of Digital Equipment Corporation.
‡Eight in each direction.

of S-100 buses in operation. Unfortunately, the S-100 bus is not standardized. The IEEE has established a committee to develop a standard, which should improve the situation in the future.

The 100 logic and power lines are divided into 8 data input lines, 8 data output lines, 16 address lines, 4 power supply lines, 8 interrupt lines, 2 grounds, and 38 control lines. The other lines are either unused or spares. Some of the lines are logically identical to those of the 8080A, while others are related to 8080A signals or uniquely defined by MITS.

An overall listing of the signals is provided in Table 9-3. Pins 1 through 50 are on the component side of the board and 51 through 100 on the foil side.

The power distributed on the bus is unregulated, so each board must regulate it locally. There are advantages to distributing power in this manner. The distribution circuitry is simplified and noise coupling between boards is reduced. The boards cost more, though, because individual regulators must be supplied. The +8 V is regulated to +5 V, +16 to +12 V, and −16 to −12 V.

The data bus is divided into separate input and output lines. Data input is used to transfer data to the processor (sometimes called the "master") from another module (the "slave"). Data output reverses the process. For both sets of lines, bit 0 is the least significant bit. The availability of unidirectional data buses offers no advantage, and eight additional pins on the connector are required to provide the separate buses. The separate buses are frequently wired together on many peripheral modules. Figure 9-5 shows how the output bus is enabled by $\overline{\text{DODSB}}$. Until that signal is pulled low, the three-state drivers have floating outputs.

Table 9-3
S-100 Bus Signals

Pin	Purpose	Comments	Pin	Purpose	Comments
1	+8 V	Unregulated power.	38	DO4	Data out 4.
2	+16 V	Unregulated power.	39	DO5	Data out 5.
3	XRDY	External ready input to MPU.	40	DO6	Data out 6.
4	VI0	Vectored-interrupt 0.	41	DI2	Data in 2.
			42	DI3	Data in 3.
5	VI1	Vectored-interrupt 1.	43	DI7	Data in 7.
6	VI2	Vectored-interrupt 2.	44	SM1	Machine cycle 1 (instruction fetch).
7	VI3	Vectored-interrupt 3.			
8	VI4	Vectored-interrupt 4.	45	SOUT	Output. Status signal indicating that the address bus holds the output device code.
9	VI5	Vectored-interrupt 5.			
10	VI6	Vectored-interrupt 6.			
11	VI7	Vectored-interrupt 7.	46	SINP	Input. Status signal indicating that the address bus hold the input device code.
12	···	Undefined.			
13	···	Undefined.			
14	···	Undefined.	47	SMEMR	Memory read. Status signal indicating that a memory read will occur.
15	···	Undefined.			
16	···	Undefined.			
17	···	Undefined.	48	SHLTA	Halt. Status signal in response to an HLT instruction.
18	$\overline{\text{STATDSB}}$	Status disable. Strobe for three-state buffers on status lines.			
			49	$\overline{\text{CLOCK}}$	Inverted Φ2 clock.
19	$\overline{\text{C/CDSB}}$	Command/control disable. Strobe for the three-state command/control buffers.	50	GND	Ground.
			51	+8 V	Unregulated +5-V power (same as pin 1).
20	UNPROT	Unprotect. Input to memory protect flip-flop.	52	−16 V	Unregulated power.
21	SS	MPU is executing in single step (one instruction at a time).	53	$\overline{\text{SSWI}}$	Sense switch input from panel.
22	$\overline{\text{ADDRDSB}}$	Address disable. Strobe for three-state buffers on address lines.	54	$\overline{\text{EXTCLR}}$	External clear to I/O devices.
			55	···	Undefined.
			56	···	Undefined.
23	$\overline{\text{DODSB}}$	Data output disable. Strobe for three-state output on data lines.	57	···	Undefined.
			58	···	Undefined.
			59	···	Undefined.
24	Φ2	Phase 2 clock.	60	···	Undefined.
25	Φ1	Phase 1 clock.	61	···	Undefined.
26	PHLDA	Hold acknowledge. Processor command/control signal.	62	···	Undefined.
			63	···	Undefined.
			64	···	Undefined.
27	PWAIT	Wait. Processor command/control signal.	65	···	Undefined.
			66	···	Undefined.
28	PINTE	Interrupt enable. Processor command/control signal.	67	···	Undefined.
			68	MWRITE	Memory write. Data is to be placed in memory.
29	A5	Address line 5.			
30	A4	Address line 4.			
31	A3	Address line 3.	69	$\overline{\text{PS}}$	Memory protect flip-flop status.
32	A15	Address line 15.			
33	A12	Address line 12.	70	PROT	Input to memory protect flip-flop.
34	A9	Address line 9.			
35	DO1	Data out 1.	71	RUN	Indicates that MPU is in the run mode.
36	DO0	Data out 0.			
37	A10	Address line 10.	72	PRDY	Processor ready input.

Table 9-3 *(Continued)*
S-100 Bus Signals

Pin	Purpose	Comments	Pin	Purpose	Comments
73	$\overline{\text{PINT}}$	Interrupt request.	85	A13	Address line 13.
74	$\overline{\text{PHOLD}}$	Processor command/ control input to enter hold state.	86	A14	Address line 14.
			87	A11	Address Line 11.
75	$\overline{\text{PRESET}}$	Reset processor command/ control input.	88	DO2	Data out 2.
			89	DO3	Data out 3.
76	PSYNC	Sync processor command control output.	90	DO7	Data out 7.
			91	DI4	Data in 4.
			92	DI5	Data in 5.
77	$\overline{\text{PWR}}$	Write processor command/ control output.	93	DI6	Data in 6.
78	PDBIN	Data bus input processor command/control signal.	94	DI1	Data in 1.
			95	DI0	Data in 0.
			96	SINTA	Interrupt acknowledge output.
79	A0	Address line 0.			
80	A1	Address line 1.	97	$\overline{\text{SWO}}$	Write out status signal.
81	A2	Address line 2.	98	SSTACK	Stack status signal.
82	A6	Address line 6.	99	$\overline{\text{POC}}$	Power on clear.
83	A7	Address line 7.	100	GND	Ground.
84	A8	Address line 8.			

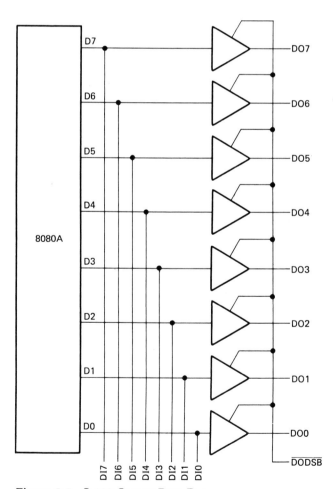

Figure 9-5. S-100 Output Data Bus.

The address bus is a standard 16-bit buffered bus. As Fig. 9-6 shows, bits A0 through A15 correspond to the 8080A address pins. A three-state buffer is used on the lines. The $\overline{\text{ADDRDSB}}$ signal enables the buffers when true.

The command/control bus, shown in Fig. 9-7, buffers six signals used to control the other bus information. Any member of the bus, and the front panel switches of the microcomputers, can originate these signals. The PINTE signal represents the status of the interrupt enable flag of the processor. "Hold acknowledge" (PHLDA) is generated by the processor when it enters the hold state. A low $\overline{\text{PWR}}$ signal means that write operation to memory or an I/O device will occur. Data on the address and output buses must not change while this signal is low. When the processor is in the wait state, PWAIT is high. PDBIN is used to indicate that the addressed device should place its data on the data input bus. PSYNC corresponds to the 8080A SYNC signal, which indicates the beginning of a machine cycle. Figure 9-7 also shows how the command/control outputs are derived from the 8080A. $\overline{\text{C/CDSB}}$ must be true before any of these signals will appear on the bus.

The status bus signals in Fig. 9-8 are typically latched by an 8212 I/O port. All of the status signals are derived from the status byte sent by the 8080A. The SMEMR signal is used to designate that a memory read will occur next. The memory write (MWRITE) signal is derived from SMEMR. A true SINP signal means that the address bus is set to

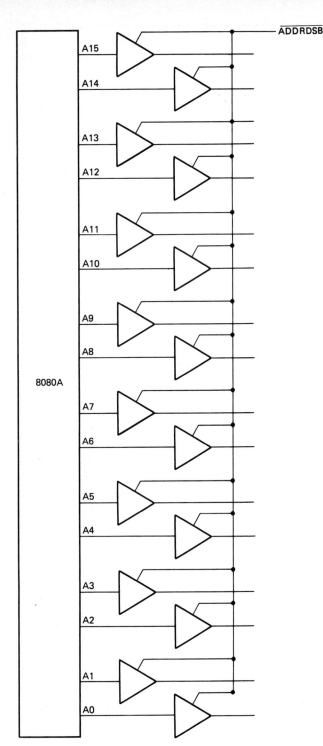

Figure 9-6. S-100 Address bus.

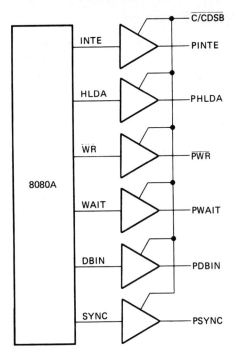

Figure 9-7. S-100 Command/Control Bus.

PRDY/XRDY corresponds to the READY output of 8080A, PHOLD to HOLD, PINT to INT (interrupt request), and PRESET to RESET. All of these S-100 signals are identical to the 8080A signals.

Some other signals are the two clock phases, Φ1 and Φ2, and $\overline{CLOCK}$ (Φ2 inverted). The $\overline{POC}$ signal indicates that power is being applied to the processor when true. The vectored interrupts, VI0 through VI7, are intended to reference the eight vector addresses in the 8080A using the RST instruction.

The original computer, which the bus was designed for, had a series of switches on the front panel that controlled some of the bus signals. Data in memory could be altered if UNPROT were true and was protected against change when PROT was true. Momentary contact switches to originate the $\overline{PRESET}$ or $\overline{EXTCLR}$ were also provided. The mode of operation depended on the state of the RUN and SS switch. A final signal, $\overline{SSWI}$, is used to coordinate data transfer to the front panel sense switch.

the input device address. Similarly the SOUT signal indicates that the output device code is on the address bus. An instruction fetch cycle (M1) is indicated by SM1 going high. When the processor halts, it sets SHLTA high. The stack pointer address is on the address bus when SSTACK is true. A write operation is indicated by $\overline{SWO}$ and an interrupt request acknowledged by use of SINTA.

The control signals are buffered and latched also.

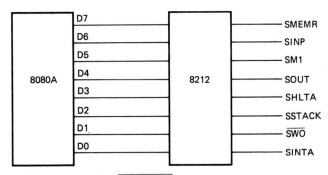

All signals are enabled by $\overline{STATUSDSB}$

Figure 9-8. S-100 Status Bus.

Electrical Specifications

The voltages and currents for high and low levels on the bus are listed in Table 9-4. Because the levels are not specified, the values listed should be considered typical of what one would expect for TTL compatibility. Capacitive loading on any signal line should not exceed 25 pF. Positive current means that the module is acting as a sink. Bus drivers and receivers on each PC board should be placed close to their S-100 bus connectors.

Mechanical Specifications

The S-100 is implemented by use of a *motherboard* consisting of 100 parallel foil strips which interconnect several 100-pin receptacles. The individual printed circuit cards plug into the motherboard by use of an edge connector.

Figure 9-9 shows the S-100 mechanical configuration. The S-100 bus connector consists of a 100-pin plug with conductors at 1/8-in (0.3-cm) spacing. There are 50 pins on each side of the board. Boards are separated by 3/4 in (1.9 cm) along the motherboard, with component height restricted to 0.55 in (1.4 cm). The board thickness is 0.062 in (0.16 cm).

S-100 Timing

The S-100 bus timing is quite similar to that of the 8080A. Timing diagrams for memory read and write are shown in Figure 9-10. The read operation is signaled by the true state of SMEMR and false state of $\overline{PWR}$. The data is accepted by the memory cell addressed by A0 through A15 when DBIN goes high.

A write operation requires that SMEMR be low. The addressed memory will respond with the data when PWR becomes true. (Write operations may also be controlled by MWRITE.) The status codes appear on the data lines during T1 of the instruction cycle, as with normal 8080A operations.

Other operations that use the bus are those for exchanging bus control and interrupting the processor. To request bus control, the device forces $\overline{PHOLD}$

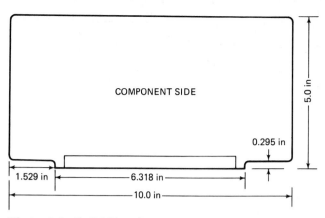

Figure 9-9. S-100 Board.

true. When the processor has entered the hold state, it relinquishes the bus with the acknowledgement, PHLDA. Then the requesting device disables the processor bus drivers (Figs. 9-5 through 9-8) with $\overline{DODSB}$, $\overline{ADDRDSB}$, $\overline{C/CDSB}$, and $\overline{STATDSB}$ signals. The device then has complete control of the bus. The bus is surrendered by raising the disable signals and PHOLD. The processor will regain control of the bus at that time. Unfortunately, two devices can request and gain control of the bus at once in this manner. To correct this shortcoming, the user must provide bus arbitration logic.

Interrupts are signalled with a low $\overline{PINT}$ signal. When the current instruction is completed, the MPU sets the interrupt acknowledge status, SINTA. The interrupted device then supplies the next instruction (usually RST or CALL) on the data input bus.

Example of an S-100 System

A microcomputer which uses the S-100 bus is shown in Fig. 9-11. There are three modules plus the power supply which form the computer. The processor is provided with the control and status buses and the normal address and data buses.

The memory is controlled by the status of MWRITE and SMEMR, while the I/O controller module requires SOUT, $\overline{PWR}$, PDBIN, and SINP for its operations. As you will notice, two modules may use

Table 9-4
S-100 Electrical Characteristics

	Voltage, V		Current	
	Max	**Min**	**Max**	**Min**
Driver				
High	+5.5	+2.4		−1.2 mA
Low	0.5	0		+24 mA
Receiver				
High	+5.5	+2.0	+40 μA	
Low	+0.8	−0.6	−0.8 mA	

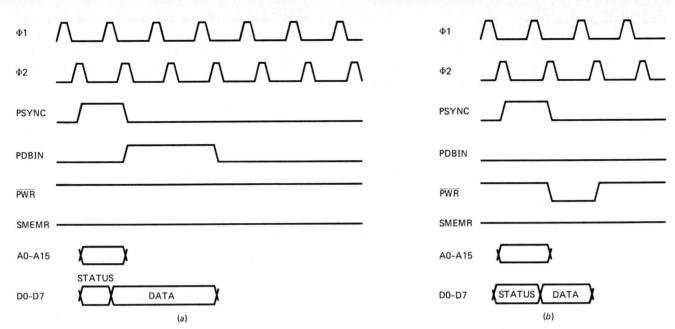

Figure 9-10. S-100 Timing (*a*) Read (*b*) Write.

quite different status and control signals to communicate with the processor. In addition to the control, status, address, and data lines, power will be distributed to each module by means of the bus.

Weaknesses of the S-100 Bus

In spite of the S-100 popularity, the technician must be aware of its shortcomings to be able to properly service equipment built with it. The most serious problem likely to be encountered is the power

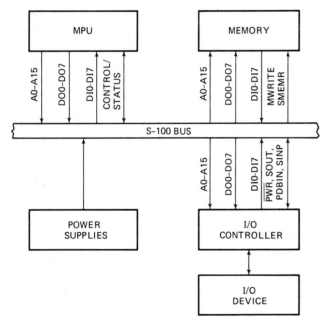

Figure 9-11. S-100 Microcomputer.

distribution pins. Unplugging a board with power applied provides the opportunity to touch −18 V (pin 1) to the +8-V (pin 2) line with subsequent spectacular, though expensive, results. At the least, the regulators will be damaged, but every IC with a +5-V power input could be wiped out.

Variations in power level for the boards located more distantly from the supply can sometimes induce current variations. A module may work properly in one slot of the motherboard, but not in another.

Manufacturers have picked up some of the unassigned pins on the bus and applied special signals to them. The use of the undefined pins can make two boards incompatible. Because the bus was designed prior to the 8228 system controller, many of the S-100 control signals are now redundant. There is no specification for the use of the vectored interrupts (pins 4 through 11). Because the rapidly changing clock lines run parallel to control signals, a great deal of noise is coupled into the control lines, often requiring that shielding be provided and good design practices be followed. No signals should use a frequency equal to the clock rate or double that rate, for example.

Because the bus is not buffered, capacitive loading can severely degrade the signals. The designer must derive such simple 8080A signals as $\overline{MEMR}$ and $\overline{MEMW}$ because they are not on the bus. Making some signals true high and others true low is a confusing convention and makes it difficult to OR two or more signals of opposite polarity together. The lack of arbitration when two devices request bus control is a serious obstacle in direct memory access designs.

S-100 Bus Review

1. True or false? The S-100 bus provides separate unidirectional input and output data lines.

2. Explain how the output data bus in enabled.

3. What is the purpose of the PINTE control signal?

4. Which signal on the bus corresponds to the 8080A SYNC pulse?

5. How is the memory write signal, MWRITE, derived?

6. Distinguish between SINP and SOUT.

7. List the maximum and minimum driver voltage levels.

8. Explain the method used to transfer bus control.

THE MULTIBUS

The *Multibus* provides a mechanism for quickly connecting single-board computers, memory, digital or analog I/O boards, and peripheral controllers. This bus is specified and supported by Intel Corporation. Table 9-5 lists some of the modules available for operation on the Multibus. In building a microcomputer, one simply selects the mix of components that will satisfy the requirements of the application. Card cages, power supplies, and cabinets are produced by the manufacturer as well.

The Multibus carries five types of signals: There is a 20-line address bus, a 16-line bidirectional data bus, 8 multilevel interrupt lines, control and timing lines, and power distribution lines. The address and data bus are three state, while the interrupt lines are open collector.

Modules on the bus operate as either masters or slaves. A master module transmits commands and designates addresses. Another way of defining this relationship is to say that a master module can control the bus; a slave cannot. Arbitration logic is built in to handle requests from multiple masters. The

speed of data transfer is not synchronous with the bus clock, so a faster rate is possible. The data rates of the master and slave are the controlling factors. For that reason a slow master unit can have the same opportunity to gain bus access as a fast master module. Once a master has bus control, either single or multiple-word transfers are allowed.

Table 9-6 lists the signals carried by the Multibus. The signals are assigned to pins in the P1 primary connector or the P2 secondary connector. The P1 signals include address, data, control, interrupt, and power lines. The P2 signals in the auxiliary connector are optional and are used for battery (back up) power and memory protection. Most of the signals on the bus use negative logic; that is, they are true when low. With negative logic, the possibility of issuing an incorrect command is lessened because TTL devices produce high outputs when not driven. Therefore, invalid true outputs will not be issued when one bus master takes control from another.

Primary Signal Lines

The initialization signal is the system reset command. Most often used in startup operations, the $\overline{INIT}$ signal would probably be a result of the operator pressing a front panel switch.

The address bus, $\overline{ADR0}$–$\overline{ADR13}$, is numbered in the hexadecimal (0_{16} through 13_{16}), so there are 20 lines in all. An 8-bit microprocessor would normally only use 16 address lines ($\overline{ADR0}$–$\overline{ADRF}$) for memory operations and 8 address lines ($\overline{ADR0}$–$\overline{ADR7}$) for I/O port addressing. The Multibus can also support 16-bit microprocessors. Then all 20 address lines are needed for referencing memory, and 12 lines are used for I/O port designation ($\overline{ADR0}$–$\overline{ADRB}$).

Inhibit lines are provided so that both RAM and ROM can be assigned identical memory addresses. The $\overline{INH1}$ signal inhibits the read/write memory from responding to the memory address. The $\overline{INH2}$ signal performs an identical function for ROM. Some uses for the inhibit signals are to allow either ROM or RAM to share the same memory addresses, to

Table 9-5
Typical Multibus Modules

| Designation | Description | Power requirements | | | |
		+5 V	+12 V	−5 V	−12 V
80/10	Microcomputer	4.4 mA	150 mA	2 mA	175 mA
80/20-4	Microcomputer	5.2	90	2	20
016	16K RAM	1.5	1000	3.2	
032	32K RAM	3.2	600	40	
416	16K PROM	0.91	1040	750	
116	Combination 16K RAM				
	and 8K PROM	4.0	450	3	60

Table 9-6
Multibus Signals

Name	Symbol	Source	Purpose
P1 signals:			
Initialization	$\overline{\text{INIT}}$	Master/external switch	Resets system.
Address line	$\overline{\text{ADR0}}$–$\overline{\text{ADR13}}$ (numbered 0–13_{16})	Master	Memory and I/O address.
Inhibit RAM signal	$\overline{\text{INH1}}$	Master	Prevents RAM response.
Inhibit ROM signal	$\overline{\text{INH2}}$	Master	Prevents ROM response.
Data lines	$\overline{\text{DAT0}}$–$\overline{\text{DATF}}$	Master/slave	Bidirectional data to or from memory/I/O port.
Byte high enable	$\overline{\text{BHEN}}$	Master	Used with 16-bit memory and I/O transfers.
Bus clock	$\overline{\text{BCLK}}$	Bus control	Negative edge is used to sync bus priority resolution circuits.
Constant clock	$\overline{\text{CCLK}}$	Bus control	General-purpose clock.
Bus priority in	$\overline{\text{BPRN}}$	Bus control	Indicates to a particular master that it has highest priority.
Bus priority out	$\overline{\text{BPRO}}$	Master	Used in daisy chain priority resolution schemes.
Bus busy	$\overline{\text{BUSY}}$	Master	Indicates bus is in use.
Bus request	$\overline{\text{BREQ}}$	Master	Indicates that a master requires use of the bus.
Common request	$\overline{\text{CREQ}}$	Master	Informs current bus master that another master wants to use the bus.
Memory read	$\overline{\text{MRDC}}$	Master	Address of a memory location to be read is on the address bus.
Memory write	$\overline{\text{MWTC}}$	Master	Address of a memory location to be written is on the address bus.
I/O read command	$\overline{\text{IORC}}$	Master	Address of an input port to be read has been placed on the address bus.
I/O write command	$\overline{\text{IOWC}}$	Master	Address of an output port to be written has been placed on the address bus.
Transfer acknowledge	$\overline{\text{XACK}}$	Slave	Response when specified read/write operation has been completed.
Interrupt request	$\overline{\text{INT0}}$–$\overline{\text{INT7}}$	Slave	Multilevel parallel interrupt request lines.
Interrupt acknowledge	$\overline{\text{INTA}}$	Master	Requests transfer of interrupt information.
P2 signals:			
AC low	ACLO	Power supply	AC input voltage too low.
Power fail interrupt	$\overline{\text{PFIN}}$	External power fail circuit	Power failure.
Power fail sense	$\overline{\text{PFSN}}$	External power fail circuit	Output of a latch indicating that a power failure has occurred.
Power fail reset	$\overline{\text{PFSR}}$	External power fail circuit	Resets the power failure sense latch.
Address latch enable	ALE	Master	From 8085 or 8086 as an auxiliary address latch.
Halt	$\overline{\text{HALT}}$	Master	MPU has halted.

Table 9-6 *(Continued)*
Multibus Signals

Name	Symbol	Source	Purpose
Wait state	$\overline{\text{WAIT}}$	Master	Master processor is in the wait state.
Auxiliary reset	$\overline{\text{AUXRESET}}$	External	Initiates power up sequence.
Memory protect	$\overline{\text{MPRO}}$	External	Prevents memory operations when power is uncertain.

allow for an auxiliary ROM with the same addresses as the primary ROM, or to allow memory-mapped I/O ports to override ROM.

The bidirectional data lines are the paths for data moving between the processor and memory or an I/O port. A 16-bit-wide bus is available, but 8-bit microprocessors use only the least significant 8 bits. The byte high enable signal must be true when the upper 8 bits of the data bus are being used.

Seven bus lines are dedicated to priority resolution. The negative edge of the bus clock synchronizes the bus arbitration (also called "priority resolution") circuits. The constant clock has a 100-ns period and is intended for general-purpose use by any module. The priority in and out lines are used for priority resolution; they are connected in daisy chain fashion, as shown in Fig. 9-12. With this arrangement, the physical card position establishes the priority for a given master. When a master gains control, it uses $\overline{\text{BUSY}}$ as an indication to other masters, preventing them from requesting the bus. When the bus is not busy, the module wanting to use it makes its requirement known with the $\overline{\text{BREQ}}$ signal. The master currently in control is made aware of another master needing the bus with the $\overline{\text{CREQ}}$ line.

Another group of bus lines is assigned to coordinate transferring of information. Two sets of read and write signals are available: one set for memory operations and the other for I/O devices. The $\overline{\text{MRDC}}$ and $\overline{\text{MWTC}}$ signals are associated with strobing memory, while $\overline{\text{IORC}}$ and $\overline{\text{IOWC}}$ do the same for an input or output port. When the slave completes the read or write operation, it sends the transfer acknowledgement. Interrupt requests are made by the slave using the multilevel lines and granted by the processor sending $\overline{\text{INTA}}$.

The power-supply bus carries voltage to all modules. The design of each board must provide bulk decoupling capacitors on the board to prevent current surges on the power bus. High-frequency decoupling is also recommended. Values of 22 μF for +5- and +12-V pins and 10 μF for −5- and −12-V pins are typical.

Optional Signal Lines

The optional P2 signals are not bussed to the backplane, so a separate connector is required for each board that uses these signals. A power failure warning is provided by the ACLO signal. Normally this signal becomes true 3 ms before the dc power will fall below acceptable levels. Restoring the power to within 95 percent of rated voltage disables this signal. An external power source (battery) provides the voltage to interrupt the processor with $\overline{\text{PFIN}}$ and to indicate that power has failed with $\overline{\text{PFSN}}$. The latter signal remains true until reset by $\overline{\text{PFSR}}$.

Memory contents cannot be altered if $\overline{\text{MPRO}}$ is low. This signal is used when the dc voltage level is unreliable. An auxiliary address latch, ALE, is available if the microprocessor is an 8085 or 8086. When the MPU halts, it produces a low on the halt line. The $\overline{\text{WAIT}}$ signal indicates that the processor is in the wait state. Finally, an auxiliary reset signal is available to initiate the power up sequence.

Data Transfer

Reading and writing of data on the Multibus are limited to a maximum rate of 5 MHz. More typical times are 2 MHz to allow for bus arbitration and memory access time. The timing diagram for reading data is shown in Fig. 9-13. Depending on whether memory or an input device is to supply the data, the $\overline{\text{IORC}}$ or $\overline{\text{MRDC}}$ line is selected. The address must be stable 50 ns before either of these commands goes low. The slave replies by placing the data on the bus and pulling the acknowledge signal low.

Write timing resembles the read in many ways. Figure 9-14 shows that $\overline{\text{IOWC}}$ or $\overline{\text{MWTC}}$ signal the addressed memory or output port that the data is

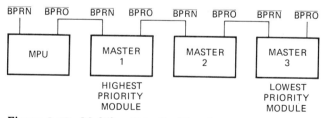

Figure 9-12. Multibus Priority Signals.

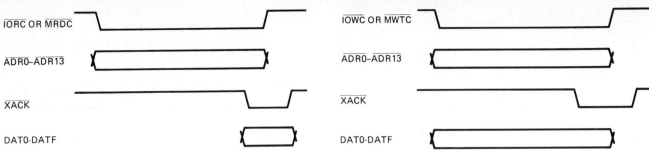

Figure 9-13. Multibus Read Timing.

Figure 9-14. Multibus Write Timing.

ready to be sampled. Data is applied to the bus at the same time as the address. When the data has been sampled, the slave signals with $\overline{XACK}$.

The interrupt lines $\overline{INT0}$–$\overline{INT7}$ allow a slave to interrupt the processor. There are two schemes for interrupting possible. Bus vectored interrupts transfer the vector address over the Multibus address lines from the slave to the master using the $\overline{INTA}$ command for synchronization. The other type of vectored interrupt requires that the interrupt controller of the master generate the vector address and transfer it to the processor over the local bus. No address appears on the Multibus.

Electrical Specifications

The output voltage levels for all drivers on the bus must be in the range of 2.0 to 5.25 V for a high

and 0 to 0.45 V for a low. The receivers must accept a range of 2.0 to 5.5 V as a high, and −0.5 to 0.8 V as a low. The drive current, output stage, and termination for all signals are specified and listed in Table 9-7. Almost all bussed signals are three state. The tolerance of all power-supply voltages is ±1 percent with the ripple not to exceed 25 mV (P-P). Drivers and receivers should be located as close as possible to their Multibus pin connections.

Mechanical Specifications

The motherboard supports the 86-pin receptacles that mate with the plug on each board. The auxiliary connector is not connected into the system bus. Board thickness is 0.062 in (0.16 cm) and spacing between board is 0.6 in (1.5 cm). Component height is limited to 0.4 in (1.12 cm). Figure 9-15 is a diagram of

Table 9-7
Multibus Electrical Specifications

Signals	Output stage	Minimum driver current, mA	Maximum receiver current, mA	Termination, Ω
$\overline{DAT0}$–$\overline{DATF}$	Three state	16	−0.8	2200
$\overline{ADR0}$–$\overline{ADR13}$	Three state	16	−0.8	2200
$\overline{MRDC},\overline{MWTC}$	Three state	32	−2	1000
$\overline{IORC},\overline{IOWC}$	Three state	32	−2	1000
$\overline{XACK}$	Three state	32	−2	510
INH1,INH2	Open collector	16	−2	1000
BCLK,CCLK	Three state	48	−2	220 and 330
$\overline{BREQ}$	Three state	5	2	100
$\overline{BPRO}$	Three state	5	−1.6	⋯
$\overline{BPRN}$	Three state	5	−2	⋯
BUSY,CBRQ	Open collector	32	−2	1000
$\overline{INIT}$	Open collector	32	−2	2200
$\overline{INTA}$	Three state	32	−2	1000
$\overline{INT0}$–$\overline{INT7}$	Open collector	16	−1.6	1000
PFSR,PFSN	Three state	16	−1.6	1000
ACLO	Open collector	16	−1.6	1000
$\overline{PFIN}$	Open collector	16	−1.6	1000
$\overline{MPRO}$	Three state	16	−1.6	1000
$\overline{AUXRESET}$	⋯	⋯	−2	⋯

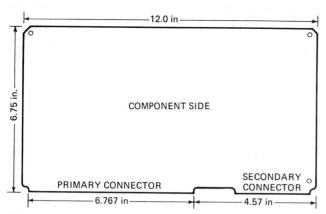

Figure 9-15. Multibus Board.

the most important dimensions. The Multibus connector is an 86-pin plug and the secondary bus connector has 60 pins.

Multibus Review

1. Distinguish between P1 and P2 Multibus signals.

2. Which signal indicates a system reset has occurred?

3. Explain how both 8- and 16-bit microprocessors can effectively communicate over the Multibus.

4. Why is it possible to assign identical addresses to ROM and RAM?

5. Describe the bus arbitration scheme. What establishes the priority of a master module?

CHAPTER SUMMARY

1. A microcomputer bus is a collection of wires used to communicate between modules of the computer. Any member can be the transmitter or receiver of data or control signals. Power is also distributed by the bus.

2. The bus is implemented on a motherboard or backplane which accepts the plugs of PC cards.

3. A daisy chain bus is unidirectional, so it cannot be used to carry data. The bidirectional party line bus can be used for data exchange.

4. Arbitration or priority resolution logic selects one of the modules competing for bus access.

5. The processor controls the timing on a synchronous bus, while handshaking is necessary on an asynchronous bus.

6. Several types of drivers including logical OR, wired-OR, and three state are found on multiplexed buses.

7. The proper receiver can substantially enhance bus performance by reducing capacitive loading.

8. The S-100 bus is the basis for many personal computers. This bus features unidirectional data paths. Many of the S-100 signals correspond to those of the 8080A. Remaining signals can be grouped into an address bus, command/control bus, status bus, and power bus. No standard presently exists for this bus.

9. The Multibus is a standardized computer bus used with 8- and 16-bit processors. Five groups of signals are carried on the bus. These groups include address, data, interrupt, control, and power distribution buses.

KEY TERMS AND CONCEPTS

Multiplexed bus	Bus arbitration	Transceiver
Motherboard	Synchronous bus control	Bidirectional driver
Backplane	Asynchronous bus control	S-100 bus
Daisy chain multiplexed bus	Drivers	Multibus
Party line bus		

PROBLEMS

9-1 Assume that you are checking the operation of a Multibus slave module and find that its interrupt output is attached to $\overline{INT2}$. What address in an 8080A will be referenced when the interrupt occurs?

9-2 If the processor shown in Fig. 9-1a is sending an output to the I/O controller, what delays will be encountered if propagation times are as listed below?

	Receive, μs	Transmit, μs
MPU	0.5	0.7
ROM	0.2	0.2
RAM	0.3	0.35
I/O port	1.5	1.0

9-3 Compute the delay time between the processor and I/O port of Prob. 9-2 if the party line bus shown in Fig. 9-1b is substituted for the daisy chain.

9-4 What is the bus level in Fig. 9-2a if the inputs are as listed below?

Inputs		Selection	
1	H	1	L
2	H	2	H
3	L	3	L

9-5 If the inputs to all gates shown in Fig. 9-2b are high, but no gate is selected, what is the level of the bus?

9-6 If the bus shown in Fig. 9-2c is in the low state, what can you say about the state of the selection lines?

9-7 Let the input to the bidirectional driver shown in Fig. 9-4b be high. What effect does a low input on the bus have if the enable input line is true?

9-8 What can be said about the levels of the command/control signals on the S-100 bus if the following 8080A signal levels exist?

INTE	L
$\overline{WR}$	H
WAIT	L
SYNC	H
$\overline{C/CDSB}$	H

9-9 All three masters shown in Fig. 9-12 issue a low signal on $\overline{BREQ}$. Assume that the $\overline{BPRN}$ input to master 3 is grounded by a malfunction. Which master(s) is (are) granted bus control?

9-10 The memory addresses for a ROM and RAM on the Multibus are identical. What value appears in the accumulator in the situation described below?

Program counter	RAM	ROM
1051	1051 3A	1051 3A
	1052 54	1052 54
	1053 10	1053 10
	1054 00	1054 FF

$\overline{BHEN}$	H
$\overline{INH1}$	L
$\overline{INH2}$	H
BCLK	L

PURPOSE: To investigate a data bus.

PARTS LIST:

Item	Quantity
8212	1
5082–7340 display	1
74LS00	1
74LS20	1
*Logic Analyzer	1

*A logic analyzer is an optional piece of equipment for this experiment. If you have a logic analyzer available, follow Steps 1–4. If not, go to Step 5.

PROCEDURE:

STEP 1. Write a program to count from 00_{16} to FF_{16} and output each value to device 37_{16}. After the final count is reached, jump back to the beginning of the program.

STEP 2. Connect the data bus to the logic analyzer input channels. Switch to the pulse train display mode. Start the program and record the signals. What is the meaning of each channel (1–16)? (Trigger the display on the $\overline{I/OW}$ signal.)

STEP 3. Repeat the experiment using the binary display mode. Explain the results.

STEP 4. Now perform the experiment with the analyzer in the map mode. Sketch the image. Run the experiment again. Does the map change? Explain why it should or should not change.

STEP 5. If you do not have a logic analyzer, wire the parallel interface shown in Figs. 4-37 and 4-38. Change the program in Step 1 to delay 1 s between each count. Change the device code to 07.

STEP 6. Connect the data bus to the parallel interface. Start the program and record the first 16 outputs by observing the hexadecimal display.

STEP 7. Draw a diagram of how each of these outputs would appear as digital pulse trains. (For example, a value of 00_{16} would be a parallel sequence of eight low outputs, 01_{16} of seven lows and one high, and so on.)

10

ANALOG INTERFACES

A major class of microcomputer applications requires that the computer control, interpret, monitor, or generate signals for analog devices. Bridging the gap between the digital signals of the processor system and the varying voltages or currents of the analog equipment is the objective of analog interfacing. These systems call for solutions that are compatible with the timing, voltage, current, and loading requirements on both sides of the interface.

At times we may be fortunate enough to find that the analog component can accept the same levels that are used by the microprocessor. This method can generally only be used with simple devices. More complex analog equipment calls for a conversion process before signals can be exchanged with the computer. In this chapter we will investigate various means of using interfaces to satisfactorily couple the computer to analog equipment.

CHAPTER OBJECTIVES

Upon completion of this chapter you should be able to:

1. Show how to directly connect a microcomputer to simple analog components.
2. Draw a block diagram of a digital-to-analog converter.
3. List the basic types of digital-to-analog converters.
4. Explain the operation of a multiplying digital-to-analog converter.
5. Calculate the output voltage of a digital-to-analog converter.
6. Program a microcomputer to generate a variety of analog waveforms.
7. Explain the purpose for double buffering a digital-to-analog converter.
8. List typical types of analog-to-digital converters.
9. Compare the output waveforms of counter and successive approximation analog-to-digital converters.
10. Program a microcomputer to perform data sampling.
11. Describe the characteristics of analog interface devices.
12. Explain the purpose of sample-and-hold integrated circuits.
13. Explain the principles of operation for voltage-to-frequency converters.

THE SIMPLE ANALOG INTERFACE

Sometimes we find that the job of interfacing to an analog device is straightforward because the digital voltages can be used without change. Such a case is shown in Fig. 10-1. Here the speaker is our analog device. We simply want the computer to produce a series of signals that generate a tone from the speaker.

There is not even a data output in this circuit. The device code on the address bus acts as a trigger for each tone sample. When the correct device code is recognized, the low output of the decoder is NORed with the $\overline{OUT}$ signal clocking the D flip-flop. On each clock pulse, the previous output is fed back and complemented. The TTL flip-flop acts as a driver for the speaker. By complementing the output in this way, we avoid the necessity of a data output. The speaker input is therefore a series of square waves. By adjusting the time between output instructions, we can change the tone of the sound generated.

A program for this interface is listed below in Table 10-1. By changing the delay interval, the speaker output frequency can be varied. Decreasing the value in locations 1003_{16} and 1004_{16} increases the frequency and increasing that value lowers the frequency.

We can calculate the approximate frequency by the formula

$$F = \frac{1}{\text{delay interval}}$$

$$= \frac{1}{(n)\,(7.5\ \mu s)} \qquad (10\text{-}1)$$

where n = the value in cells 1003_{16} and 1004_{16} (in decimal).

Simple Analog Interface Review

1. How is the drive current for the speaker produced in this circuit?

2. Why is there no need for a data output?

3. Describe the relationship between the computer program and the audio frequency from the speaker.

4. What causes the signal to alternate between the high and low voltage?

DIGITAL-TO-ANALOG CONVERTERS

A key element in a *digital-to-analog (D/A) converter,* as well as many of the other devices we will study in this chapter, is an operational amplifier. The op amp serves the dual purpose of buffering the output and decoupling from the load. As a buffer, the amplifier acts to collect and store the output signal. Loading effects of the downstream circuitry are eliminated by the decoupling of op amp. Figure 10-2 shows a generalized D/A converter. A digital input consisting of several bits is applied to the decision matrix. The matrix is, in fact, a collection of logic gates. Voltage is connected to the resistor stage for one state of the input and not connected for the other state. The matrix can be thought of as switches which open or close as directed by the digital input. If there are *n* bits of the input, then there are *n* switches in the matrix. The number of switches determines the *resolution* of the converter. The more bits in the input means the smaller increments that the output voltage can be divided into.

The resistor network is arranged to weight the incoming current that is passed through the closed switches in the decision matrix. Common weighting schemes accommodate either binary or BCD inputs. The reference voltage is the source of the drive for the resistor network. This reference must be accurately maintained at its assigned voltage if an accurate conversion is to be accomplished. A Zener diode is often used to provide a constant voltage level.

D/A converters with input level compatible with TTL or CMOS integrated circuits are readily available. With these characteristics, interfacing with 7400 TTL integrated circuits or microcomputers is easy. The converter itself is an integrated circuit

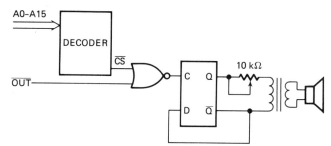

Figure 10-1. Audio Generator.

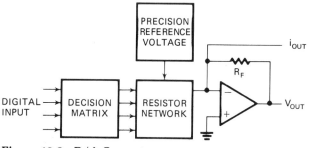

Figure 10-2. D/A Converter.

Table 10-1
Audio Generator Program

Label	Mnemonic	Operand	Address	Code	Comment
NEXT	OUT	10	1000	D3	Device code is 10
			1001	10	
	LXI H	FFFF	1002	21	
			1003	FF	Delay
			1004	FF	
LOOP	DCX H		1005	2B	
	MVI A	00	1006	3E	
			1007	00	
			1008	85	Test for zero bit
	ADD L		1008	85	
	ADD H		1009	84	
	JNZ	LOOP	100A	C2	
			100B	05	
			100C	10	Repeat
	JMP	NEXT	100D	C3	
			100E	00	
			100F	10	

which can be ordered in flatpack, TO "cans," or dual-in-line package configurations.

Converters that accept supply voltages of 5 to 35 V, or more, are available. Almost all of them operate reliably over a wide range of temperatures.

D/A Converter Output

The output range of a D/A converter can be found if the number of input bits and the reference voltage are known. Assuming a binary input is used,

$$V_{out} = \frac{\text{binary input}}{2^n} \cdot V_{ref} \qquad (10\text{-}2)$$

where n = number of input bits.

For example, consider a 3-bit converter which uses a reference voltage of 4 V. Table 10-2 lists the output values resulting from any input. As the table shows, the least significant bit (001_2) represents 0.5 V. This voltage is the resolution of the converter. No smaller voltage steps can be produced. Each output level is exactly that voltage increment above the preceding

Table 10-2
D/A Outputs

Binary input	Output voltage, V
000	0
001	0.5
010	1.0
011	1.5
100	2.0
101	2.5
110	3.0
111	3.5

one. Also note that the full-scale output (when the input is all ones) is not 4 V. The D/A full-scale output is always one LSB less than the reference voltage.

Input Coding

The number of steps in the output is related to the digital *input code*. In our example, binary coding was used. As was mentioned above, BCD is frequently encountered as well. In that case, each decimal digit is represented by 4 bits. Those bits must always fall within the limits of 0000 to 1001 for each decimal digit. If a converter had a two-digit BCD input, the lowest input value expressed in bits would be 0000 0000 and the full scale input would be 1001 1001, representing 99.

Other converters use complement number systems. Both 1's and 2's complement binary converters can be obtained. Depending on the converter, the output may or may not be negative voltage. Two examples of 1's complement converters are provided below. Both use references of 8 V.

Converter	1's Complement binary input	Output voltage, V
A	0000 0000	0
	1111 1111	− 7.5
B	0000 0000	0
	1111 1111	+ 7.5

Yet another popular coding scheme is *offset binary*. In it, some midpoint value is selected as the zero voltage output. In this way both positive and negative (bipolar) outputs can be produced. Table 10-3 gives an example.

Types of D/A Converters

The most frequently encountered converters use either *weighted resistor* or *resistor ladder networks*. The weighted resistor converters use a series of resistors to develop current from each input bit. The resistors values are obtained by doubling their value in going from one bit to the next. If the resistor for the most significant bit is 10 kΩ, then the resistor for the next lower bit would be 20 kΩ, and so on. The LSB resistor is then $(10K)(2^{n-1})$. The resistor ladder uses only two values for its resistors. If R represents one value, then the other is $2R$.

MULTIPLYING D/A CONVERTERS. *Multiplying D/A Converters (MDACs)* are equivalent to digitally controlled potentiometers. The MDAC has both an analog and digital input. The analog input is multiplied by a fraction represented by the digital input to yield the output voltage:

$$V_{out} = \frac{\text{digital input}}{2^n} \cdot V_{analog} \qquad (10\text{-}3)$$

The digital input is assumed to have a radix point to the left of the MSB. Let an 8-bit MDAC have an analog input of 12 V and a digital input of 1100 0000. Placing the radix point to the left of the MSB,

therefore
$$0.1100\ 0000_2 = 0.75_{10}$$
$$V_{out} = (12\ \text{V})(0.75) = 9\ \text{V}$$

Multiplying D/A converters are classed as either *two- or four-quadrant devices*, with a further subdivision made in two-quadrant devices. *Digital two-quadrant MDACs* are most common, but they are not as versatile as the other types. The output voltage always either increases or decreases from zero. The digital input ranges over positive and negative values (bipolar).

Analog two-quadrant MDACs are analogous to a three-terminal pot. The digital codes are limited to

Table 10-3
Offset Binary Converter

Binary input	Output voltage, V
000	−1.0
001	−0.75
010	−0.50
011	−0.25
100	0
101	0.25
110	0.5
111	0.75

either an increasing or decreasing range, but the amplitude of the output signal includes positive and negative values.

Four-quadrant devices allow the digital controlling input and the output signal both to take on positive and negative values. In addition to varying the amplitude, the four-quadrant MDAC can change the signal phase by 180° as well.

A circuit for a digital two-quadrant MDAC is shown in Fig. 10-3. At the maximum limit, the signal is at its negative extreme. When the digital count reaches zero, the output also goes to zero.

COMPANDING D/A CONVERTERS. A variation of the MDAC is the *companding (compression/expansion function) D/A converter*. The companding converter permits the 8-bit input from a microcomputer to achieve a low signal-to-quantizing error over a 40-dB range, which would be impossible by just using linear coding. This type of converter is an implementation of the Bell System μ-255 logarithm companding law. The output can be expressed as

$$y = 0.18 \ln (1 + \mu x) \qquad (10\text{-}4)$$

where y = output
x = normalized input
μ = 255

Obviously the law is named for the constant, μ.

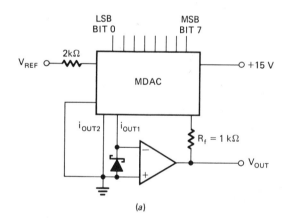

(a)

(b)

Figure 10-3. Digital Two-Quadrant MDAC (a) Circuit (b) Configuration (Helipot Division, Beckman Instruments, Inc.).

The operation of the converter is best shown by an example. Let the 8-bit input be defined as

Bit number	7	6 5 4	3 2 1 0
	Sign	Chord number	Step size

The sign bit denotes positive or negative values (1 = negative). The chord is one of the eight line segments which symmetrically form a linear approximation of the transfer function. See Fig. 10-4. The 3 bits allow us to specify which of the eight chords is currently being designated. The last 4 bits indicate one of 16 step sizes for the designated chord. The cumulative transfer function is usually tabulated in a form similar to that given in Table 10-4. Assume that we input a positive chord designator of 3 and a step size of 1. Reading from the chart, we see that the length of that chord in the transfer function will be 247 units. (This length means that the output will be 247/8031 times the positive full-scale value.) By changing the chord designator and step size, the shape of the transfer function can be modified.

To show the equivalence of the units used on the chart, we note that the maximum length is 8031. Therefore one unit represents

$$\frac{1}{8031} = 0.0125\%$$

of full scale, so incrementing by two units in the 0 chord column is the same as 0.025 percent of full scale (2 × 0.0125 percent) and the 256 units in the 7 chord column represent 3.2 percent of full

scale (256 × 0.0125 percent). These same units result for the resolution indicated.

$$\text{Chord 0:} \quad \frac{1}{2^{12}} = 0.025\%$$

$$\text{Chord 7:} \quad \frac{1}{2^{5}} = 3.2\%$$

Thus an input of a step size 1 and chord of 0 (represented as 1,0) will give us a resolution of 0.025 percent, which is the same as would be produced by a 12-bit D/A converter. The increment using chord 7 is 3.2 percent—the same as that of a 5-bit D/A converter.

Let us continue this example using the notation V_{out} (step, chord) to indicate the output. The output voltage can be calculated as

$$V_{out}\text{(step, chord)} = \frac{\text{chart (step, chord)}}{8031} \cdot V_{ref}$$

(10-5)

Let the output voltage range be −12 to 12 V. (That means V_{ref} is either −12 or +12 V, depending on sign.)

$$V_{out}(1,0) = \left(\frac{2}{8031}\right)(12\text{ V}) = 0.003\text{ V}$$

equivalent to $V_{out} = 0.00025\,(12\text{ V}) = 0.003$ V

$$= 0.025\%\text{ full-scale voltage}$$

Another case showing the step-size increment is

$$V_{out}(0,7) = \frac{(4191)}{(8031)}(12\text{ V}) = 6.26\text{ V}$$

$$V_{out}(1,7) = \frac{(4447)}{(8031)}(12\text{ V}) = 6.64\text{ V}$$

$$V_{out}(1,7) - V_{out}(0,7) = \text{voltage increment}$$

$$= 0.38\text{ V}$$

$$= 3.2\%\text{ of full scale}$$

$$= (2^{1/5})(12\text{ V})$$

A summary of the variety of D/A converters on the market appears in Table 10-5. The resolution range of from 6 to 12 bits covers most ordinary requirements.

Programming for D/A Converters

Once the digital-to-analog interface has been constructed for the microcomputer, a variety of wave-

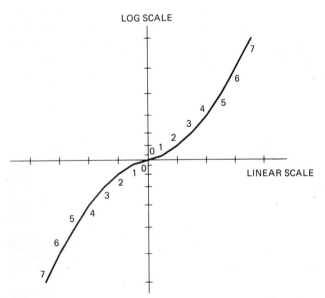

Figure 10-4. Companding D/A Converter Transfer Function.

Table 10-4

Step size	Chord							
	0	1	2	3	4	5	6	7
0	0	33	99	231	495	1023	2079	4191
1	2	37	107	(247)	527	1087	2207	4447
2	4	41	115	263	559	1151	2335	4703
.	.	.	.	.	.	.	.	.
.	.	.	.	.	.	.	.	.
.	.	.	.	.	.	.	.	.
.								maximum
15	30	93	219	471	975	1983	3999	(8031)
Increment	2	4	8	16	32	64	128	256
Resolution (bits)	12	11	10	9	8	7	6	5
Increment as a percent of full scale	0.025	0.05	0.1	0.2	0.4	0.8	1.6	3.2

Table 10-5
Typical D/A Converters

Manufacturer	Model	Bits	Conversion time, ns	Range
PMI	DAC-01	6	3000	±5 V
PMI	DOC-03	10	1500	0.10 V
Analog devices	AD 7522 (multiplying)	10	500	±5 mA
Motorola	1406L	6	150	±1 mA
Motorola	MC1408L8	8	300	±1 mA
National	DA1200	12	1500	10 V

forms and functions can be generated by simply changing the program in the computer. Figure 10-5 shows an interface to an 8-bit D/A converter that uses a 74100 8-bit latch. The 74100 is composed of eight identical D flip-flops. Data placed on the input of any latch is transferred to the output terminal and the level maintained until the next input is received.

The inputs to the latch are the data bus bits. When the latch is enabled by the device select and $\overline{\text{OUT}}$ signals, the information on the data bus is fed to the D/A converter. The converter transforms the

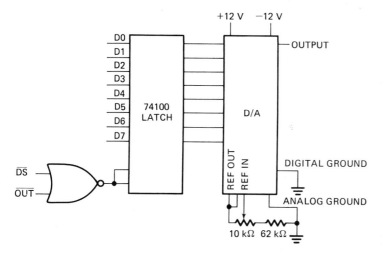

Figure 10-5. D/A Converter Interface.

digital input into an analog voltage. The analog output will track the values sent by the microcomputer.

The waveform generated depends on two aspects of the program. The period of the signal results from the time it takes to execute one complete pass through the program, as shown in Fig. 10-6. The amplitude is determined by the maximum value of the output.

SQUARE WAVE GENERATION. The program to produce a square wave from the circuit shown in Fig. 10-5 is listed in Table 10-6. The program relies on the complement instruction.

The accumulator is zeroed initially and that value is sent to the converter. After a delay (instructions in addresses 1004_{16} to $100E_{16}$), the accumulator is changed to its 1's complement (FF_{16}). This value is equivalent to the maximum full-scale output of the D/A converter. Thus the square wave alternates between zero and full-scale output with a period of twice the delay loop. We can calculate this delay knowing the time it takes to execute the instructions in the loop. (We will assume that the microprocessor is running with a 2-MHz clock.)

DCX	2.5 μs
MVI	3.5
ADD L	2.0
ADD M	2.0
JNZ	5.0
	15.0 μs

and $FFFF_{16} = 65535_{10}$

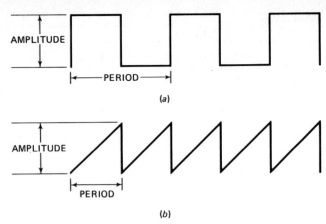

Figure 10-6. Waveforms (a) Symmetrical Square Wave (b) Sawtooth Wave.

so $$65535 \times 15 \text{ μs} = 0.98 \text{ s}$$

The period of the square wave will be approximately 2 s.

SAWTOOTH WAVE GENERATION. A sawtooth or ramp function can be generated almost as easily. In this program, we simply increment the accumulator, letting it overflow. (See Table 10-7.) Every time it goes from FF_{16} to 0, the output changes from its maximum to its minimum value. In this case, the delay is placed between each step to control the slope of the ramp. See Fig. 10-7.

In actuality the wave is a stairstep function, but the resolution of the D/A converter is sufficiently small to approximate a linearly increasing slope.

Table 10-6
Square Wave Program

Label	Mnemonic	Operand	Address	Code	Comments
	MVI A	0	1000	3E	Zero the accumulator
			1001	00	
NEXT	OUT	12	1002	D3	Output the next value
			1003	12	
	LXI H	FFFF	1004	21	
			1005	FF	Loop count A HL
			1006	FF	
LOOP	DCX H		1007	2B	Decrement
	MVI A	00	1008	3E	
			1009	00	
	ADD L		100A	85	
	ADD H		100B	84	Test for zero bit
	JNZ	LOOP	100C	C2	
			100D	07	
			100E	10	
	CMA		100F	2F	Complement accumulator
	JMP	NEXT	1020	C3	
			1021	02	
			1022	10	

Table 10-7
Sawtooth Wave Program

Label	Mnemonic	Operand	Address	Code	Comments
NEXT	OUT	12	1000	D3	Output the next value
			1001	12	
	MVI B	7F	1002	06	Loop count → B
			1003	7F	
LOOP	DCR B		1004	05	Decrement
	JNZ	LOOP	1005	C2	Delay loop
			1006	04	
			1007	10	
	INR A		1008	3C	Increment accumulator
	JMP	NEXT	1009	C3	Repeat
			100A	00	
			100B	10	

In this situation the period can be found by multiplying the delay in each step by the number of steps, which is FF_{16} (255_{10}). The delay at each step is 127_{10} ($7F_{16}$) $\times$ 7.5 μs.

We have

$$255 \text{ steps} \times (127 \times 7.5 \text{ } \mu\text{s/step}) = 0.24 \text{ s}$$

This time means that the period is about a quarter of a second. The amplitude increases to full-scale, then drops to zero and begins to count up again at the completion of each period.

We can easily make this program generate a decreasing sawtooth instead. Just changing the instruction at cell 1008 to DCR A accomplishes this modification. Now the accumulator decrements to zero and underflows to all 1s.

DOUBLE BUFFERING. The scheme we described above works fine with D/A converters that have inputs not exceeding the data bus width, that is, 8 bits or less. What if we have a 10- or 12-bit A/D converter, though? A thought that comes immediately to mind is to address the low 8 bits and upper bits of input separately and output the two sets of bits to separate devices.

Consider how this approach would work with a 12-bit D/A converter producing a sawtooth output.

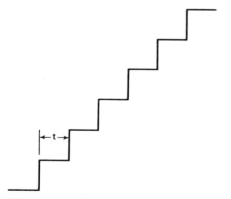

Figure 10-7. Incrementing Ramp.

Assuming that the accumulator starts at zero, we have Table 10-8. This method seems to work fine. But consider what happens in going from $0000 \text{ } 1111 \text{ } 1111_2$ to $0001 \text{ } 0000 \text{ } 0000_2$. The lower half is changed to zero before the upper becomes 0001. Therefore the output will drop to zero, causing a *glitch* every time the lower 8 bits increment to zero. A related difficulty is observed when the counter is going from all 1s back to zero. We could observe that the data lines change as follows:

$1111 \text{ } 1111 \text{ } 1111_2$	Initial
$1111 \text{ } 0000 \text{ } 0000_2$	Lower half increments
$0000 \text{ } 0000 \text{ } 0000_2$	Upper half becomes zero

We can prevent both of these problems by use of a *double buffer,* as shown in Fig. 10-8.

Latches 1 and 2 hold the new value for the D/A converter, but they are not applied to the input terminals until latches 3 and 4 are strobed. By assuring that both the upper and lower set of bits have been assigned their correct values prior to applying either to the D/A converter, the glitches that previously were a problem are eliminated. A program fragment to output the value $17F7_{16}$ to the 12-bit D/A converter is given below.

MVI A, F7	Lower bits
OUT 12	Output to latch 2
MVI A, 17	Upper bits
OUT 13	Output to latch 1
OUT 14	Enable latches 3 and 4

Only on the last output do the data bits change the D/A converter input. Double buffering is so frequently necessary that many D/A converters have the twin sets of latches built into the package.

Digital-to-Analog Converters Review

1. Explain the purpose for each component of a D/A converter.

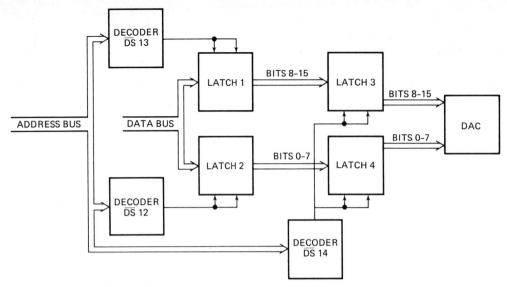

Figure 10-8. Double Buffer.

2. Distinguish between binary and offset binary input coding.

3. Describe the operation of a multiplying D/A converter.

4. Why is the companding D/A converter considered to be an implementation of the μ-255 law?

5. What determines the period of a waveform generated by a computer program? How is the amplitude defined?

ANALOG-TO-DIGITAL CONVERTERS

Now let us discuss devices that can provide inputs to the computer that are samples of analog voltages. With an *analog-to-digital (A/D) converter*, physical processes can be monitored by the computer program. The program simply inputs data from the converter at some interval to obtain its readings. These readings could represent a temperature, vol-

Table 10-8

Action	Accumulator	B Register (temporary storage)	Bits											
			11	10	9	8	7	6	5	4	3	2	1	0
Output lower 8 bits	00	?	?	?	?	?	0	0	0	0	0	0	0	0
Save value	00	00												
Output upper 4 bits	00	00	0	0	0	0	0	0	0	0	0	0	0	0
Switch A and B	00	00												
Increment A	01	00												
Output lower	01	00	0	0	0	0	0	0	0	0	0	0	0	1
Switch A and B	00	01												
Output upper	00	01	0	0	0	0	0	0	0	0	0	0	0	1
Switch A and B	01	00												
Increment A	10	00												
Output lower	10	00	0	0	0	0	0	0	0	0	0	0	1	0
Switch A and B	00	10												
Output upper	00	10	0	0	0	0	0	0	0	0	0	0	1	0
.	.	.												
.	.	.												
.	.	.												

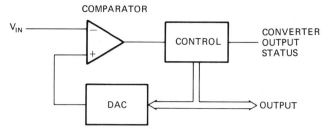

Figure 10-9. A/D Converter Concept.

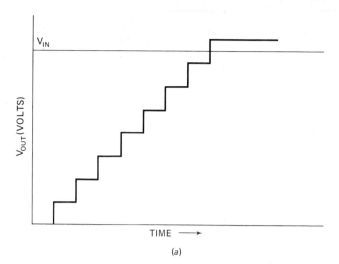

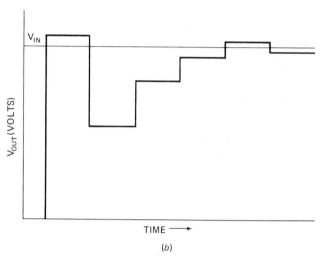

Figure 10-10. A/D Converter Outputs (*a*) Counter (*b*) Successive Approximation.

tage, current, pressure, or some other important parameter of the system being controlled.

Several types of integrated A/D converters are manufactured. Two of them use a feedback loop which has a D/A converter in the loop. Figure 10-9 illustrates their principle of operation. The *counter* A/D converter feeds the output of a comparator to the control circuitry that senses when the digital estimate equals or exceeds the analog input. A counter is used to produce the digital estimate, giving the converter its name. The output is produced slowly in stairstep manner, as Fig. 10-10*a* shows. The counter A/D converter is popular despite its slowness because of its simplicity and low cost.

Another widely used converter is the *successive approximation* converter. Here the comparator inputs are also the unknown analog voltage and the output of a D/A converter. A bit-by-bit comparison is made, starting with the most significant bit set high. If the resulting digital value exceeds the analog 1, that bit is turned off. Then the process continues with the next lower bit and so on, until all bits have been used. Figure 10-10*b* shows how the output develops. A good voltage reference and D/A converter are required in the successive approximation converter, but the cost is justified by the speed of conversion, which is in the range of 10 to 20 μs.

The *parallel* A/D converter performs the process simultaneously. The digital result is a summation from many separate comparators, so operation can be continuous with new samples of the analog signal being constantly fed into the converter. This type of converter is used for sampling rates in excess of 10 MHz, although it is costly. The resolution of the parallel A/D converter is related to the number of comparators:

$$C = 2^{n/2+1} - 2 \qquad (10\text{-}6)$$

where C = number of comparators
         n = number of bits of resolution

A *tracking* A/D converter operates on the principle of a servo loop. In fact, it is also called a "servo A/D converter." The converter tracks the analog input, but it takes considerable time to acquire and

lock the signal. This time lag is especially pronounced if the input makes large jumps. Even so, this style of converter is very accurate.

An op amp integrator forms the basis of the *integrating* A/D converter. Here a reference time is compared with a variable time, which is proportional to the analog voltage. The output can be derived from a count of the time intervals:

$$V_{in} = \frac{T_{in}}{T_{ref}} \cdot V_{ref} \qquad (10\text{-}7)$$

This converter is quite insensitive to component values, so it can be built inexpensively and has good noise rejection. Its disadvantage is the slow time for conversion—about 10 ms. Integrating A/D converters are frequently used as panel voltmeters.

Data Sampling

A straightforward A/D converter that can be used in a computer sampling system is shown in Fig.

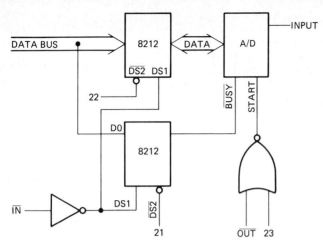

Figure 10-11. Data Sampling.

10-11. The two 8212 I/O ports interface the data bus to the converter.

The program used to drive this circuit is given in Table 10-9. The output to device 23 starts the converter and causes it to convert one sample. As long as the $\overline{\text{BUSY}}$ is low, the device is performing the conversion, so the program loops until that signal (received as data bit 0) goes high. Finally, a sample is accepted by the input from device 22.

A list of typical A/D converters is provided in Table 10-10. This collection suggests some of the ranges in resolution, conversion time, and voltage range that can be found today.

Analog-to-Digital Converters Review

1. Distinguish between counter, successive approximation, parallel, tracking, and integrating A/D converters.

2. Give another name for a servo A/D converter?

3. Explain the purpose of the $\overline{\text{BUSY}}$ input of the A/D converter shown in Fig. 10-11.

4. How is the program in microprocessor able to determine that the conversion process has been completed in a data sampling system?

CHARACTERISTICS OF CONVERTERS

Specifications for converters are usually expressed in terms that have a specialized meaning. Knowing this terminology makes it possible for you to read and understand data books for the converters. An appreciation of the limits and capabilities of a particular converter model will allow you to judge whether a specific use is within its design limits or if a different model could be used as a substitute.

Most of the specifications are expressed as errors in the output. These errors are generally determined by measuring the deviation of the actual output from the idealized value expected. Some of these errors, such as gain and zero scale, can be removed or reduced by adjustment. The others are inherent limits of the device. Probably the most important of the latter is *linearity,* followed closely by *drift.*

The *gain* or full-scale error is the difference in the actual full-scale range from the ideal full-scale range. This range is the span of voltage or current values over which the converter can be used, such as 1 to 10 V. Zero-scale (sometimes called *offset*) error is the shift in the transfer function by some DC bias. See Fig. 10-12a. As we stated above, the offset error can be removed by adjustment so the output is zero when the input is grounded.

Linearity, more than any other parameter, is the measure of converter quality. It is the limit of performance. Linearity is measured by finding the deviation of the transfer function from a straight

Table 10-9
A/D Conversion Program

Label	Mnemonic	Operand	Address	Code	Comments
	OUT	23	1000	D3	Start conversion
			1001	23	
LOOP	IN	21	1002	DB	Input $\overline{\text{BUSY}}$
			1003	21	
	ANI	01	1004	E6	Get bit 0
			1005	01	
	JZ	LOOP	1006	CA	If still busy, check again
			1007	02	
			1008	10	
	IN	22	1009	DB	Sample A/D converter output
			100A	22	

Table 10-10
A/D Converters

Manufacturer	Model	Bits	Conversion time, ms	Voltage range, V
Analog Devices	ADC 1100	10(BCD)	42	± 0.1999
Analog Devices	ADC 14I	14	40	±10
Analogic	AN 2313	10	6.7	± 2
Datel	ADC E10B	10	1.25	±10

line extending from zero to full scale. The maximum deviation is expressed as a percent of full-scale range or in terms of the least significant bit value. Almost any converter should limit its linearity error to less than 1 percent.

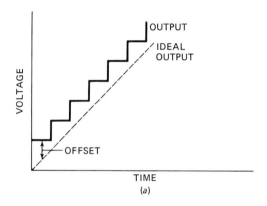

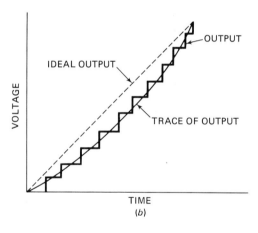

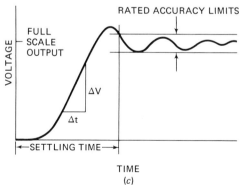

Figure 10-12. Converter Characteristics (*a*) **Offset Error** (*b*) **Linearity Error** (*c*) **Slew Rate.**

Drift results from the variation in the output as a result of temperature. Changes in temperature can effect linearity, offset, and gain. The total drift can be calculated from the temperature coefficients provided in manufacturer's data sheets.

$$D = (TC_L + TC_O + TC_G) \times \Delta T \qquad (10\text{-}8)$$

where
D = drift in parts per million (ppm)
TC_L = linearity temperature coefficient
TC_O = offset temperature coefficient
TC_G = gain temperature coefficient
ΔT = change in temperature, °C

Low values for the coefficients are required for accurate conversion over any spread of temperatures.

A monotonic converter is one for which the output always increases or remains at the last value for an increase in the input. The monotonic parameter is especially important for successive approximation and counter A/D converters.

Resolution should be a familiar concept to you by now. It can be expressed as the number of states that the digital input or output can be divided into. It can be expressed as

$$\text{Resolution} = \frac{\text{full-scale range}}{2^n} \qquad (10\text{-}9)$$

$$= \text{value of the LSB} \qquad (10\text{-}10)$$

where n = number of digital bits. Naturally the full-scale analog input range is used to calculate resolution of A/D converters and output units for D/A converters. A useful formula for the value of the most significant bit is

$$\text{MSB} = \frac{(2^{n-1})\,(\text{full-scale range})}{2^n - 1} \qquad (10\text{-}11)$$

Absolute accuracy expresses the difference between an ideal full-scale output and that measured. (Do not confuse this value with the relative accuracy, which is another term for linearity.)

How fast does a converter respond to a change of input? This question is answered by the *slew rate, settling time,* and *aperture error* specifications. The slew rate of a D/A converter is expressed as the rate of change in output for large input signal changes, as shown in Fig. 8-12*c*. This change of output per unit time is often rated in volts per microsecond:

$$\text{Slew rate} = \Delta v / \Delta t \qquad (10\text{-}11)$$

The time elapsed before the output of a D/A converter remains within its rated accuracy limits is the settling time. You can think of the settling time as the period needed for overshoots to damp out. This parameter is one of the best indications of the converter speed.

Aperture errors of an A/D converter result from variations in the input during the sampling time. Because every converter has a nonzero slew rate, the input signal may change its value before the conversion has been completed. (The aperture error of an A/D converter is a counterpart of the slew rate in the D/A converter.) The sample-and-hold circuit described in the following section is frequently used to overcome the aperture error.

Characteristics of Converters Review

1. List the errors that can usually be adjusted out of a converter.

2. Which is the most important characteristic in rating a D/A converter?

3. True or false? Large temperature coefficients are required for accurate conversion.

4. Define the term "monotonic."

5. Distinguish between absolute and relative accuracy in a converter.

6. How does slew rate affect the speed of conversion? In what way does settling time enter into the question?

7. Would a small aperture time be desirable in an A/D converter? Explain.

SAMPLE-AND-HOLD CIRCUITS

As noted in the discussion on A/D converter aperture time, a rapidly varying input signal cannot be accurately converted. In that case, we need a voltage memory device that can "freeze" the input level for some specified period. The *sample-and-hold (S/H) circuit* performs this function when it is used as a *front end* for a converter. As Fig. 10-13 shows, there are two intervals of interest. During the sample period, the S/H obtains an estimate of the incoming signal. This value is then held at a constant level until the clock indicates the next sample is to be taken.

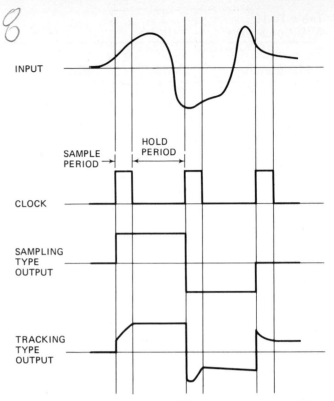

Figure 10-13. Sample-and-Hold.

As you can see, there are two techniques used in constructing a sample-and-hold circuit. The *sampling* type of S/H abruptly changes to the new output value, while the *tracking* type of S/H follows the signal to its new value.

There are many other uses for the S/H besides holding the signal steady for the A/D converter. The sample-and-hold can also be used to eliminate transients on the output of a D/A converter (Fig. 10-14a). Yet another use is to increase fan-out of the voltages generated by a D/A converter.

A common problem that occurs in process control is monitoring many sensors by a microcomputer. Figure 10-14c shows how many sensors can be sampled with a single A/D converter and one computer I/O port. With this configuration, a minimal amount of hardware is used to do the job. The computer program signals the analog multiplexer, which allows only one of the sensor inputs to pass through to the converter at any time. The processor accepts the digital input knowing that that value is to be associated with the sensor requested from the multiplexer.

Sample-and-Hold Characteristics

Just as with converters, performance of a S/H can be assessed by investigating its characteristics. Linearity is the most important measure for the S/H

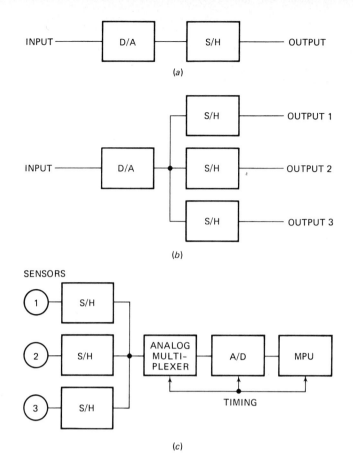

Figure 10-14. S/H Applications (*a*) Eliminate D/A Transients (*b*) Fan-Out D/A Converter (*c*) Multiplexing.

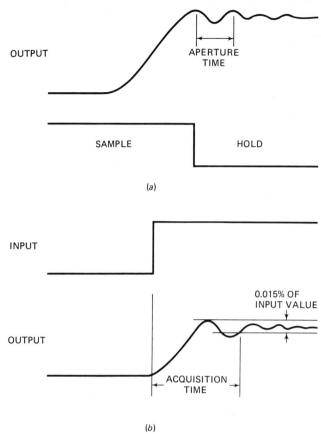

Figure 10-15. Aperture and Acquistion Time (*a*) Aperture Time (*b*) Acquisition Time.

and, like the converter, linearity of a S/H is the variation of its output from an ideal straight line. The *DC offset* is the difference in input and output voltages with the input terminal grounded. Just as with converters, the offset error can be removed by adjustment.

Slew rate for a S/H is measured similarly to that for a converter. The rate of change in voltage with time is a key element in the speed of sampling. Aperture time is, however, measured a little differently. As Fig. 10-15*a* shows, the aperture time is the duration required for switching from the sample mode to the hold mode. Another timing measure is the *acquisition time* shown in Fig. 10-15*b*. This measure specifies the time required to obtain a sample from the hold mode until the new output is within 0.01 percent of the input voltage.

Sample-and-Hold Circuits Review

1. Explain the purpose of the S/H circuit.

2. Distinguish between sampling and tracking S/H devices.

3. How can the S/H be used to remove transient voltages from a D/A converter output?

4. Describe how an analog multiplexer can be used with several S/H circuits to monitor many sensors.

5. How does the aperture time definition for a S/H differ from that of an A/D converter.

6. True or false? Short acquisition times are not demanded of most sample-and-hold circuits.

VOLTAGE-TO-FREQUENCY CONVERTERS

Converters that work on an entirely different principle can also be used for analog to digital conversion. The *voltage-to-frequency (V/F) converter* changes an input voltage to a frequency that is proportional to the input. This output frequency is TTL-compatible. A microprocessor program estimates the analog voltage by counting the pulses per unit time.

Because some time must elapse while a count is made, V/F conversion is a relatively slow process. The converter is, however, useful for many purposes in spite of this limitation. Integration of the input signal is readily achieved, as is summing out random noise (which is integrated to zero). With the V/F

Table 10-11
V/F Converters

Manufacturer	Mode	Full-Scale accuracy, %	Frequency range, KHz	Output drive, mA
Intech	A-8400	±15	100	2
Analog Device	AD537J	±7	150	20
Teledyne	9400	±10	100	10
Raytheon	RC4151	±10	100	3
Burr Brown	VFC32	±5	500	8

converter, the TTL output simplifies interfacing to the processor. Another characteristic that makes V/F converters highly effective is their accuracy. Table 10-11 lists some V/F converters available at low cost.

The components of a charge-balancing V/F converter are shown in Fig. 10-16. The input signal combined with the common input causes the integrator to generate a ramp waveform. When the negative-going ramp drops below the threshold voltage, the trigger fires. The trigger, in turn, causes the one-shot to produce a pulse that saturates the output transistor and also forces the integrator to output a positive-going ramp. When the ramp again reaches the input level, the cycle repeats.

The time necessary for the ramp voltage to complete one cycle depends on how much difference exists between the input signal voltage and trigger voltage. If these voltages are close in value, little time is required for the ramp to transit between them, and the output frequency is high. If those voltages are far apart, the duration is longer, making the output frequency lower.

A microcomputer circuit using a V/F converter is shown in Fig. 10-17. A pullup resistor is used to interface the V/F converter to the 7400 gate. The reset line (a 1-bit output line) from the processor synchronizes the V/F output with the counting program.

Voltage-to-Frequency Converters Review

1. List some advantages of V/F converters.

2. True or false? The V/F converter is well suited for circumstances calling for rapid conversion.

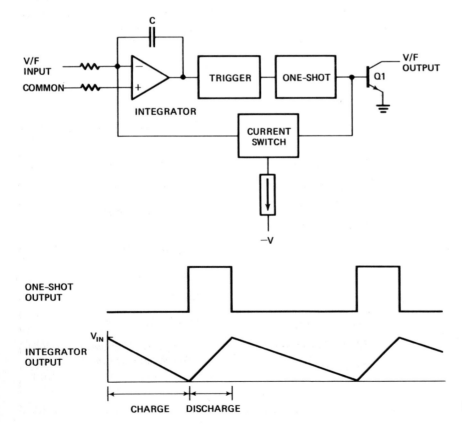

Figure 10-16. V/F Converter.

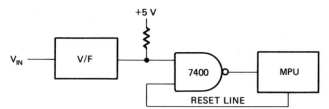

NOTE: The reset line is a control output from the microprocessor (not to be confused with the RESET signal used to initialize the 8080A).

Figure 10-17. Microcomputer with V/F Converter.

3. Explain the operation of the charge-balancing V/F converter.

CHAPTER SUMMARY

1. If the analog system is a simple one, the processor may be directly connected to it. Only in cases when the voltages and currents are compatible can this method be applied.

2. A D/A converter can be thought of as being constructed from a decision matrix, voltage reference, resistor network, and an op amp. Outputs of the converter are TTL or CMOS levels which readily accommodate microprocessor interfacing.

3. D/A converter outputs are coded as binary, BCD, 1's or 2's complement, and offset binary.

4. Multiplying D/A converters combine the analog input with a digital fraction to extend their range. Digital and analog two- and four-quadrant MDACs are available. Companding converters are a special class of multiplying converters.

5. By changing the program in the microcomputer, the same circuit can be used to generate many different waveforms.

6. Double buffering is needed to prevent glitches in D/A converters that have inputs wider than the data bus.

7. The families of A/D converters include counter, successive approximation, parallel, tracking, and integrating converters.

8. Errors in converters can be classed as adjustable and inherent. Errors such as offset and gain can be eliminated by adjustment. Inherent errors limit the accuracy of conversion. Most important of the inherent errors is linearity.

9. Sample-and-hold circuits are employed to eliminate aperture errors of A/D converters. These circuits are also useful for eliminating transients, providing fan-out, and sampling many sensors. Errors of S/H devices include DC offset, acquisition time, slew rate, aperture time, and linearity.

10. Voltage-to-frequency converters offer accurate, noise-free A/D conversion. These converters are easy to interface to a processor.

KEY TERMS AND CONCEPTS

Digital-to-analog (D/A) converter	Double buffer	Settling time
Resolution	Analog-to-digital (A/D) converter	Aperture error
Input coding	Linearity	Sample-and-hold (S/H) circuit
Offset binary	Drift	Sampling S/H
Multiplying D/A converters (MDACs)	Gain	Tracking S/H
Two- or four-quadrant devices	Offset	DC offset
Companding (compression/ expansion function) D/A converter	Monotonicity	Acquisition time
	Absolute accuracy	Voltage-to-frequency (V/F) converters
Waveform generation	Slew rate	

PROBLEMS

10-1 What is the resolution of a 10-bit D/A converter with an output range of 0 to 5 V?

10-2 If the binary input to the converter in Prob. 10-1 is $1001\ 0111_2$ and the reference voltage is 5 V, what is the output?

10-3 The output voltage of the MDAC in Fig. 10-3 is equal to the product of I_{out1} with R_f. What is the current into the inverting terminal of the op amp if the reference voltage is 10 V and the digital input is $11\ 1010_2$?

10-4 What is the output of the companding D/A converter discussed in this chapter if its range is -12 to $+12$ V and the input is $1010\ 0000_2$?

10-5 If the input to the companding D/A converter is increased from $0001\ 0110_2$ to $0010\ 0110_2$, how large an increment is produced in the output as a percent of full scale?

10-6 Change the square wave program to generate a wave with a period of $\frac{1}{2}$ s and an amplitude of one-quarter the full-scale output of the converter.

10-7 How many comparators are required in a 10-bit parallel A/D converter?

10-8 What is the input voltage to an integrating A/D converter with a reference time of 1 μs and reference voltage of 12 V if the measured time interval is 397 ns?

10-9 Find the D/A converter drift resulting from the temperature decreasing from 75 to 68°F. The manufacturer lists the following characteristics for the converter.

Temperature coefficient

Linearity	2.94
Offset	1.72
gain	1.03

10-10 Find the slew rate for the converter with a switching characteristic as shown in Fig. 10-18.

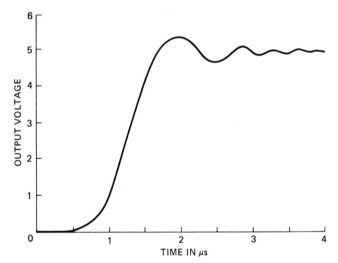

Figure 10-18. Problem 10-10.

PURPOSE: To investigate digital-to-analog interfacing.

PARTS LIST:

Item	Quantity
74LS02	1
74LS30	1
74LS100	1
Precision Monolithics DAC-03	1
10 kΩ potentiometer	1
62 kΩ resistor	1

IC DIAGRAMS:

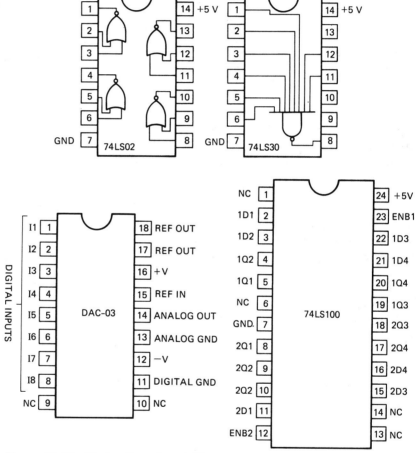

Figure 10-19. ICs for Experiment 10.

PROCEDURE:

STEP 1. Construct the circuit shown in Fig. 10-20. Note that you only use one of the four gates of the 74LS02.

STEP 2. Load the program below into the microcomputer. The device address for the D/A converter will be FF_{16}.

Label	Mnemonic	Operand	Address	Code	Comments
	MVI A	FF	1000	3E	All 1s → A
			1001	FF	
LOOP	OUT	FF	1002	D3	Output on port FF
			1003	FF	
	JMP	LOOP	1004	C3	Repeat
			1005	02	
			1006	10	

This program will constantly output a full-scale value to the D/A converter.

STEP 3. Execute the program and while it is running adjust the pot for a 5-V output on the D/A converter.

STEP 4. Now use the programs given in this chapter for generating a square wave and sawtooth wave to produce those waveforms. Observe the patterns on an oscilloscope. Relate the timing and voltage levels to specific instructions in each program.

STEP 5. Using the program in this chapter as a model, produce a square wave that has its output high half as long a time as it is low. Sketch the waveform you observe on an oscilloscope when you run the program.

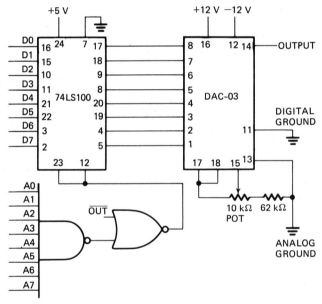

Figure 10-20. D/A Converter Circuit.

11

SUPPORT DEVICES

The range of tasks that a microcomputer can perform need not be limited to those supported by custom-built interface circuits. There are hundreds of supporting chips available to supplement the more basic types of input/output devices. These supporting chips provide special functions such as encrypting and decrypting the digital information or producing audio signals. Peripheral controllers are another large class of supporting ICs. The peripheral controllers simplify the job of interfacing the processor to a floppy disk drive, CRT terminal and keyboard, printers, and cassette recorders. There are even interfacing circuits for games that are driven by microprocessors.

CHAPTER OBJECTIVES

Upon completion of this chapter you should be able to:

1. Explain the principles of data encryption.
2. Describe the operation of an encryption/decryption support chip.
3. Discuss the generation of audio signals by means of a programmable sound generator.
4. Explain the operation of a floppy disk controller.
5. List the requirements for interfacing to the keyboard and CRT of a display terminal.

DATA ENCRYPTION UNIT

In many cases, the information being processed by the computer is quite sensitive. For example, banks may wish to prevent unauthorized people from gaining knowledge of electronic funds transfers or businesses may want to protect their trade secrets from competitors. Encryption of the data can mask the information content from those not authorized to have access to it, yet allow those with the key to readily read the data.

Data encryption is based on a reversible algorithm that can use one of a large number of possible mathematical transforms that scramble, or encrypt, the original bit sequence. By converting the data to an apparently random pattern, the algorithm makes reading it impossible without reversing the process. Decryption requires knowledge of that specific transform which encrypted the bit stream to convert the data back to the original message. The *key* identifies the specific transform to be used.

The *data encryption unit* (*DEU*) incorporates a product-cipher developed by IBM. The cypher is based on the work of Horst Feister. The cryptographic procedure requires 16 alternate rounds of key-controller substitutions and permutations of the original bits. The crypto process was accepted by the National Bureau of Standards in July 1977. A complete description of the *NBS algorithm* is given in the NBS algorithm publication, *Federal Information Processing Data Encryption Standard.*

Although a person has complete knowledge of the algorithm, the cipher cannot be broken without the *key* because there are such a large number of possible sequences. In some ways the cipher can be compared with a combination lock. Knowing how the lock works internally makes it no easier to open without the combination.

Encryption or decryption groups 8 bytes into 64-bit data blocks, then operates on the block as a unit. The key consists of 56 bits. The resulting transformed data is also a 64-bit block. Figure 11-1 illustrates the rounds of encryption. There are 16 rounds required in all. In the first, the right-most 32 bits of data are transformed by the kernel function as specified by a value derived from the key. The results are summed with the left-most 32 bits and a swap of the right and left half of the bits is made. In round 2 a similar process occurs, and so on until round 16. After the last round one more data switch is needed before the final output is developed. Decrypting uses exactly the same key and algorithm.

Although a microprocessor could implement the algorithm, the time required to do all the arithmetic would be excessive, resulting in quite slow encryption. A more efficient means of accomplishing the

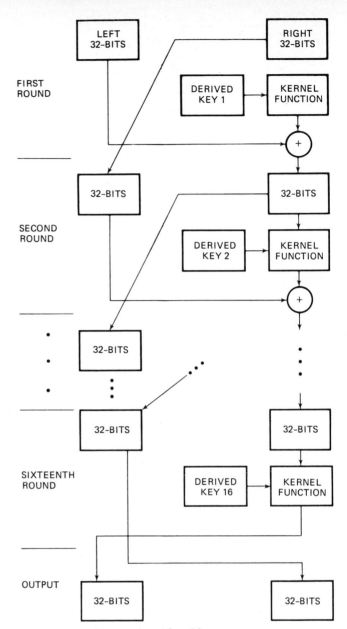

Figure 11-1. Encryption Algorithm.

encryption is to use an integrated circuit developed to implement the NBS standard.

One such device is the 8294 data encryption unit. Its pin diagram is shown in Fig. 11-2. The 40-pin DIP requires only a single +5-V power supply. A brief description of each signal is listed in Table 11-1.

Timing for the transforms is supplied by an external crystal or LC oscillator through the X1 and X2 inputs. The chip is enabled for reading or writing with the $\overline{CS}$ true input. The unit is forced to an idle condition whenever $\overline{RESET}$ becomes low. A high-frequency SYNC signal, with a frequency equal to the clock divided by 15, is supplied for use by external circuits, if desired.

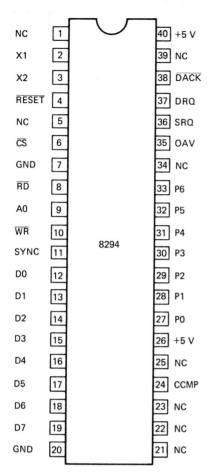

Figure 11-2. Data Encryption Unit.

The most efficient way of moving data through the device is by direct memory access, by means of the DMA request (DRQ), and acknowledge ($\overline{\text{DACK}}$) provided for use with the 8257 DMA controller, as explained earlier in Chap. 4.

When the data encryption unit is awaiting data or commands at the input buffer, the service request interrupt (SRQ) is issued to inform the processor.

When data or status information is available to be read by the microprocessor from the 8294 output buffer, an OAV interrupt occurs. After the encrypting or decrypting conversion on a 64-bit block has been completed, the encryption unit sends a CCMP interrupt. A 7-bit output port, which is completely independent from the crypto process, is provided in the 8294. The output pins P0 through P6 can be used in this fashion.

To program the 8294, one must follow the steps outlined in Fig. 11-3. First, the mode of operation command must be issued and interrupts enabled. Then the key is entered. Although the key is only 56 bits long, each 7-bit segment is sent with a parity bit, so sending 64 bits is required to change the key. Next the unit is told to run the data through the transforms. Upon completion, the data encryption unit interrupts the processor, which then reads the results and can transform another block. The process continues until the processor runs out of data.

A more detailed breakdown of the data encryption unit will better describe the steps in the program. There are several registers in the 8294 that can be read or written. The command input buffer receives all of the instructions. Each command is tabulated in Table 11-2. The command for setting the mode and enabling interrupts permits the user to individually control the output available, service request, and conversion completion interrupts. At any point these interrupts can be allowed or locked out. DMA transfers can be enabled or disabled in a like manner.

When a key is to be entered, it must be preceded by the appropriate command. The key is entered most significant byte first, with odd parity on each byte. Either the encrypt or decrypt mode is selected prior to beginning operation. With DMA transfers, the unit then can automatically obtain its data from memory once the processor initializes the DMA read and write channels.

Table 11-1
Data Encryption Unit Signals

Signal name	Purpose	Input or output
D0–D7	Data bus	Bidirectional
$\overline{\text{RD}}$	Read strobe	Input
$\overline{\text{WR}}$	Write strobe	Input
A0	Control/data select	Input
$\overline{\text{RESET}}$	Initialization	Input
X1, X2	Frequency reference	Input
SYNC	High frequency	Output
DRQ	DMA request	Input
$\overline{\text{DACK}}$	DMA acknowledge	Output
SRQ, OAV, CCMP	Interrupt requests	Output
P0–P6	Output port	Output
$\overline{\text{CS}}$	Chip select	Input

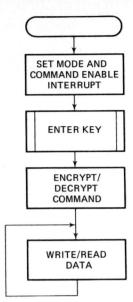

Figure 11-3. 8294 Programming.

Table 11-3
Accessing Registers

Register	Signal			
	$\overline{RD}$	$\overline{WR}$	$\overline{CS}$	A0
Data input buffer	1	0	0	0
Data output buffer	0	1	0	0
Command input buffer	1	0	0	1
Status output buffer	0	1	0	1

interrupt, and in conjunction with the key parity error (KPE) flag indicates the parity correctness of key entries.

Figure 11-4 shows the use of the various registers in entering a key. First, the program waits until the input buffer is full. Next, an enter key command is sent. Again, a delay is allowed while the command is read, then 1 byte of the key is entered. After all key bits are sent, the CF and KPE flags are checked to assure that the new key was received correctly.

The encryption and decryption flowchart is shown in Fig. 11-5. Here the sequence of sending the data bytes out is much the same as sending key bytes. After all bytes have been sent, a wait for either the completion flag or interrupt is incurred. Then the processed data is retrieved 1 byte at a time.

Reading of the registers to obtain data or status and writing of data or commands is controlled by four pins, as Table 11-3 shows. Use of these registers will be demonstrated by entering a key and encrypting/decrypting. The data input buffer is used for inserting a key, data for encryption or decryption, and the DMA block count. The output buffer is the register for results.

The status buffer consists of five flags that indicate the states within the chip. The output buffer full flag (OBF) is set when there is data to be read, reset when the buffer is empty. The input buffer full flag (IBF) is a 1 when writing is in progress and a 0 afterward. The mode is indicated by the DEC flag that is 0 for decryption and 1 for encryption. The completion flag (CF) is used to signal the end of an 8-byte block data transfer, can replace the CCMP

Data Encryption Review

1. Define the term "data encryption."

2. What are desirable characteristics of an encryption algorithm?

3. Explain how the data is transposed in 32-bit units on each round of the NBS encryption process.

Table 11-2
Data Encryption Unit Commands

Command	Function
40	Enter new key. Followed by 8-byte key (each key byte must have odd parity using LSB).
30	Encrypt data.
20	Decrypt data.
0X	Set mode, enable interrupts, or allow DMA transfers for value of X.

0	none		8	OAV
1	CCMP		9	OAV, CCMP
2	DMA		A	OAV, DMA
3	DMA, CCMP		B	OAV, DMA, CCMP
4	SRQ		C	OAV, SRQ
5	SRQ, CCMP		D	OAV, SRQ, CCMP
6	SRQ, DMA		E	OAV, SRQ, DMA
7	SRQ, DMA, CCMP		F	all

Command	Function
*Various	Write to output port. (MSB* of command must be a 1, remaining bits are output on P6–P0, respectively.)

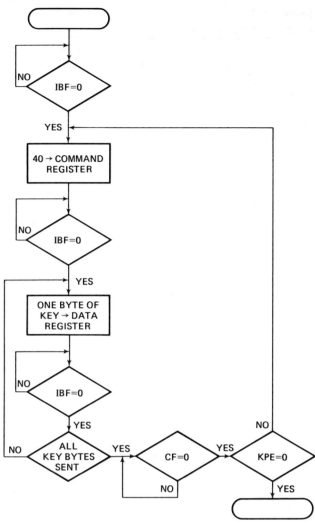

Figure 11-4. Entering a Key.

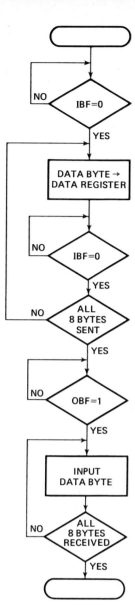

Figure 11-5. Encryption and Decryption Flowchart.

4. What is the purpose of the SRQ interrupt?

5. Describe the steps a program for the data encryption unit must execute.

6. How do the read, write, chip select, and A0 pins control the reading or writing of register data?

SOUND GENERATOR

A variety of sounds ranging from musical notes to cannon shots can be created with a *sound generator* IC. Although the processor could synthesize the sound with software and output the resulting waveform to a D/A converter, the sound effects would be limited to slowly changing values. The MPU would be tied up for long periods of time with sound production, so it may not have available time to control other events.

Instead, a sound generator such as the General Instruments Corporation AY-3-8912 could be substi-tuted to generate the sound. The sound generator is a versatile device that contains its own D/A converter and provides programmed control of the frequency and amplitude of three separate tones. The pin configuration is shown in Fig. 11-6.

The signals are grouped by function in Table 11-4. The bidirectional data bus passes data and address information between the processor and generator. The upper address bit permits the memory-mapped address space of the sound generator to be assigned to a 512-word memory area. An idle condition is established with the reset signal. The timing input requires a TTL-compatible oscillator as a reference to synthesize the tones. Control of the bus is exercised with three signals. The sound of each tone is picked up on channels A, B, or C. An independent bidirectional I/O port is also supplied by the chip.

A block diagram, shown in Fig. 11-7, illustrates how the audio signal is produced. The register array

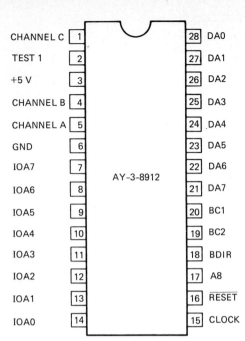

CHANNEL C — 1   28 — DA0
TEST 1 — 2   27 — DA1
+5 V — 3   26 — DA2
CHANNEL B — 4   25 — DA3
CHANNEL A — 5   24 — DA4
GND — 6   23 — DA5
IOA7 — 7   22 — DA6
IOA6 — 8   21 — DA7
IOA5 — 9   20 — BC1
IOA4 — 10   19 — BC2
IOA3 — 11   18 — BDIR
IOA2 — 12   17 — A8
IOA1 — 13   16 — RESET
IOA0 — 14   15 — CLOCK

AY-3-8912

Figure 11-6. Sound Generator.

Table 11-5
Register Usage

Register	Function
0 ⎫	Channel A
1 ⎬	Tone period
2 ⎫	Channel B
3 ⎬	Tone period
4 ⎫	Channel C
5 ⎬	Tone period
6	Noise period
7	Enable
8	Channel A amplifier
9	Channel B amplifier
10	Channel C amplifier
11 ⎫	
12 ⎬	Envelope period
13	Envelope shape
14	I/O port buffer
15	Not used

controls the analog circuitry as directed by the processor. The array contains 15 control registers plus the I/O port buffer. These registers are memory-mapped so the processor can change the status of any channel by writing in them or inspect the status by reading. The lower 4 bits of data and address bus select one of the registers while the 5 high-order bits act as a chip selection address.

The function of each register is listed in Table 11-5. The first six registers are used in pairs to specify each channel's *tone period*. (Specifying the period is equivalent to specifying frequency.) Register 6 controls the *noise period* and register 7 enables output. Each of the three amplifiers is controlled by registers 8 through 10. The *envelope* period and shape depend on the next three registers. The last register is a buffer for the I/O port.

The tone generators produce a square wave with a frequency of the tone to be produced by that channel. The noise generator produces a frequency-modulated, pseudorandom pulse width square wave which is combined with the tone outputs in each of the mixers. The amplitude control varies the amplitude pattern of the D/A converter.

The frequency of the tone generator is dependent on the oscillator clock frequency input. The oscillator frequency is divided by 16, then counted down by the 12-bit value formed from the 8 bits of the lower register and the lower 4 bits of the upper register for that channel—for instance, registers 0 and 1 for channel A. The tone frequency is therefore

$$f_{tone} = \frac{f_{clock}}{(16)(TP)} \qquad (11\text{-}1)$$

where TP = 12 bits from the tone period registers (in decimal).

As an example, let the 12-bit value in R0 and R1 be 1250_{10} and the clock frequency be 2 MHz:

$$f_{tone} = \frac{2 \times 10^6}{16\,(1250)} = 100 \text{ Hz}$$

Table 11-4
Sound Generator Signals

Signal	Purpose	Input or Output
DA0–DA7	Data and address bus	Bidirectional
A8	Upper address bit	Input
RESET	Power-on initialization	Input
CLOCK	Timing reference	Input
BDIR, BC1, BC2	Bus control	Input
Analog channels A, B, C	Sound signal	Output
IOA0–IOA7	I/O port	Bidirectional
TEST 1, 2	Not used	

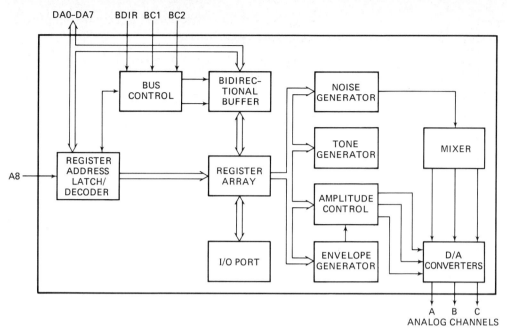

Figure 11-7. Sound Generator Block Diagram.

The noise generator frequency also depends on the input oscillator. The equation for that frequency is

$$f_{\text{noise}} = \frac{f_{\text{clock}}}{16\,(NP)} \qquad (11\text{-}2)$$

where NP = lower 5 bits of register 6 (in decimal).

Suppose the value in register 6 is $1A_{16}$. What is the noise frequency? Converting the contents of R6 to decimal gives 26_{10}, so

$$f_{\text{noise}} = \frac{2 \times 10^6}{16\,(26)} = 4.8\text{ kHz}$$

Mixer control is derived from R7, which also enables or disables the I/O port. A zero in any control bit position enables that function.

Bit number	7	6	5	4	3	2	1	0
	$\cdots$		C	B	A	C	B	A

I/O port enable   Noise enable   Tone enable

The amplitude of the D/A converters (controlled by R8, R9 or R10 respectively) may be either fixed or variable. If the microprocessor controls the amplitude directly, it must be fixed. The variable amplitude allows the envelope generator to control the value. If bit 4 of the channel amplitude is zero, fixed amplitude is used. The lower 4 bits specify the level when fixed amplitude is specified. Maximum amplitude is represented by F_{16}, half-amplitude by 7, one-quarter by 3, and so on.

Use of envelope control allows more complex sound patterns to be produced. The envelope frequency signifies how many times per second the envelope pattern will repeat:

$$f_{\text{env}} = \frac{f_{\text{clock}}}{256\,(TE)} \qquad (11\text{-}3)$$

where TE = the 16 bits in R11 and R12 (R12 is the most significant half) in decimal. With the same clock frequency as our previous examples, the envelope frequency for a TE value of $15DC_{16}$ is

$$f_{\text{env}} = \frac{2 \times 10^6}{256\,(5596)} = 1.4\text{ Hz}$$

The shape of the envelope is specified by 4 bits in R13, bit 0 is the hold parameter, bit 1 alternate, bit 2 attack, and bit 3 continue. Figure 11-8 shows the resulting envelopes for all values of these 4 bits.

A complete audio interface for the sound generator is shown in Fig. 11-9. From the figure, you can see how simple this interface is. In this circuit the outputs of all three channels are summed, but they could have been used individually. In the latter situation, three separate speaker circuits would be required.

A program that generates a siren which alternates between two frequencies is given in Table 11-6. The first frequency has a period of 2.27 ms, the second a period of 5.346 ms. Only channel A is used and the D/A converter outputs are at maximum amplitude. A subroutine (not supplied) which delays for 350 ms is called by this program. If we want to stop the output, we merely set R8 to 0. (Note that

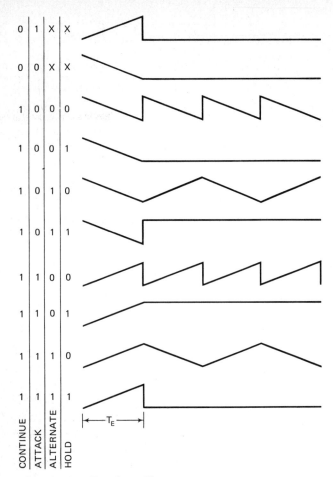

CONTINUE	ATTACK	ALTERNATE	HOLD
0	1	X	X
0	0	X	X
1	0	0	0
1	0	0	1
1	0	1	0
1	0	1	1
1	1	0	0
1	1	0	1
1	1	1	0
1	1	1	1

Figure 11-8. Envelope Shapes.

memory-mapped I/O is used. Before this program is executed, the HL register pair must be set to the address of R0.)

Sound Generator Review

1. True or false? A separate I/O port is supplied by the sound generator.

2. How is the frequency of the tone to be generated specified?

3. What is the purpose of register 6?

4. Explain the method used to vary the amplitude of the D/A converter.

5. Why is an envelope generator used with this device?

FLOPPY DISK CONTROLLER

Floppy disks are one of the most common peripherals used to load and store microcomputer programs, as was explained in Chap. 3. *Floppy disk controller* devices can interface from one to four drives to the microprocessors. The chips can also unload many error detection and correction tasks from the processor. Examples of these devices include the Motorola 6843 FDC, Rockwell 10936 FDC, and Intel 8271. We will select the Intel device to illustrate the important concepts of floppy disk control.

The Intel 8271 can read, write, or scan the disk for a specified bit pattern. The controller is packaged as a 40-pin DIP and requires a +5-V supply. A 2- or 4-MHz square wave clock input is necessary for timing.

A block diagram of the controller is shown in Fig. 11-10. The data buffer supports the 8-bit data bus input and output. A DMA controller is supplied to fetch or store data from memory. The disk interface is composed of a serial controller and a drive controller. A description of all signals is provided by Table 11-7.

Many of the signals are the same as we have seen on other microprocessor support ICs. In particular, the data bus, reset, chip select, interrupt request, read, write, and DMA lines perform the usual functions. The microprocessor interface has five registers used with A0, A1, $\overline{RD}$, and $\overline{WR}$.

The registers are selected by the settings of A0 and A1. The operation code for the command to be performed and the number of the drive to be used are placed in the command register. Up to five amplifying parameters for a command can be used by sending them to the parameter register. The results register returns the outcome of the last command such as successful or unsuccessful completion.

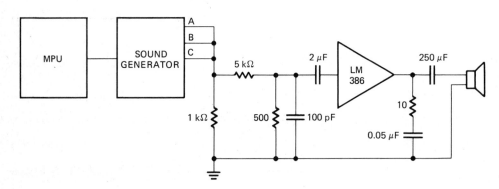

Figure 11-9. Audio Interface.

Table 11-6
Siren Program

Label	Mnemonic	Operand	Comment
	MVI A	FE	Channel A period 1
	MOV M, A		Store in R0
	INX H		Increment address to R1
	MVI A	0	Channel A period 1
	MOV M, A		Clear R1
	MVI B	0	} Increment address to R7
	MVI C	6	
	DAD B		
	MVI A	3E	Only channel A
	MOV M, A		Store in R7
	INX H		Increment address
	MVI A	F	Maximum amplitude
	MOV M, A		Store in R8
	CALL	DELAY	Wait 350 ms
	LHLD	R0ADDRL	Put R0 address in HL
	MVI A	56	Channel A period 2
	MOV M, A		Store in R0
	MVI A	1	Channel A period 2
	MOV M, A		Store in R1
R0ADDRL			} Address of R0
R0ADDRH			

Status of the controller can be read from the status register. Such conditions as register full or empty, requests for DMA or interrupts, and busy state can be determined from the contents of that register.

Transfer of data to the disk is usually by DMA (though not required by the 8271) because of the data rate. One byte can be sent or received in 32 μs, so an entire block of 128, 256, or 512 bytes can be exchanged rapidly. The use of DMA request and acknowledge signals is the same as was explained in Chap. 4.

Drive commands rely on clock pulses to reconstruct input data. All data is written between clock pulses. Figure 11-11a is a timing diagram of the combined signal. If the data bit is a 0, there will be a full-bit time between high pulses. However, if data is a 1, there is only a half-bit time from one high pulse to the next. This sequence makes

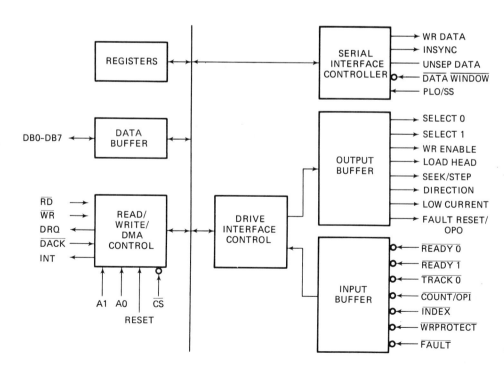

Figure 11-10. Floppy Disk Controller Block Diagram.

Table 11-7
Floppy Disk Controller Signals

Name	Function	Direction
DB0–DB7	Three-state data bus	Bidirectional
RESET	Select idle state	Input
$\overline{CS}$	Chip select	Input
A0–A1	Interface register select	Input
INT	Service request interrupt	Output
DRQ	DMA request	Output
$\overline{DACK}$	DMA acknowledge	Input
$\overline{WR}$	Write command	Input
$\overline{RD}$	Read command	Input
WR DATA	Write disk data	Output
INSYNC	Input data sync has been achieved	Output
UNSEP DATA	Unseparated data (the combined clock and data input)	Input
$\overline{DATA\ WINDOW}$	Data window established	Input
PLO/SS	Data separator specifier	Input
SELECT 0, SELECT 1	Drive select	Output
WR ENABLE	Write enable	Output
LOAD HEAD	Signal drive to press the head against the disk	Output
SEEK/STEP	Seek control	Output
DIRECTION	Seek direction (high means inward, low means outward)	Output
LOW CURRENT	Track 43 or higher selected	Output
FAULT RESET/OPO	Error condition reset	Output
$\overline{READY\ 0}$, READY 1	Specified drive ready	Input
$\overline{TRACK\ 0}$	Head is positioned over track 00	Input
$\overline{COUNT}$/OPI	Stepping pulse	Input
$\overline{INDEX}$	Disk index position	Input
WR PROTECT	Disk is write protected	Input
FAULT	Unsafe condition	Input

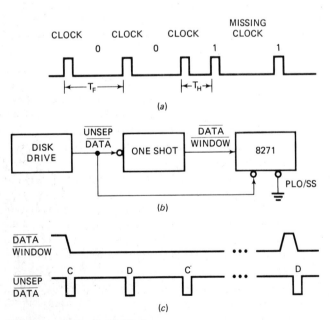

Figure 11-11. Data Timing.

it possible to detect missing clock pulses, as the figure shows.

The data window signal is separated from the data stream using a circuit such as that shown in Fig. 11-11b. The window is sampled on the leading edge of unseparated data to detect whether the delay since the previous pulse was a half- or full-bit time. As the block is read, the controller automatically establishes sync using the sync field in the identification or data portion of the block. It also computes and verifies the ID information and CRC for both identification and data fields.

In writing data, the controller builds the composite (unseparated) data block by interleaving clock pulses

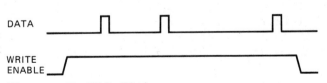

Figure 11-12. Write Timing.

with data bits. Computation of the identification and CRC fields are done for each block, and these codes are appended to the data field. Figure 11-12 shows a timing diagram for writing. When WR ENABLE is high, the electronics in the drive will pass the data stream to the write head. When that signal is low, the head reads the magnetically recorded information.

Other control functions that must be performed include generation of the head step rate, load time, setting time delay, unload delay, and monitoring of the drive. To initialize the drive, the controller pulses the seek/step high and the direction line for the desired movement (high is inward). The head then steps in or out one track for each seek/step pulse. Alternatively, the count line can supply the pulses and the seek/step line be held high until the head is in position. When the head reaches its maximum outward limit (track 00) the track 0 line becomes true.

Head seek setting time, that is, the time from the last step until reading or writing is possible, can be programmed to be from 0 to 255 ms for 8-in drives and to 510 ms for minidrives. Head load settling time, when the head is placed in contact with the disk, can also be programmed for 0 to 60 ms for large disks, and for 0 to 120 ms for minis.

The drive being selected is specified by the select 0 and select 1 lines. When recording on the inner tracks (track numbers higher than 43), the low-current pin output is active to compensate for the lower velocity of disk surface (as compared with the outer tracks).

Every disk has a write protect notch. When the floppy disk is write protected, the WR PROTECT signal becomes true, preventing the controller from writing. An interrupt is also sent to the processor to inform it of the incorrect situation. Another signal that detects problems in writing is the write fault, which indicates that data integrity is questionable. The processor is also interrupted for this condition, which is reset with the write fault reset signal.

Each drive signals its readiness for operation with the READY 0 and READY 1 lines. The drive selected must be ready before data is read or written. If not, a processor interrupt results and the operation terminates. One other quite useful service provided by the controller is alternate track recording. If one of the tracks is found to be bad, the controller will automatically record on tracks 75 or 76. Whenever the processor requests to input that data, the correct alternate track will be read.

Operating the disk drives requires that a command be issued, then the operation is carried out. Last, the results must be checked for proper conditions. To send a command, the status register is checked to ensure that the command busy bit is not set. The

DMA channel is initiated and a write op code transmitted to the command register followed by the necessary parameter. (Between each parameter write, the status register is examined and a wait incurred as long as the parameter full bit is set.)

The operation is carried out under DMA, so the processor need not involve itself with the data transfer. After the operation, the command byte is examined for a successful result. If not successful, the status and result registers allow the program to interpret the type of error that occurred. A failure could be caused by a clock error, DMA late timing, drive not ready, or attempting to write on a protected disk.

Floppy Disk Controller Review

1. Describe how the number of a floppy disk drive to be read is specified.

2. Explain the format for unseparated data.

3. How does the controller detect a missing clock pulse?

4. How is the head moved to the correct track?

5. What is an alternate track?

KEYBOARD CONTROLLER

The keyboard on a display terminal is in actuality a matrix of single-throw, normally open keys. Each key is a switch across a node in the matrix which shorts a horizontal to a vertical line when depressed. By scanning the matrix, one can detect which node is shorted. *Keyboard controllers* provide the circuitry to find key closures and also to prevent erroneous or duplicate selections.

Examples of keyboard interface chips are the National 8244, Intel 8278, and TI TMS1976. The 8278 will serve as the device for our discussion. This circuit can scan a 128-key contact or capacitive-coupled keyboard arranged in 16 columns by 8 rows. The IC also supports a multiple-digit LED display.

The 8278 block diagram is shown in Fig. 11-13. The microprocessor interface is practically identical to that of other controllers. The scan counter, key detect logic, and key FIFO (first in, first out buffer) detect the key which is closed and save the position until it can be passed to the processor. The interface signals are listed in Table 11-8.

The scan counter steps through the column scan sequence. The output values of M3 through M6 designate which column is to be scanned. This output is converted to one of 16 lines using a 4-to-16 decoder, such as the 74154, as shown in Fig. 11-14.

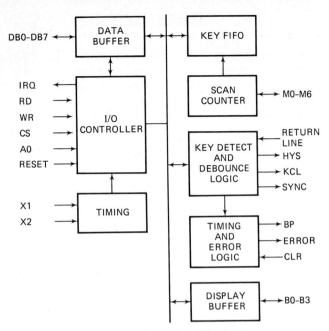

Figure 11-13. Keyboard Interface Block Diagram.

(This figure shows a contact keyboard configuration.) The row return lines are multiplexed on M0 through M2. The return line input indicates whether the key currently being scanned is closed.

If a capacitive-coupled keyboard is used, an analog multiplexer replaces the digital one, and the KCL signal enables the detector before each key is scanned. Debouncing of the keys is accomplished

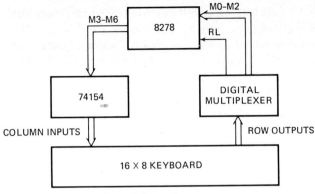

Figure 11-14. Keyboard Scanning.

by scanning twice to assure the key has remained down for a full cycle before passing the data to the processor. If two or more keys are pressed at once, a multiple-key error is detected and the data not accepted. The data format returned to the processor identifies keys by row and column intersections.

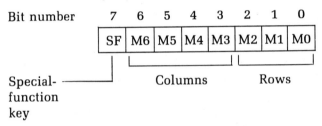

The FIFO buffer is 8 bytes long, allowing a series of keys to be depressed in succession without losing

Table 11-8
8278 Keyboard Interface Signals

Signal	Purpose	Direction
DB0–DB7	Three-state data bus	Bidirectional
IRQ	Interrupt request	Output
$\overline{\text{RD}}$	Read strobe	Input
$\overline{\text{WR}}$	Write strobe	Input
$\overline{\text{CS}}$	Chip select	Input
A0	Control or data indicator	Input
$\overline{\text{RESET}}$	Idle signal	Input
X1, X2	Clock	Input
M0–M6	Matrix scan	Output
RETURN LINE	Input from multiplexer indicating key closure	Input
$\overline{\text{HYS}}$	Hysteresis signal to analog detector (used with capacitive keyboard)	Output
KCL	Key clock to analog detector	Output
SYNC	High frequency signal used in capacitive key scan	Output
B0–B3	Binary coded data for seven-segment display	Output
BP	Tone enable	Output
ERROR	Multiple-key closure	Input
CLR	Clear error condition	Input

the information. This feature is called *rollover*. The FIFO can be tested to find out if it is full, empty, or has overrun. Status of the buffers (input for keyboard, output for LED display) can be checked as well.

Keyboard Controller Review

1. Explain the purpose of the key FIFO of the keyboard controller.

2. How is a key closure detected?

3. Discuss the method of key debouncing used by the controller.

4. What happens if three keys are pressed at once on the keyboard?

CRT CONTROLLER

A general-purpose interface to a CRT terminal can greatly simplify the output of character information from the microprocessor. Such a *CRT controller* is used with raster scan displays, which were described in Chap. 3. The controller refreshes the display by buffering information from the computer memory. As the character is buffered out, the controller keeps track of where it is writing on the screen. Examples of such controllers are the National 8350, Motorola 6845 CRTC, and Intel 8275. We will investigate the latter controller.

The 8275 is composed of a DMA controller and data buffer for the computer interface together with timing and control logic for the video terminal. The processor interface is a conventional DMA input/output controller. Figure 11-15 is a block diagram of the 8275. The signals are listed in Table 11-9.

Each display character is retrieved from memory on a row-by-row basis. The character counter determines the number of characters to be written on a row, while the line counter maintains the number of horizontal lines (sweeps) in a row. See Fig. 11-16 for an example. The number of rows that make up the entire screen is programmed using the row counter.

The display format, as shown in Fig. 11-17, is variable and under program control. The number of characters can range from 1 to 80 in a row, and up to 64 rows can be displayed on the screen. As Fig. 11-16 indicated, the line counter increments as each line of the character is sent to the screen. The 8275 controller can use from 1 to 16 lines to draw a character, and underlining is provided. The line counter simply cycles through its count repeatedly for each character. The line counter increments during the horizontal retrace after the character

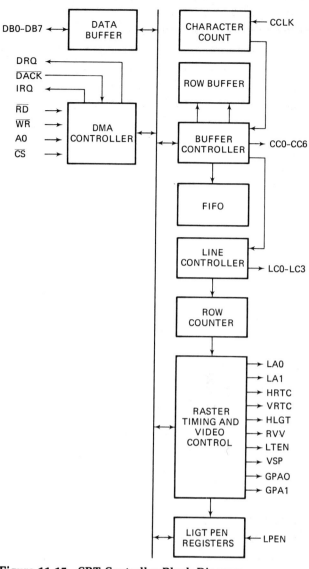

Figure 11-15. CRT Controller Block Diagram.

counter has reached the maximum value for the number of characters in a row. A timing diagram is shown in Fig. 11-18. When the retrace signal goes high, the line counter takes on its next value.

The CRT controller requires a character generator and dot timing interface to produce the video, sync, and intensity voltages for the CRT. Figure 11-19 shows a typical system. The line counter and character codes select the position on the screen and type of character that the character generator supplies. The dot timing logic supplies a clock so all of the devices can stay synchronized with the scan position on the terminal screen.

CRT Controller Review

1. How is the number of characters per row on the CRT screen specified?

Table 11-9
8275 CRT Controller Signals

Signal	Purpose
DB0–DB7	Three-state data bus
DRQ, $\overline{\text{DACK}}$	DMA control signals
IRQ	Interrupt request
$\overline{\text{RD}}$, $\overline{\text{WR}}$	Read/write strobes
A0	Select command registers or parameter registers
$\overline{\text{CS}}$	Chip select
CCLK	Character clock from the dot timing
CC0–CC6	Character codes
LC0–LC3	Line count
LA0–LA1	Line attribute codes
HRTC	Horizontal retrace interval
VRTC	Vertical retrace interval
HLGT	Highlight (to intensify the display at the current position)
RVV	Reverse video (black characters on a white background)
LTEN	Light enable (to underline)
VSP	Video suppression (blank video signal)
GPA0–GPA1	General-purpose attribute codes
LPEN	Light pen input

2. Distinguish between the line counter and row counter.

3. True or false? Up to 64 characters can be displayed on each of the 80 rows of the terminal by the CRT controller.

4. Explain how a character is drawn line by line.

CHAPTER SUMMARY

1. Data encryption is useful in preventing disclosure of sensitive material. Encryption is based on a reversible transform of the bit sequence. To perform the proper transform, one must

Figure 11-16. 10-Line Character.

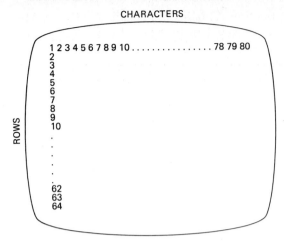

Figure 11-17. CRT Format.

know the key. Otherwise the cipher cannot be decrypted.

2. The data encryption unit is an implementation of the NBS encryption algorithm. The mathematical processes of encryption and decryption are automatically performed by this circuit.

3. Sound generators can produce a variety of audio signals under program control. The generator incorporates frequency and noise generators, envelope generators and shapers, and D/A converters.

4. The floppy disk controller can direct one of several drives to read or write on the rotating magnetic surface. Important disk operations include separating data from clocking signals, stepping the head to the correct track, loading the head against the surface, calculating identification and CRC data, and maintaining correct time relationships.

5. A keyboard controller scans the key matrix to find a closure. If multiple keys are depressed, an error condition exists, and the controller does not accept the input. The controller also debounces the keys.

6. A CRT terminal interface can be constructed more easily by use of an interface chip. The CRT controller has logic to clock out the proper

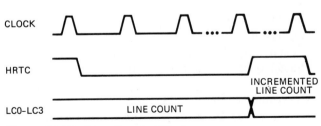

Figure 11-18. Line Counter Timing.

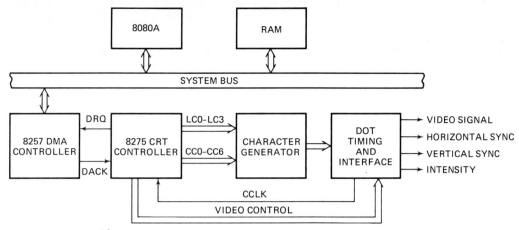

Figure 11-19. CRT System.

dot pattern for each line of characters. The controller will maintain a count of the proper number of characters in one row and the total number of rows on the screen. Signals required to time the trace on the screen are provided by the controller as well.

KEY TERMS AND CONCEPTS

Data encryption unit (DEU)	NBS algorithm	Key
Sound generator	Tone period	Noise period
Envelope	Floppy disk controller	Keyboard controllers
CRT controller		

PROBLEMS

11-1 What values would be required in the tone period registers of channel B of the sound generator to produce an audio frequency of 30.5 Hz? Of 125 kHz? (Let the clock frequency be 2 MHz.)

11-2 Given the key below, calculate the proper parity for each byte for entry into the data encryption unit.

Byte	Value$_{16}$
1	E8
2	12
3	76
4	FC
5	CC
6	BA
7	04
8	56

11-3 If the value in R6 of the sound generator is $0D_{16}$, what is the period of the noise generator? (Remember that the period is the reciprocal of the frequency.) Clock frequency is 2 MHz.

11-4 If the sound generator envelope frequency is to be 15 Hz, what values are in R13 and R14? Clock frequency is 2 MHz.

11-5 What program change is necessary to lengthen the period of the first tone in the siren program to 400 ms?

11-6 In checking the unseparated data for the first 4 bits of input, the floppy disk controller notes the following sequence of bit times. Following the true $\overline{\text{DATAWINDOW}}$ signal:

Full-bit time
Full-bit time
Half-bit time
Full-bit time
Full-bit time
Half-bit time

Key	Row	Column
A	3	1
B	4	6
C	4	4
X	4	3
Y	2	7
Z	4	2

What are the values for the first 4 bits? Were any clock pulses missing? If so, which one(s)?

11-7 If the option of pulsing the seek/step signal is used to move the head from track 07 to track 39, how many pulses of the signal are required?

11-8 A portion of the keyboard matrix row and column assignments is listed above. Which key is indicated when M0 through M6 is 24_{16}?

11-9 The sound generator is to produce a 2-kHz tone on channel B using a noise frequency of 5-kHz. What values are to be placed in the registers if the D/A amplitude is to be 50 percent of maximum?

11-10 Assume that instead of fixed D/A amplitude, we want the tone produced in Prob. 11-9 to have the last envelope shape shown in Fig. 11-8. What values must be placed in the registers?

EXPERIMENT 10

PURPOSE: To investigate keyboard scanning.

PARTS LIST:

Item	Quantity
Keyboard	1
Schematic for keyboard	1

PROCEDURE:

STEP 1. From the schematic of the keyboard, explain its row and column matrix arrangement.

STEP 2. Write a program to scan the keyboard to detect which key is pressed. You can either store the key identity in memory, or display it at a terminal.

STEP 3. Change your program to detect multiple-key errors. (Until only a single key is pressed no input is to be accepted.) Why is this program modification a good idea?

12
TROUBLESHOOTING

Skills in troubleshooting microcomputer interfaces will become one of your most important assets as you continue to work in the electronics field. A variety of new test equipment has been developed to assist you in isolating circuit failures, but the standard voltmeter and oscilloscope that you have been using for years will continue to be important aids in servicing microcomputers. Diagnostic programs are another significant type of problem identification support. More than any of these tools, however, your judgment and experience will become the prime means you should rely on in repairing these circuits. Often a few minutes spent thinking logically about the symptoms can find the problem hours earlier than would be possible if you immediately start connecting test equipment and pulling ICs from their sockets.

CHAPTER OBJECTIVES

Upon completion of this chapter, you should be able to:

1. List the steps in logically troubleshooting a microcomputer.
2. Explain how a pulser can be used to inject signals into microprocessor circuits.
3. Describe the use of a logic probe in analyzing digital circuitry.
4. Discuss the modes of operation for logic analyzers and specify when each mode should be used.
5. Explain how in-circuit emulators can be used for fault isolation.
6. Give examples of software diagnostic programs and describe their advantages and disadvantages.

AN APPROACH TO MICROCOMPUTER TROUBLESHOOTING

When confronted with the problem of tracking down a fault in a microcomputer, a technician may well feel bewildered. Just think of how many things can go wrong! Luckily the types of errors can be classified to let you proceed in an orderly fashion to isolate the general problem to a specific chip.

Some of the test equipment you will use with a microcomputer is the same as that required in general electronics troubleshooting. The oscilloscope and voltmeter can be as helpful here as in any other electronics equipment.

Before you pull out the scope and meter, however, consider an even better tool first—your eyes. Table 12-1 lists the problems you are likely to encounter by increasing order of difficulty. *Always* begin at the top of the table. You may not even need test equipment. As you can see, no equipment is needed until halfway down the list, if you look carefully instead.

If the circuit board looks OK, compare the chip placement to a logic diagram. Should this be a wire-wrapped breadboard for a prototype, check the wiring for continuity against the wire list and also be sure that the power and ground buses are properly isolated. Either a voltmeter or a buzzer (in series with a battery) can be used for these tests. Also verify that the power supply outputs are correct.

Logic probes and pulsers will readily detect stuck or floating lines. These small testers are also a good way to find shorts. If you have gotten this far and still have not found the problem, heavy artillery is called for. An oscilloscope may be of help in tracking down noisy lines, an incorrect clock period, or glitches. More than likely a logic analyzer or in-circuit emulator may be needed, especially if the computer being tested is a prototype.

Do not forget that the computer can be programmed to isolate faults also, that is, provided it is operating at least in a partial fashion. If the front panel of the computer allows you to inspect register and memory contents, use it also as a diagnostic aid.

Approach to Microcomputer Troubleshooting Review

1. What is the first step in troubleshooting any microprocessor-based equipment?

2. List the most common, and easiest to find, microcomputer faults.

3. How would you test the continuity of a prototype breadboard?

4. Explain a method for identifying lines that are stuck in a high state.

5. What faults are best found with an oscilloscope?

PULSERS

The *pulser* is a hand-held signal generator with a metal tip that is to be touched to the pin of an IC. Usually about 5 in (12.5 cm) long and weighing a few ounces, the pulser can generate a signal of either positive or negative polarity. The pulser comes with alligator clips to connect to the power supply, as shown in Fig. 12-1. Any voltage in the region of +4 to +18 V is suitable, provided only that it match V_{cc} of the chip.

To operate the pulser, simply touch the tip to the pin, then press the button (for less than 1 s). A pulse will be produced at the tip. If the button is held down continuously, a series of pulses at about 100 Hz is produced. The LED on the case flashes each time a pulse is generated. For TTL circuits, pulse width is in the 1- to 2-μs range, and it is lengthened to 10 μs in the CMOS mode.

As small as it is, the pulser has considerable drive. It can fan out to at least 50 TTL loads. Furthermore, a pulser can withstand overvoltages, pulse into short circuits, and even let you reverse the polarity on the power-supply inputs by mistake—all without damage. The three-state output is isolated from the circuit by better than 250 kΩ.

Table 12-1
Troubleshooting Guide

Level	What to look for
Easy	Not plugged in
	IC in socket backwards
	Wrong type of IC in socket
	Lead on IC bent underneath or broken off
Moderate	Solder bridge
	Cold solder joint
	Broken trace
	Power supply voltage out of tolerance
	Stuck line (high or low)
	Floating line
Difficult	Noisy switch
	Bad connector
	Bad socket
	Timing glitch
	Bus conflict (especially data bus)
	Loading
	Noise

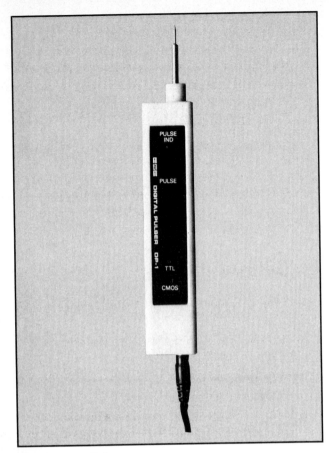

Figure 12-1. Pulser.

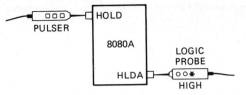

Figure 12-2. Testing the HOLD input to the 8080A.

Its operation is based on a comparator circuit. The polarity-sensing circuit selects either sink or source pulses which will activate the test point (cause it to change state). A comparator matches the voltage at the point to the power-supply voltage. If the test point is higher, the output of the pulser goes low. Otherwise a positive going pulse is produced. After each pulse has been sent out, another comparison is made. If the test point changed state, the next pulse will have reversed polarity. In this way a continuous trigger can be produced.

In use, the power-supply cable acts as the return path for the output pulse as well as providing operating voltage. Always clip the power leads close to the test point to prevent ground loops. (Ground loops can cause false triggering of the circuit being tested.) Some pulsers come with an auxiliary ground clip to be used next to the tip to prevent such problems. If the auxiliary clip is used, the pulser is not to be grounded at the power supply.

Fig. 12-2 shows an example of the pulser in use. It triggers the HOLD input of the 8080A. The test for a response (HLDA) uses a logic probe, which is described in the next section. Because the pulser has such a high fan-out, it will override any inputs to the HOLD input—regardless of the states of downstream logic. This handy feature of the pulser

makes it unnecessary to disconnect other signals being fed to the pin being pulsed.

The pulser can also be used to replace the system clock in single-phase circuits. (Because the 8080A requires two-phase clock, it cannot be tested in this way.) By clocking the circuit, you can step the logic through an entire cycle of its states. Logic probes can then sample the outputs at several key test points.

Pulsers Review

1. What voltage range can the pulser be used with?

2. What would happen if you reversed the polarity of the power-supply leads to a pulser?

3. Distinguish between the effects of pressing the pulser button for less than a second and holding it down continuously.

4. How can the pulser trigger a circuit even though downstream gates are holding the input in the low state?

LOGIC PROBES

Logic probes are capable of detecting and storing pulses from digital circuits. The pulse is latched by a flip-flop which controls the display of three LEDs, as Fig. 12-3 shows. A transition from negative to positive causes the high LED to light, while a change in the opposite direction lights the low LED. High-frequency signals blink the pulse LED.

Just as with the pulser, the logic probe has alligator clips to attach to the power supply. The power leads should be connected as close as possible to the circuit under test. The probe is set to either the TTL level, which defines a high-signal level as greater than 2.25 V and a low as less than 0.8 V, or MOS level, for which a high is a level greater than 70 percent of the power-supply voltage and a low is less than 30 percent of that voltage. Levels in the region in between are not defined.

To use the probe, choose the level appropriate for the IC being tested, then touch the output pin. In the pulse mode, the LEDs will light on each pulse. For short pulses, switch to the memory mode, in which the latch can catch pulses as narrow as 100

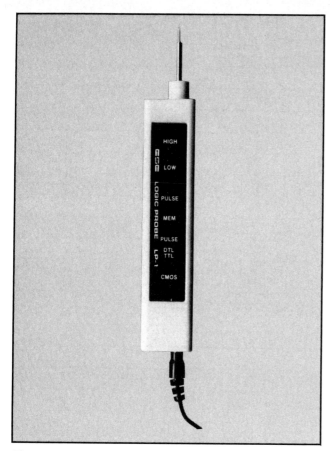

Figure 12-3. Logic Probe.

ns. When using the memory mode, first contact the pin, then switch the memory on. If the probe is not in contact when the memory is switched on, the floating tip will trigger an erroneous indication when brought into contact.

The LEDs can give more information than just the level of the signal, as shown in Table 12-2. Of course, a steady light on the high or low LED means that the signal is not changing. If all LEDs are off, the tip is in contact with an open circuit. Pulse trains cause the high and low LEDs to light with the pulse LED blinking, if the frequency is less than 100 Hz. The duty cycle of the pulse train can be estimated by the ratio of the time the pulse LED

Table 12-2
Logic Probe Indications

LED indicator			
High	Low	Pulse	Meaning
On	Off	Off	Steady high signal
Off	On	Off	Steady low signal
Off	Off	Off	Open circuit
On	On	Blink	Pulse train (frequency less than 100 kHz)
Off	Off	Blink	High-frequency pulse train

is on and off. For pulses above 100 Hz to 10 MHz, only the pulse LED is blinking.

The logic probe is quite simple to work with, so figuring out why it does not give the proper indications is straightforward. If none of the LEDs gives an indication, first check that power is applied to the equipment. Next, verify that the power-supply cable of the probe is properly connected. (If leads are crossed, the probe will not be damaged by the reverse polarity, but it will not indicate either.) A final possibility to consider is that the signal exceeds the measuring ability of the probe. In that case, select a different piece of test equipment, such as an oscilloscope.

Logic Probes Review

1. Why can logic probes be used with either TTL or MOS circuits?

2. Explain the meaning of each of the LED indicators on the probe.

3. Why must the probe tip be in contact with the pin before switching on the memory mode?

4. How can you distinguish a 90 kHz pulse train from a 900 kHz pulse train using a logic probe?

LOGIC ANALYZERS

A *logic analyzer* is a recording device that accepts a multiple number of input channels of data. Each channel represents the signals from any digital device. The devices can be either TTL, ECL, or CMOS technologies, and the analyzer will correctly interpret the logic levels. Typical analyzers can accept eight to sixteen channels of data up to 50 MHz or more. Once recorded in the random-access memory of the analyzer, the data can be displayed in many different ways. No data is lost when it is viewed on the built-in CRT or on an external scope.

The display is able to present the stored information in several formats. Each display is useful for detecting a particular type of fault. The choices of formats include pulse trains, binary, map, and computer output.

Pulse train format displays are well suited for finding timing faults. Because many channels are recorded simultaneously, the timing relationship between the pulses is available as well as the time of transition. Many times faults in microcomputers are caused by a particular signal changing levels just a little too early or late. Such a problem can easily be spotted on the display. The horizontal dimension of the display represents the duration (time) of the recording, as Fig. 12-5a shows. The

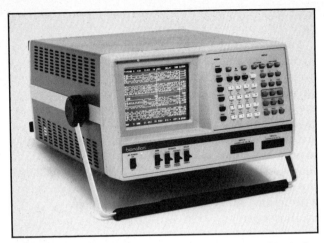

Figure 12-4. Logic Analyzer *(Gould Inc., Biomation Division).*

vertical dimension represents each of the 16 channels. By designating a point on the horizontal scale with the cursor, the user can expand the display by a factor of 10 or 20 times to examine fine details or time relationships (Fig. 12-5*b*).

The *binary data format* display is simply a listing of the logic analyzer memory contents, as Fig. 12-6 shows. The left-hand area of the display is the memory address. Any consecutive 16 memory locations can be viewed at once. The middle of each row lists the 2-byte memory contents in binary. The same value is converted to hexadecimal or octal and displayed to the right. This display format is best suited for software checkout.

The *map format* display gives an *x-y* presentation of the memory contents. Each word is divided into two equal group of bits. For example, if the memory word length is 16 bits, the upper byte is displayed on the *y* axis and the lower byte on the *x* axis. See Fig. 12-7. The image that results is a *signature* for the circuit in its present state. If any output changes value, there will be a difference in the map. Normally the map format is used at the beginning of a troubleshooting session to find out where the error might be, then the pulse train or binary mode is used for a detailed analysis of the problem.

Many analyzers also provide a serial output channel. The memory contents of the analyzer can be read directly by a computer using this channel. Testing of complicated circuitry can be computer-driven, with the responses to the test inputs being monitored on this channel.

Some analyzers provide a comparison mode to further enhance the diagnostic power of the equipment. In the *comparison mode*, the data recorded in memory is matched against each new recording of the same data. Any difference between the stored value and the latest reading is highlighted on the display. In this manner, a cyclic check for a fault can be run until its next occurrence is detected.

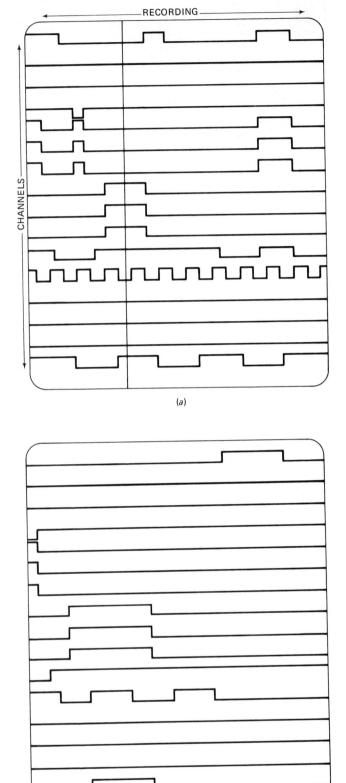

(a)

(b)

Figure 12-5. Pulse Train Display (*a*) Normal Scale (*b*) ×20 Magnification.

001	1111	1111	1111	1100	FFFC
002	1111	1111	1111	1101	FFFD
003	0111	0101	0000	0000	7500
004	1000	0000	0000	0100	8004
005	1000	0000	0000	0011	8003
006	1000	0000	0000	0010	8002
007	1000	0000	0000	0001	8001
008	1000	0000	0000	0000	8000
009	0111	0000	1100	0000	70C0
010	0111	0000	1101	0000	70D0
011	0111	1111	0000	0000	7F00
012	0111	0000	0000	0110	7006
013	1111	1111	1111	1111	FFFF
014	0101	0101	0101	0101	5555
015	0000	0000	0000	0000	0000
016	0111	0000	0100	0000	7040

Figure 12-6. Binary Display.

The analyzer readily allows the technician control of the sampling process. Sampling can begin at a selected time to cover the period that precedes and follows a specific event if *pretrigger recording* is chosen. With *delayed recording*, information is gathered after the event, similar to delay sweep triggering of an oscilloscope (except the timing of the analyzer can be controlled more precisely).

The input probes for the analyzer must present a low capacitive load, as well as a high impedance, to the circuit under test. Values in the neighborhood of 1 MΩ and 10 pF can be considered typical. The probes for each channel often have spring-loaded hooks to clip on the output lead. Cables about 10 ft (3 m) long connect the probes to the analyzer chassis.

Data is recorded as a binary value. The threshold voltage is established by a comparator which converts any input voltage above the threshold to a 1. All other inputs become 0s. The threshold can

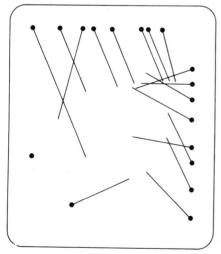

Figure 12-7. Map Display.

be set to the correct value for TTL, ECL, or MOS circuits.

In the *sampling mode*, 1 bit of data is recorded for each channel on each clock pulse. This method of sampling is best for synchronous circuits. Any signal change between clock pulses is ignored (as it should be in a synchronous circuit). For testing asynchronous circuits, the *latch mode* is provided. By latching, the data noise spikes or glitches can be detected. The analyzer records a bit and flags the event whenever there is a change in any channel that exceeds the threshold in between clock pulses. Although a bit is recorded when the noise spike occurs, the duration of the spike is not detectable using the logic analyzer. Only that a transition has taken place on one of the input channels can be read.

Another flexible feature of analyzers lies in the methods available for *clocking*. With *manual* clocking, a sample is made every time the operator pushes a button. *External* clocking permits a single event to dictate the time to sample. Most variation is provided by the *internal* clock, which responds to a particular bit pattern combination of the input data. Each bit can be set for on, off, or don't care. For example, we may be monitoring the address bus and want to sample when the address reaches $3B_{16}$. By simply dialing in the number, the technician causes the analyzer to sample when the address is $3B_{16}$. Another variation of the same idea is to cause the data to be sampled as long as it does *not* equal the preset value.

Logic Analyzers Review

1. List the display formats of the logic analyzer.

2. Which format is best for debugging software?

3. Explain the structure of the map display.

4. What is a circuit signature?

5. When should the sampling mode be used? The latch mode?

6. How is the analyzer clock derived?

IN-CIRCUIT EMULATORS

An *in-circuit emulator* (*ICE*) is a module that plugs into the socket of the microcomputer as a replacement for the processor. By removing the microprocessor and inserting the emulator in its place, a powerful diagnostic capability is provided. A cable runs from the ICE to a microprocessor development system, as Fig. 12-8 shows. This system also simu-

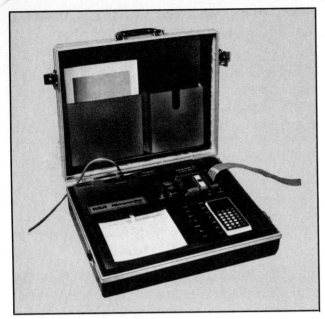

Figure 12-8. The COSMAC Micromonitor is an Example of an In-Circuit Emulator *(RCA)*.

lates ROM, RAM, and I/O operations to check out the hardware and software of a prototype system.

With the emulator in place, the MPU registers and RAM contents can be examined or modified. The program can be run in single step (one instruction at a time) or at full speed. *Breakpoints* can be inserted to cause the program to stop whenever a predefined event occurs. Such events may include reading or writing in a specified memory address or executing a particular instruction. After the breakpoint, the operator gains control from the program and may inspect or change register and memory values. Input or output of data can also be carefully monitored.

When the ICE is to be used, only a few actions are needed to change over from the normal microcomputer configuration to one with the emulator installed. First, the computer is unplugged. Next, the computer system clock or the ICE clock is selected. The microprocessor is removed and the in-circuit emulator put in, then the ground connection from the ICE to computer ground is made. In the powerup sequence, the microcomputer is turned on first, followed by applying power to the ICE development system. After forcing a reset signal, the computer is ready to begin running the program. Results will be shown on the development system display.

In-Circuit Emulators Review

1. List the test capabilities that an in-circuit emulator provides.

2. What steps are required before an emulator can be used?

3. If you wanted to step through a program one instruction at a time, would a logic analyzer or an ICE be more appropriate?

4. Define the term "breakpoint."

SOFTWARE DIAGNOSTICS

With the versatility of the microcomputer, faults can often be detected with computer programs (*software diagnostics*). Unfortunately, software checkout utility programs cannot be run unless at least a portion of RAM is operating reliably and much of the control and arithmetic logic is also usable. Some microcomputers are equipped with a microprogram ROM program to verify that enough of the circuits are operable to begin running the diagnostics programs.

These programs can thoroughly exercise the processor by executing every instruction, then examine memory functions, and finally verify peripheral equipment operation. Some RAMs have been known to experience a sensitivity to certain bit patterns. When one of these patterns is stored, incorrect values are obtained when the data is read later. Sometimes writing into one address will change the value of another location.

Because the number of bit patterns that can be stored in microcomputer memory is large, for practical purposes an exhaustive test of every pattern cannot be made. The number of possible patterns is

$$\text{Number of memory patterns} = 2^W \times M \quad (12\text{-}1)$$

where W = word size
            M = memory size

For example, a 32K memory on an 8-bit computer can store a possible

$$(2^8)(32{,}768) = 8{,}388{,}608$$

different patterns. If we could verify one pattern in 30 ms, it would take almost 70 hours just to test one memory. Obviously a short cut is needed.

Most often, patterns that represent worst-case conditions are used for memory testing. Patterns of all 0s, all 1s, and alternating 1s and 0s are frequently used. Some diagnostic programs divide the memory into zones and apply the patterns in a checkerboard fashion.

A Microprocessor Diagnostic Program

As an example of the type of program used for diagnostic work, Table 12-3 lists a test program for

Table 12-3
8080A Shift Diagnostic Program

Label	Mnemonic	Operand	Address	Machine Code	Comments
	LDA	PATTERN	1000	3A	Shift pattern → A
			1001	33	
			1002	10	
	RLC		1003	07	Rotate left
	CPI	55	1004	FE	
			1005	55	Compare with correct value
	JZ	TEST 2	1006	CA	Go to TEST 2 if OK
			1007	0C	
			1008	10	
	MVI A	01	1009	3E	Error code → A
			100A	01	
	HLT		100B	76	Stop
TEST 2	LDA	PATTERN	100C	3A	Shift pattern → A
			100D	33	
			100E	10	
	RRC		100F	0F	Rotate right (clear carry)
	CPI	55	1010	FE	Compare with correct value
			1011	55	
	JZ	TEST 3	1012	CA	Go to TEST 3 if OK
			1013	18	
			1014	10	
	MVI A	02	1015	3E	Error Code → A
			1016	02	
	HLT		1017	76	Stop
TEST 3	LDA A	PATTERN	1018	3A	Shift pattern → A
			1019	33	
			101A	10	
	RAL		101B	17	Rotate left through carry (set carry)
	CPI	54	101C	FE	
			101D	54	Compare with correct value
	JZ	TEST 4	101E	CA	Go to TEST 4 if OK
			101F	24	
			1020	10	
	MVI A	03	1021	3E	Error code → A
			1022	03	
	HLT		1023	76	Stop
TEST 4	LDA	PATTERN	1024	3A	Shift pattern → A
			1025	33	
			1026	10	
	RAR		1027	1F	Rotate right through carry
	CPI	55	1028	FE	Compare with correct value
			1029	55	
	JZ	END	102A	CA	End test if OK
			102B	30	
			102C	10	
	MVI A	04	102D	3E	Error code → A
			102E	04	
	HLT		102F	76	Stop
END	MVI A	00	1030	3E	Clear A
			1031	00	
	HLT		1032	76	Stop
PATTERN		AA	1033	AA	

the 8080A shift logic. The four rotate instructions (RAL, RAR, RLC, and RRC) are each used one time to verify that the proper result is produced. If so, the program then tests the next instruction in sequence. Otherwise, the program stops with a code number in the accumulator indicating which instruction failed. If all instructions execute correctly, the program stops with the accumulator cleared. The error indications are as follows:

A register	Instruction which failed
1	RLC
2	RRC
3	RAL
4	RAR

A Memory Diagnostic Program

Next, an example of a memory diagnostic program will be given. (Refer to Table 12-4.) The program starts the test at the location stored in the LOWER LIMIT variable location and ends the test at the cell which is one less than the UPPER LIMIT variable location. (For example, if the LOWER LIMIT is 1005 and the UPPER LIMIT 1015, the cells tested will be those in the range 1005 to 1014.) All zeros are written and read from each cell. If the test fails, the HL register pair contains the address and the accumulator value is the number that is supposed to be in the memory cell. If the test is successful, the program halts with a value of 01 in the accumulator. Obviously this program cannot test the

Table 12-4
Memory Diagnostic Program

Label	Mnemonic	Operand	Address	Machine Code	Comments
	LHLD	LOWER LIMIT	0000	2A	Lower limit → HL
			0001	1D	
			0002	00	
LOOP	MVI A	00	0003	3E	0 → A
			0004	00	
	MOV M, A		0005	77	Store value in memory
	CMP M		0006	BE	Compare memory value to A
	INX H		0007	23	
	JZ	NEXT	0008	CA	Increment count
			0009	0C	Go to next cell if OK
			000A	00	
	HLT		000B	76	Otherwise stop (error)
NEXT	LDA	UPPER LIMIT	000C	3A	Check L value. Is this the last cell?
			000D	1F	
			000E	00	
	CMP L		000F	BD	
	JNZ	LOOP	0010	C2	If not, repeat test.
			0011	03	
			0012	00	
	LDA	UPPER LIMIT + 1	0013	3A	Check H value.
			0014	20	
			0015	00	
	CMP H		0016	BC	
	JNZ	LOOP	0017	C2	Is this the last cell? If not, repeat the test.
			0018	03	
			0019	00	
	MVI A	01	001A	3E	1 → A
			001B	01	
	HLT		001C	76	Stop
LOWER LIMIT			001D		
			001E		
UPPER LIMIT			001F		
			0020		

memory area where the diagnostic routine itself resides.

Software Diagnostics Review

1. Describe the type of testing that software diagnostic programs can support.

2. Why is exhaustive pattern testing of memories not practical?

3. What patterns are frequently used for memory tests?

4. What would happen if the memory diagnostic program given in this chapter were used between the limits of 0000_{16} and $1A2F_{16}$?

5. Why does the shift diagnostic program not need to check the contents of the carry register?

CHAPTER SUMMARY

1. Logicical troubleshooting can save you time. Look first for the "obvious" failures before using test equipment. Proceed in a step-by-step manner.

2. A pulser can generate a signal to trigger a logic circuit at any point. Its high fan-out overwhelms the effects of downstream gates. Either single pulses or a series can be produced.

3. Logic probes can indicate the presence of a large number of different signals in digital circuits. Based on the indicator LEDs, the technician can readily identify signal levels.

4. Logic analyzers record signals obtained from many channels at once. This feature makes analyzers invaluable in diagnosing problems on the data, address, or control buses of a microcomputer. Display formats for pulse train, binary data, and maps are provided.

5. An in-circuit emulator replaces the processor to permit inspection and changing of register or memory contents, controlling I/O, or inserting breakpoints in the program. Any RAM, ROM, or I/O operation can be simulated with this test equipment. The program can be run in single-step or full-speed modes when the emulator is in place.

6. Software diagnostics can provide almost limitless troubleshooting assistance, provided enough memory and processor circuits are operable to execute the instructions. Even using the speed of the computer, however, exhaustive tests are not practical.

KEY TERMS AND CONCEPTS

Pulser	Logic probes	Logic analyzer
Pulse train format	Binary data format	Map format
Signature	Comparison mode	Pretrigger recording
Delayed recording	Sampling mode	Latch mode
Clocking	In-circuit emulator (ICE)	Breakpoints
Software diagnostics		

PROBLEMS

12-1 How many different memory patterns could be stored in a 16-bit memory with a capacity of 64 K?

12-2 If each pattern of the memory in Prob. 12-1 could be tested in 25 ms, how long would it take to completely test the memory?

12-3 If the pattern for the shift diagnostic program were to be changed to 55_{16}, what modification would be necessary in the listing?

12-4 Change the memory diagnostic program so that it tests the ability of the RAM to store all 1s in each cell.

12-5 How would the memory diagnostic program have to be changed to store alternate 1 s and 0 s (AA_{16}) in each cell?

12-6 Assume that the shift diagnostic program is being run and a logic analyzer is attached to the address bus. Show the contents of the binary display after the first three instructions have been executed (that is, the instructions in cells 1000_{16} through 1005_{16}).

12-7 Repeat Prob. 12-6, but show the pulse train display instead.

12-8 If a pulser and logic probe are applied to the circuit shown in Fig. 12-9, what indications would the probe give?

12-9 Assume that a logic probe is to be used to test a CMOS circuit that has a V_{CC} of +12 V. What minimum voltage must a pulse have to register as a high level on the probe? As a low level?

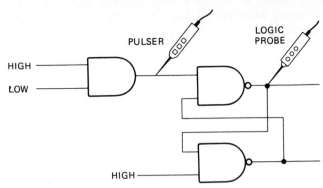

Figure 12-9. Problem 12-8.

12-10 A logic probe is connected to a TTL circuit and gives the following indications:

1. All LEDs off except that high is steady.

Followed by:

2. The high and low LEDs are steady while the pulse indicator is blinking.

Draw the pulse train that produced these indications. (Show voltage levels and time intervals.)

APPENDIX

While the experiments and examples given in the text are based on the 8080A microprocessor, with little or no change most apply to the 8085 or Z80 processors as well. The following sections will comment on the differences between the 8080A and the other processors to indicate how the experiments or examples might be modified for those machines.

THE 8085 MICROPROCESSOR

The architecture of the 8085 is extremely similar to that of the 8080A. For this reason, 8080A programs can be run on the 8085 without modification. Considerable savings in software costs can be realized in this manner, even though the hardware itself is upgraded if a commercial product is converted from being based on the 8080A to an 8085 system.

Many of the 8085 signal lines, however, do not correspond to those of the 8080A. As can be seen in the diagram of Fig. A-1, and as listed in Table A-1, the pin arrangement differs considerably from that in the 8080A. Immediately obvious is the requirement for only a single +5-V power supply. This refinement makes using the 8085 in a circuit less costly. Another modification is inclusion of clock logic on the microprocessor chip. Providing the clock on the chip eliminates the need for the 8224 clock generator. Timing signals for the 8085 consist of a more straightforward single-phase clock. The standard clock period in the 8085 is 320 ns, as compared to the slower 500 ns of the 8080A.

The lower 8 bits of the address (A0 through A7) and data (D0 through D7) are multiplexed on the same bus. These dual-purpose lines are designated AD0 through AD7. The remaining address bits (A8 through A15) use dedicated lines. The memory or I/O device can distinguish data from addresses on AD0 through AD7 by the level of the ALE signal. It is high when data is on the bus and low when the bus signals represent an address.

In reading and writing of data, the 8085 employs new signals. The $\overline{RD}$ signal is used to read either memory or input data, and $\overline{WR}$ is used for writing memory or output data. Another signal is necessary to distinguish between the two types of reading and writing. When memory operations are in progress, the auxiliary signal, IO/$\overline{M}$, is low. For input or output, IO/$\overline{M}$ is high.

The purpose of the signals currently on the data bus can be interpreted by referring to the S0 and S1 control signals. These two signals specify whether the intent is data reading, data writing, instruction fetching, or a halt state. The meanings of these signals are listed here:

S1	S0	Meaning
0	0	Halt
0	1	Memory or output write
1	0	Memory or input read
1	1	Instruction fetch

Serial input and output are supported by the 8085 as well. With the SIO instruction, the program can transmit only the most significant bit of the accumulator. A serial input is provided by the SID instruction. The data bit is received in the MSB of the accumulator.

Peripherals can coordinate functions with the control bus signals. If a memory or I/O device needs more time to respond to an I/O request from the processor, the READY signal can be used. External logic can request control of the address bus with the HOLD signal; the processor acknowledges with HLDA. The microprocessor is reset by the $\overline{RESETIN}$ signal, which need not be synchronized with the clock. The processor then provides a reset signal for the remainder of the system with RESETOUT.

The interrupt structure of the 8085 is quite powerful. General-purpose interrupt requests are handled with the INTR input. (This input corresponds to the 8080A interrupt request.) The TRAP interrupt cannot be disabled and has the highest priority. For this reason, the TRAP is best suited to be a power failure interrupt. Three other interrupts are supplied for hardware vectoring. Each (as well as INTR) can be individually enabled or disabled with the SIM instruction. (All interrupts, except TRAP, can be enabled or disabled as a group with the EI and DI

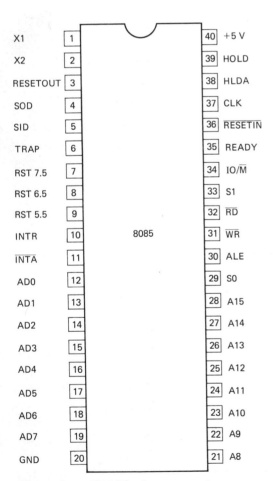

Figure A-1. 8085 Pin Arrangement.

Table A-1
8085 Signals

Signal	Description
AD0–AD7	Multiplexed three-state address and data bus
A8–A15	Three-state high-order bits of address bus
ALE	Address latch enable
$\overline{RD}$, $\overline{WR}$	Read, write strobe
IO/$\overline{M}$	I/O or memory indicator
S0, S1	Bus status indicators
READY	Wait state request
SID, SOD	Serial data input, output
HOLD, HLDA	Hold request, acknowledgement
INTR	Interrupt request
TRAP	Nonmaskable interrupt request
RST 5.5, RST 6.5, RST 7.5	Hardware vectored-interrupt requests
$\overline{INTA}$	Interrupt acknowledgement
$\overline{RESETIN}$	System reset input
RESETOUT	Peripheral reset output
X1, X2	Crystal inputs
CLK	Clock signal output

instructions, like on the 8080A.) The TRAP interrupt will respond to either edge or level triggering. The RST 5.5 and RST 6.5 interrupts are level-triggered, while RST 7.5 is edge-triggered. All interrupts are acknowledged by the processor issuing a true $\overline{INTA}$ signal.

THE Z80 MICROPROCESSOR

All of the 8080A instructions are a subset of the Z80 repertoire. This provision means that the 8080A programs will also run on the Z80. (The Z80 instructions number 158, while the 8080A has 78.) Although the operation codes are identical, you will note that different mnemonics are used in Z80 manuals. The Z80 requires only a +5-V power supply and uses a single-phase clock. Clock logic is on the chip.

As shown in Fig. A-2 and listed in Table A-2, the Z80 does not separate read and write into memory or I/O operations. An I/O or memory selection pulse is provided to distinguish between them, as with the 8085. A nonmaskable interrupt, which is usually used to detect power failure, is supported. The Z80 also supplies a dynamic memory refresh signal, simplifying the interface to dynamic RAM.

This processor has more registers than the 8080A and has expanded the addressing modes. The additional registers are indicated in Fig. A-3. The alternate set of registers (indicated by prime marks, such as A' and E') can be used in exactly the same way

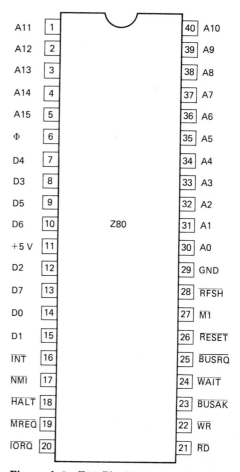

Figure A-2. Z80 Pin Arrangement.

Table A-2
Z80 Signals

Signal	Description
D0–D7	Three-state data bus
A0–A15	Three-state address bus
$\overline{RD}$, $\overline{WR}$	Read, write strobes
$\overline{M1}$	Instruction fetch cycle
$\overline{MREQ}$	Memory access indicator
$\overline{IORQ}$	I/O operation indicator
$\overline{RFSH}$	Dynamic memory refresh indicator
$\overline{HALT}$	MPU in halt state
$\overline{WAIT}$	Wait state request
$\overline{INT}$	Interrupt request
$\overline{NMI}$	Nonmaskable interrupt request
$\overline{RESET}$	Reset MPU input
$\overline{BUSRQ}$	Request for control of the data, address, and control buses
$\overline{BUSAK}$	Bus acknowledge
Φ	Clock input

as the main set, doubling the number of programmable registers. The alternate set is also convenient to reserve for interrupt servicing routines. Then no registers need be saved before processing the interrupt.

The interrupt vector register extends the interrupt processing capacity of the MPU. The refresh counter indexes the address when rewriting the values into dynamic memories which is necessary to prevent data loss. Thus separate memory refresh circuitry is eliminated from the microcomputer.

The index registers allow the address of the operand to be offset by a displacement value. This programming feature is frequently applied to table or list processing and also frees the register pairs for other purposes. The operand address in an indexed instruction is calculated as

$$address = (IX) + D$$

or

$$address = (IY) + D \tag{A-1}$$

where (IX) = contents of the X index register
      (IY) = contents of the Y index register
        D = displacement, a signed 8-bit value to be added to the index; the data can be located within ±128 bytes of the index register contents

The relative jump instruction also uses a displacement. This instruction allows the programmer to branch to an address equal to

$$address = (PC) + 2 + D \tag{A-2}$$

where (PC) = contents of the program counter
        D = displacement

Individual bits can be manipulated by a group of instructions that can set or reset any single bit in a word. Block move instructions can transfer any number of contiguous memory cells to another memory area or to an output port. The block compare can scan a memory area for a specific data value. The Z80 status register provides a subtraction indicator, so the DAA instruction used in BCD arithmetic programs is simplified.

Main Register Set

A	PSW
B	C
D	E
H	L

Alternate Register Set

A′	PSW′
B′	E′
D′	E′
H′	L′

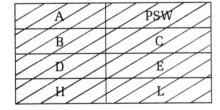

SP	
PC	
IX	
IY	
IV	R

IX   X index register
IY   Y index register

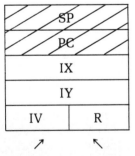

Interrupt vector address   Dynamic memory refresh counter

Legend

▨   Equivalent to the 8080A

▢   Unique to the Z80

Figure A-3. Z80 Registers.

Table A-3
Numerical Listing of 8080 Operation Codes

Most Significant Digit	Least Significant Digit															
	0	**1**	**2**	**3**	**4**	**5**	**6**	**7**	**8**	**9**	**A**	**B**	**C**	**D**	**E**	**F**
0	NOP	LXI B	STAX B	INX B	INR B	DCR B	MVI B	RLC	X	DAD B	LDAX B	DCX B	INR C	DCR C	MVI C	RRC
1	X	LXI D	STAX D	INX D	INR D	DCR D	MVI D	RAL	X	DAD D	LDAX D	DCX D	INR E	DCR E	MVI E	RAR
2	X	LXI H	SHLD	INX H	INR H	DCR H	MVI H	DAA	X	DAD H	LHLD	DCX H	INR L	DCR L	MVI L	CMA
3	X	LXI SP	STA	INX SP	INR M	DCR M	MVI M	STC	X	DAD SP	LDA	DCX SP	INR A	DCR A	MVI A	CMC
4	MOV B,B	MOV B,C	MOV B,D	MOV B,E	MOV B,H	MOV B,L	MOV B,M	MOV B,A	MOV C,B	MOV C,C	MOV C,D	MOV C,E	MOV C,H	MOV C,L	MOV C,M	MOV C,A
5	MOV D,B	MOV D,C	MOV D,D	MOV D,E	MOV D,H	MOV D,L	MOV D,M	MOV D,A	MOV E,B	MOV E,C	MOV E,D	MOV E,E	MOV E,H	MOV E,L	MOV E,M	MOV E,A
6	MOV H,B	MOV H,C	MOV H,D	MOV H,E	MOV H,H	MOV H,L	MOV H,M	MOV H,A	MOV L,B	MOV L,C	MOV L,D	MOV L,E	MOV L,H	MOV L,L	MOV L,M	MOV L,A
7	MOV M,B	MOV M,C	MOV M,D	MOV M,E	MOV M,H	MOV M,L	HLT	MOV M,A	MOV A,B	MOV A,C	MOV A,D	MOV A,E	MOV A,H	MOV A,L	MOV A,M	MOV A,A
8	ADD B	ADD C	ADD D	ADD E	ADD H	ADD L	ADD M	ADD A	ADC B	ADC C	ADC D	ADC E	ADC H	ADC L	ADC M	ADC A
9	SUB B	SUB C	SUB D	SUB E	SUB H	SUB L	SUB M	SUB A	SBB B	SBB C	SBB D	SBB E	SBB H	SBB L	SBB M	SBB A
A	ANA B	ANA C	ANA D	ANA E	ANA H	ANA L	ANA M	ANA A	XRA B	XRA C	XRA D	XRA E	XRA H	XRA L	XRA M	XRA A
B	ORA B	ORA C	ORA D	ORA E	ORA H	ORA L	ORA M	ORA A	CMP B	CMP C	CMP D	CMP E	CMP H	CMP L	CMP M	CMP A
C	RNZ	POP B	JNZ	JMP	CNZ	PUSH B	ADI	RST 0	RZ	RET	JZ	X	CZ	CALL	ACI	RST 1
D	RNC	POP D	JNC	OUT	CNC	PUSH D	SUI	RST 2	RC	X	JC	IN	CC	X	SBI	RST 3
E	RPO	POP H	JPO	XTHL	CPO	PUSH H	ANI	RST 4	RPE	PCHL	JPE	XCHG	CPE	X	XRI	RST 5
F	RP	POP A	JP	DI	CP	PUSH A	ORI	RST 6	RM	SPHL	JM	EI	CM	X	CPI	RST 7

X = not assigned.

Mnemonic	Operation Code	Bytes	Description	Clock Periods
ACI	CE	2	$(A)+(DATA)+(CARRY) \to A$	7
ADC A	8F	1	$(A)+(A)+CARRY \to A$	4
ADC B	88	1	$(A)+(B)+(CARRY) \to A$	4
ADC C	89	1	$(A)+(C)+(CARRY) \to A$	4
ADC D	8A	1	$(A)+(D)+(CARRY) \to A$	4
ADC E	8B	1	$(A)+(E)+(CARRY) \to A$	4
ADC H	8C	1	$(A)+(H)+(CARRY) \to A$	4
ADC L	8D	1	$(A)+(L)+CARRY \to A$	4
ADC M	8E	1	$(A)+(M)+CARRY \to A$	7
ADD A	87	1	$(A)+(A) \to A$	4
ADD B	80	1	$(A)+(B) \to A$	4
ADD C	81	1	$(A)+(C) \to$	4
ADD D	82	1	$(A)+(D) \to A$	4
ADD E	83	1	$(A)+(E) \to A$	4
ADD H	84	1	$(A)+(H) \to A$	4
ADD L	85	1	$(A)+(L) \to A$	4
ADD M	86	1	$(A)+(M) \to A$	7
ADI	C6	2	$(A)+(DATA) \to A$	7
ANA A	A7	1	(A) AND $(A) \to A$	4
ANA B	A0	1	(A) AND $(B) \to A$	4
ANA C	A1	1	(A) AND $(C) \to A$	4
ANA D	A2	1	(A) AND $(D) \to A$	4
ANA E	A3	1	(A) AND $(E) \to A$	4
ANA H	A4	1	(A) AND $(H) \to A$	4
ANA L	A5	1	(A) AND $(L) \to A$	4
ANA M	A6	1	(A) AND $(M) \to A$	7
ANI	E6	2	(A) AND $(DATA) \to A$	7
CALL	CD	3	$(PCH) \to (SP)-1,$ $(PCL) \to (SP)-2,$ $(SP)-2 \to SP,$ $ADDR \to PC$	17
CC	DC	3	CALL if CARRY=1	11/17
CM	FC	3	CALL if SIGN=1	11/17
CMA	2F	1	$(\overline{A}) \to A$ (1's complement)	4
CMC	3F	1	$(\overline{CARRY}) \to CARRY$	4
CMP A	BF	1	$(A)-(A)$ set condition bits, $A_f=A_i$	4
CMP B	B8	1	$(A)-(B)$ set condition bits, $A_f=A_i$	4
CMP C	B9	1	$(A)-(C)$ set condition bits, $A_f=A_i$	4
CMP D	BA	1	$(A)-(D)$ set condition bits, $A_f=A_i$	4
CMP E	BB	1	$(A)-(E)$ set condition bits, $A_f=A_i$	4
CMP H	BC	1	$(A)-(H)$ set condition bits, $A_f=A_i$	4
CMP L	BD	1	$(A)-(L)$ set condition bits, $A_f=A_i$	4
CMP M	BE	1	$(A)-(M)$ set condition bits, $A_f=A_i$	7
CNC	D4	3	CALL if CARRY=0	11/17

Mnemonic	Operation Code	Bytes	Description	Clock Periods
CNZ	C4	3	CALL if ZERO=0	11/17
CP	F4	3	CALL if SIGN=0	11/17
CPE	EC	3	CALL if PARITY=1	11/17
CPI	FE	2	(A)−(DATA) set condition bits, $A_f = A_i$	7
CPO	E4	3	CALL if PARITY=0	11/17
CZ	CC	3	CALL if ZERO=1	11/17
DAA	27	1	Decimal adjust A	4
DAD B	09	1	(HL)+(BC) → HL	10
DAD D	19	1	(HL)+(DE) → HL	10
DAD H	29	1	(HL)+(HL) → HL	10
DAD SP	39	1	(HL)+(SP) → HL	10
DCR A	3D	1	(A)−1 → A	5
DCR B	05	1	(B)−1 → B	5
DCR C	0D	1	(C)−1 → C	5
DCR D	15	1	(D)−1 → D	5
DCR E	1D	1	(E)−1 → E	5
DCR H	25	1	(H)−1 → H	5
DCR L	2D	1	(L)−1 → L	5
DCR M	35	1	(M)−1 → M	10
DCX B	0B	1	(BC)−1 → BC	5
DCX D	1B	1	(DE)−1 → DE	5
DCX H	2B	1	(HL)−1 → HL	5
DCX SP	3B	1	(SP)−1 → SP	5
DI	F3	1	0 → INTE	4
EI	FB	1	1 → INTE	4
HLT	76	1	Stop processor	7
IN	DB	2	Input → A	10
INR A	3C	1	(A)+1 → A	5
INR B	04	1	(B)+1 → B	5
INR C	0C	1	(C)+1 → C	5
INR D	14	1	(D)+1 → D	5
INR E	1C	1	(E)+1 → E	5
INR H	24	1	(H)+1 → H	5
INR L	2C	1	(L)+1 → L	5
INR M	34	1	(M)+1 → M	10
INX B	03	1	(BC)+1 → BC	5
INX D	13	1	(DE)+1 → DE	5
INX H	23	1	(HL)+1 → HL	5
INX SP	33	1	(SP)+1 → SP	5
JC	DA	3	Jump if CARRY=1	10
JM	FA	3	Jump if SIGN=1	10
JMP	C3	3	Jump	10
JNC	D2	3	Jump if CARRY=0	10
JNZ	C2	3	Jump if ZERO=0	10
JP	F2	3	Jump if SIGN=0	10
JPE	EA	3	Jump if PARITY=1	10
JPO	E2	3	Jump if PARITY=0	10
JZ	CA	3	Jump if ZERO=1	10
LDA	3A	3	(ADDR) → A	13

Mnemonic	Operation Code	Bytes	Description	Clock Periods
LDAX B	0A	1	(Address=(BC)) → A	7
LDAX D	1A	1	(Address=(DE)) → A	7
LHLD	2A	3	(ADDR) → L,(ADDR+1) → H	16
LXI B	01	3	(DATA) → BC	10
LXI D	11	3	(DATA) → DE	10
LXI H	21	3	(DATA) → HL	10
LXI SP	31	3	(DATA) → SP	10
MOV A,A	7F	1	(A) → A	5
MOV A,B	78	1	(B) → A	5
MOV A,C	79	1	(C) → A	5
MOV A,D	7A	1	(D) → A	5
MOV A,E	7B	1	(E) → A	5
MOV A,H	7C	1	(H) → A	5
MOV A,L	7D	1	(L) → A	5
MOV A,M	7E	1	(M) → A	7
MOV B,A	47	1	(A) → B	5
MOV B,B	40	1	(B) → B	5
MOV B,C	41	1	(C) → B	5
MOV B,D	42	1	(D) → B	5
MOV B,E	43	1	(E) → B	5
MOV B,H	44	1	(H) → B	5
MOV B,L	45	1	(L) → B	5
MOV B,M	46	1	(M) → B	7
MOV C,A	4F	1	(A) → C	5
MOV C,B	48	1	(B) → C	5
MOV C,C	49	1	(C) → C	5
MOV C,D	4A	1	(D) → C	5
MOV C,E	4B	1	(E) → C	5
MOV C,H	4C	1	(H) → C	5
MOV C,L	4D	1	(L) → C	5
MOV C,M	4E	1	(M) → C	7
MOV D,A	57	1	(A) → D	5
MOV D,B	50	1	(B) → D	5
MOV D,C	51	1	(C) → D	5
MOV D,D	52	1	(D) → D	5
MOV D,E	53	1	(E) → D	5
MOV D,H	54	1	(H) → D	5
MOV D,L	55	1	(L) → D	5
MOV D,M	56	1	(M) → D	7
MOV E,A	5F	1	(A) → E	5
MOV E,B	58	1	(B) → E	5
MOV E,C	59	1	(C) → E	5
MOV E,D	5A	1	(D) → E	5
MOV E,E	5B	1	(E) → E	5
MOV E,H	5C	1	(H) → E	5
MOV E,L	5D	1	(L) → E	5
MOV E,M	5E	1	(M) → E	7
MOV H,A	67	1	(A) → H	5
MOV H,B	60	1	(B) → H	5
MOV H,C	61	1	(C) → H	5

Mnemonic	Operation Code	Bytes	Description	Clock Periods
MOV H,D	62	1	(D) → H	5
MOV H,E	63	1	(E) → H	5
MOV H,H	64	1	(H) → H	5
MOV H,L	65	1	(L) → H	5
MOV H,M	66	1	(M) → H	7
MOV L,A	6F	1	(A) → L	5
MOV L,B	68	1	(B) → L	5
MOV L,C	69	1	(C) → L	5
MOV L,D	6A	1	(D) → L	5
MOV L,E	6B	1	(E) → L	5
MOV L,H	6C	1	(H) → L	5
MOV L,L	6D	1	(L) → L	5
MOV L,M	6E	1	(M) → L	7
MOV M,A	77	1	(A) → M	7
MOV M,B	70	1	(B) → M	7
MOV M,C	71	1	(C) → M	7
MOV M,D	72	1	(D) → M	7
MOV M,E	73	1	(E) → M	7
MOV M,H	74	1	(H) → M	7
MOV M,L	75	1	(L) → M	7
MVI A	3E	2	DATA → A	7
MVI B	06	2	DATA → B	7
MVI C	0E	2	DATA → C	7
MVI D	16	2	DATA → D	7
MVI E	1E	2	DATA → E	7
MVI H	26	2	DATA → H	7
MVI L	2E	2	DATA → L	7
MVI M	36	2	DATA → M	10
NOP	00	1	No operation	4
ORA A	B7	1	(A) OR (A) → A	4
ORA B	B0	1	(A) OR (B) → A	4
ORA C	B1	1	(A) OR (C) → A	4
ORA D	B2	1	(A) OR (D) → A	4
ORA E	B3	1	(A) OR (E) → A	4
ORA H	B4	1	(A) OR (H) → A	4
ORA L	B5	1	(A) OR (L) → A	4
ORA M	B6	1	(A) OR (M) → A	7
ORI	F6	2	(A) OR (DATA) → A	7
OUT	D3	2	(A) → output	10
PCHL	E9	1	(HL) → PC	5
POP A	F1	1	(STACK) → A-PSW	10
POP B	C1	1	(STACK) → BC	10
POP D	D1	1	(STACK) → DE	10
POP H	E1	1	(STACK) → HL	10
PUSH A	F5	1	(A-PSW) → STACK	11
PUSH B	C5	1	(BC) → STACK	11
PUSH D	D5	1	(DE) → STACK	11
PUSH H	E5	1	(HL) → STACK	11
RAL	17	1	Rotate A left through CARRY, (CARRY) → A_o	4

Mnemonic	Operation Code	Bytes	Description	Clock Periods
RAR	1F	1	Rotate A right through CARRY, (CARRY) $\rightarrow$ A_7	4
RC	D8	1	Return if CARRY=1	5/11
RET	C9	1	Return	10
RLC	07	1	Rotate A left, $(A_7) \rightarrow$ CARRY	4
RM	F8	1	Return if SIGN=1	5/11
RNC	D0	1	Return if CARRY=0	5/11
RNZ	C0	1	Return if ZERO=0	5/11
RP	F0	1	Return if SIGN=0	5/11
RPE	E8	1	Return if PARITY=1	5/11
RPO	E0	1	Return if PARITY=0	5/11
RRC	0F	1	Rotate A right, $(A_0) \rightarrow$ CARRY	4
RST 0	C7	1	(PCH) $\rightarrow$ ((SP)−1), (PCL) $\rightarrow$ ((SP)−2), (SP)+2 $\rightarrow$ SP, $00_{16} \rightarrow$ PC	11
RST 1	CF	1	(PCH) $\rightarrow$ ((SP)−1), (PCL) $\rightarrow$ ((SP)−2), (SP)+2 $\rightarrow$ SP, $08_{16} \rightarrow$ PC	11
RST 2	D7	1	(PCH) $\rightarrow$ ((SP)−1), (PCL) $\rightarrow$ ((SP)−2), (SP)+2 $\rightarrow$ SP, $10_{16} \rightarrow$ PC	11
RST 3	DF	1	(PCH) $\rightarrow$ ((SP)−1), (PCL) $\rightarrow$ ((SP)−2), (SP)+2 $\rightarrow$ SP, $18_{16} \rightarrow$ PC	11
RST 4	E7	1	(PCH) $\rightarrow$ ((SP)−1), (PCL) $\rightarrow$ ((SP)−2), (SP)+2 $\rightarrow$ SP, $20_{16} \rightarrow$ PC	11
RST 5	EF	1	(PCH) $\rightarrow$ ((SP)−1), (PCL) $\rightarrow$ ((SP)−2), (SP)+2 $\rightarrow$ SP, $28_{16} \rightarrow$ PC	11
RST 6	F7	1	(PCH) $\rightarrow$ ((SP)−1), (PCL) $\rightarrow$ ((SP)−2), (SP)+2 $\rightarrow$ SP, $30_{16} \rightarrow$ PC	11
RST 7	FF	1	(PCH) $\rightarrow$ ((SP)−1), (PCL) $\rightarrow$ ((SP)−2), (SP)+2 $\rightarrow$ SP, $38_{16} \rightarrow$ PC	11
RZ	C8	1	Return if ZERO=1	5/11
SBB A	9F	1	(A)−(A)−CARRY $\rightarrow$ A	4
SBB B	98	1	(A)−(B)−CARRY $\rightarrow$ A	4
SBB C	99	1	(A)−(C)−CARRY $\rightarrow$ A	4
SBB D	9A	1	(A)−(D)−CARRY $\rightarrow$ A	4
SBB E	9B	1	(A)−(E)−CARRY $\rightarrow$ A	4
SBB H	9C	1	(A)−(H)−CARRY $\rightarrow$ A	4
SBB L	9D	1	(A)−(L)−CARRY $\rightarrow$ A	4
SBB M	9E	1	(A)−(M)−CARRY $\rightarrow$ A	7
SBI	DE	2	(A)−DATA−CARRY $\rightarrow$ A	7
SHLD	22	3	(L) $\rightarrow$ ADDR, (H) $\rightarrow$ ADDR+1	16
SPHL	F9	1	(HL) $\rightarrow$ SP	5
STA	32	3	(A) $\rightarrow$ ADDR	13
STAX B	02	1	(A) $\rightarrow$ Address=(BC)	7
STAX D	12	1	(A) $\rightarrow$ Address=(DE)	7
STC	37	1	1 $\rightarrow$ CARRY	4

Mnemonic	Operation Code	Bytes	Description	Clock Periods
SUB A	97	1	$(A)-(A) \rightarrow A$	4
SUB B	90	1	$(A)-(B) \rightarrow A$	4
SUB C	91	1	$(A)-(C) \rightarrow A$	4
SUB D	92	1	$(A)-(D) \rightarrow A$	4
SUB E	93	1	$(A)-(E) \rightarrow A$	4
SUB H	94	1	$(A)-(H) \rightarrow A$	4
SUB L	95	1	$(A)-(L) \rightarrow A$	4
SUB M	96	1	$(A)-(M) \rightarrow A$	7
SUI	D6	2	$(A)-(DATA) \rightarrow A$	7
XCHG	EB	1	$(H) \leftrightarrow (D), (L) \leftrightarrow (E)$	4
XRA A	AF	1	(A) Exclusive OR (A) $\rightarrow$ A	4
XRA B	A8	1	(A) Exclusive OR (B) $\rightarrow$ A	4
XRA C	A9	1	(A) Exclusive OR (C) $\rightarrow$ A	4
XRA D	AA	1	(A) Exclusive OR (D) $\rightarrow$ A	4
XRA E	AB	1	(A) Exclusive OR (E) $\rightarrow$ A	4
XRA H	AC	1	(A) Exclusive OR (H) $\rightarrow$ A	4
XRA L	AD	1	(A) Exclusive OR (L) $\rightarrow$ A	4
XRA M	AE	1	(A) Exclusive OR (M) $\rightarrow$ A	7
XRI	EE	2	(A) Exclusive OR (DATA) $\rightarrow$ A	7
XTHL	E3	1	$(L) \rightarrow (SP), (H) \rightarrow ((SP)+1)$	18

Legend:

( ):	Contents of register or memory location
$\rightarrow$:	Transfer
+:	Plus
$-$:	Minus
PC:	Program counter
PCL:	Lower byte of PC
PCH:	Higher byte of PC
SP:	Stack pointer
$\overline{A}$:	Complement of A
A_i:	Initial contents of A (before instruction execution)
A_f:	Final contents of A (after instruction execution)
A_o:	Least significant bit of A
A_7:	Most significant bit of A
INTE:	Interrupt enable flip-flop
ADDR:	Memory address bytes of the instruction
DATA:	Data byte of the instruction
CARRY:	Carry bit
$\overline{CARRY}$:	Complement of CARRY
M:	The memory address in HL register pair
SIGN:	Sign status bit
ZERO:	Zero status bit
PARITY:	Parity status bit
PSW:	Program status word

EXPLANATORY NOTE ON DECIMAL ADJUST ACCUMULATOR (DAA) INSTRUCTION

The DAA instruction is used to perform BCD arithmetic in the 8080A. When necessary this instruction modifies the sum of two BCD numbers to produce a correct answer. To do so requires a two-step procedure.

1. If the 4 least significant bits of the accumulator are greater than 9, or if the A_C bit is 1, six is added to the accumulator. Otherwise no change is made to the accumulator.

2. If the four most significant bits of the accumulator are now more than 9, or if the carry bit is 1, the 4 most significant bits are incremented by six. Otherwise no change is made.

If step 1 produces a carry, the A_C bit is set; otherwise it is cleared. Similarly the carry bit is set if step 2 produces a carry; if not, the bit is cleared.

☐ **EXAMPLE.** Initially the accumulator is $7A_{16}$ and both A_C and the carry bits are cleared. When DAA is executed, the following occurs:

Step 1:   A = 7A   Four least significant bits are greater than 9.

add 6   +6
————
80

Step 2:   A = 80   Four most significant bits are not greater than 9, so no further operations are performed.

SUGGESTIONS FOR FURTHER READING

Barden, William, Jr.: *The Z-80 Microcomputer Handbook*, Howard W. Sams & Co., Inc., Indianapolis, 1978.

Kane, Jerry and Osborne, Adam: *An Introduction to Microcomputers, Volume III Some Real Support Products*, Osborne & Associates, Inc., Berkeley, 1978.

Larsen, David G. and Rony, Peter R.: *The Bugbook IIA*, E & L Instruments, Inc., Derby, CT, 1977.

MCS-85™ User's Manual, Intel Corporation, Santa Clara, CA, 1978.

Pasahow, Edward: *Digital Integrated Circuits for Electronics Technicians*, McGraw-Hill Book Company, New York, 1979.

Pasahow, Edward: *Microprocessors and Microcomputers for Electronics Technicians*, McGraw-Hill Book Company, New York, 1981.

Peatman, John B.: *Microcomputer-Based Design*, McGraw-Hill Book Company, New York, 1977.

Z80^R-CPU, Z80A^R-CPU Technical Manual, Zilog, Inc., Cupertino, CA, 1977.

Z80 Microcomputer System Micro-Reference Manual, Mostek Corp., Carrollton, TX, 1978.

8080 Assembly Language Programming Manual, Intel Corporation, Santa Clara, CA, 1974.

ANSWERS TO ODD-NUMBERED PROBLEMS

(Answers not listed here may be found in the Teacher's Manual.)

2-1. 3, $0000-5FFF_{16}$.

2-3. E = 50, D = AA, PC = 4095, L = A0, H = 02.

2-5. 0002 = 0B, 0003 = 0F, PC = 4096.

2-7. (*a*) 44.

2-9. 12_{16}.

3-1. 8.800 ms.

3-3. 64.

3-5. 40,960 bits.

3-7. 548 ms.

3-9. 378 ms.

4-3. 3 and 5.

4-7.

A0			Output
0	14	ICWI	
1	43	ICW2	1
1	C0	ICW3	
0	14	ICW1	
1	51	ICW2	
1	06	ICW3	2
0	14	ICW1	
1	59	ICW2	
1	07	ICW3	
0	E0	OCW2	3
0	68	OCW3	4
1	CF	Mask	
0	00	OCW2	5
0	68	OCW3	6
1	00	New mask	
0	0C	OCW3	7

5-1. (a) Low, high, high, high, low, high, low, low.
(b) transition to low, low, low, low, transition to high, high, transition low, transition high.

5-3. 1011 0111, 0110 1110, 1101 1100, 1011 1000.

5-7. 4.8 kHz.

5-9. 7E F4 76 46CB09 21E2 7E.

6-1. Bit 1: C = 0   A = 0110   0101 = 65.
Bit 2: C = 1   A = 0011   0010 = 32.
Bit 3: C = 0   A = 1001   1001 = 99.

6-3. Increase total number of iterations of the inner loop to 1600_{10}. One possible solution is to let the inner loop count = 200_{10} and outer loop count = 8.

6-7. 0, 2, 3, and 6 closed.

6-9. 5RC = 2.35 ms.

7-1. CA, CB, and CD high while BA pulses.

7-3. CG goes low after 8 bits are received.

7-5. No, signal rate of change exceeds 30 V / μs.

7-7. R1 = 0.2 mA, R2 = 0.2 mA, R3 = 0.2 mA, R4 = 1.6 mA approximately.

7-9. −0.6 V, 5.6 V.

8-1. 6.2KΩ, has 0 mA, 3KΩ has 1.7 mA.

8-3. 3KΩ has 5.7 V, 6.2KΩ has −0.7 V, approximately 1.9 mA.

8-5. DIO = X001   0100, all others are don't care.

8-7. DIO = X110   1011.

8-9. Unlisten.

9-1. 0010_{16} corresponding to an RST2 instruction.

9-3. 2.2 μs.

9-5. Low.

9-7. The input / output line becomes low.

9-9. Masters 1 and 3.

10-1. 4.9 mV.

10-3. 2.27 mA.

10-5. 0.025 percent.

10-7. 62.

10-9. 22.1 ppm.

11-1. 1002_{16}, 0001.

11-3. 104 μs.

11-5. Increase the period of the delay subroutine.

11-7. 32.

11-9. Using a 2-MHz clock:

R2 = 0	R3 = 3F
R6 = 19	R7 = 2D
R9 = 7	R11 and R12 set for envelope period

Others zero

12-1. 16,777,216.

12-3. 1033 = 55, 1005 = AA, 1011 = AA, 101D = AB, 1029 = 2A.

12-5. 0004 = AA.

12-9. above 8.4 V, below 3.6 V.

INDEX

Counter A/D converter, 165
CRC (cyclic redundancy check), 43–44
CRT controller, 187
CRT terminal, 46–48
Current loops, 107–110, 123
Cyclic redundancy check (CRC), 43–44

D

D/A converters [see Digital-to-analog (D/A) converters]
DAC [see Digital-to-analog (D/A) converters]
Daisy chain bus, 141
Data bus, 2
  8080A, 10
Data communications equipment (DCE), 116
Data encryption unit (DEU), 176–179
Data lines, 8080A, 8–9
Data sampling, 165–166
Data terminal equipment (DTE), 116
DCE (data communications equipment), 116
Debouncing keyboards, 46
DEU (data encryption unit), 176–178
Device code, 57
Digital-to-analog (D/A) converters, 157–164
  companding, 159–160
  input coding, 158–159
  multiplying, 159
  output range of, 158
  programming, 160–163
Direct memory access (DMA), 3, 76–84
Double buffering, 90–91, 163–164
Drift, A/D converter, 166
Drivers (see Bus drivers)
DTE (data terminal equipment), 116

E

EDAC (error detection and correction codes), 42–44
EIA (Electronic Industries Association), 116
8080A:
  architecture, 8
  clock phases, 11
  control, 11
  data bus, 10
  halt state, 15
  hold state, 14
  instruction format, 24
  interrupt control, 10
  memory operations, 13–14
  pin assignment, 9
  power supply, 8

8080A (Continued):
  programmable registers, 10
  register pairs, 10, 25
  RESET signal, 15–16
  signals, 9
  timing signals, 9–10, 16
  wait state, 14
8085, 204–205
8212, 60–63
8224, 16–18
8228, 18–20, 69
8257, 78–84
8259, 70–78
8271, 182–185
8275, 187
8278, 185–187
8294, 176–178
Electronic Industries Association (EIA), 116
Encoding instructions, 29
Error detection and correction (EDAC) codes, 42–44

F

Floppy disk controller, 182–185
Floppy disks, 48–49
  format for, 50–51
Frequency shift keying (FSK), 48
FSK (frequency shift keying), 48
Full-duplex system, 48, 90, 110–111
Fully decoded address selection, 59

G

Gain, A/D converter, 166
General-purpose interface bus (GPIB), 127
  (See also IEEE-488 bus)
GPIB (see General-purpose interface bus)
Guard times, 90

H

Half-duplex system, 48, 90, 110
Halt state:
  8080A, 15
  and interrupts, 70
Handshaking, 93
  bus, 141
  IEEE-488, 128, 131–132
  output port, 63
  RS-232C, 120

Synchronous protocol, 97–98
Synchronous receiver/transmitter, 95–96
   NEC μPD379, 97–100
Synchronous serial protocol, 93
System controller, 8228, 18–19
System network architecture (SNA)
   communications, 95

T

Teletype characteristics, 107
Termination networks, 59
Timing:
   instruction execution, 11–12
   interrupt process, 67–68
   I/O instruction, 58–59
   S-100 bus, 147
Timing signals:
   8080A, 9–10, 16
   RS-232C, 119
Tracking A/D converter, 165
Transceiver, 142
Troubleshooting checklist, 193

U

Universal asynchronous receiver/
   transmitter (UART), 107
   NEC μPD369, 100–103

V

Vectored-interrupt instructions, 66
Voltage-to-frequency (V/F) converter, 169–
   170

W

Wait state, 8080A, 14
Word size, 2
Writing memory data, 8080A, 14

X

X.25 standard, ISO, 95

Z

Z80 microprocessor, 205–206